# Improved Test Scores, Attitudes, and Behaviors in America's Schools

# Improved Test Scores, Attitudes, and Behaviors in America's Schools

## *Supervisors' Success Stories*

EDITED BY Rita Dunn
AND Thomas C. DeBello

**BERGIN & GARVEY**
Westport, Connecticut • London

**Library of Congress Cataloging-in-Publication Data**

Improved test scores, attitudes, and behaviors in America's schools :
  supervisors' success stories / edited by Rita Dunn and Thomas C.
  DeBello.
    p.  cm.
   Includes bibliographical references and index.
   ISBN 0–89789–687–4 (alk. paper)
   1. School supervision—United States Case studies.  2. School
supervisors—United States Case studies.  3. Individualized
instruction—United States Case studies.  4. Academic achievement—
United States Case studies.  5. Educational change—United States
Case studies.  I. Dunn, Rita Stafford, 1930– .  II. DeBello,
Thomas C.
LB2806.4.I56  1999
371.2'00973—dc21      99–14842

British Library Cataloguing in Publication Data is available.

Library of Congress Catalog Card Number: 99–14842
ISBN: 0–89789–687–4

First published in 1999

Bergin & Garvey, 88 Post Road West, Westport, CT 06881
An imprint of Greenwood Publishing Group, Inc.
www.greenwood.com

Printed in the United States of America

The paper used in this book complies with the
Permanent Paper Standard issued by the National
Information Standards Organization (Z39.48–1984).

10 9 8 7 6 5 4 3 2 1

# Contents

*Introduction*

# Successful Supervisors: What Worked for Whom, Where, When, and Why

*Rita Dunn*

Education is a profession in which billions of federal dollars have been spent to reduce academic underachievement—particularly for minority children from poverty homes. Few funded programs have reduced failure on standardized achievement tests. Despite either repetition or innovation, most children who fail do not perform substantially better the "next time around."

On the other hand, practitioners who have used the Dunn and Dunn learning-styles approaches have reported statistically higher standardized achievement and aptitude test scores among average, poorly achieving, and Special Education students. As described in the chapters of this book, that occurred at every academic level in urban as well as suburban and rural schools (see Figure I.1).

These practitioners from geographically varied locations have succeeded in impressively increasing students' achievement and aptitude test scores and improving their behaviors. What magic did these supervisors employ? How did they know what to do? What made what they *did* do work? Are there lessons to be learned or paths to be followed?

Although presented anecdotally in this book, these stories actually have the strongest research base possible. For example:

- Researchers at more than 115 institutions of higher education have conducted studies with the Dunn and Dunn Model (*Research on the Dunn & Dunn Learning-Style Model*, 1999).

- A meta-analysis of 42 experimental studies conducted with the Dunn and Dunn Learning-Style Model between 1980 and 1990 at 13 different universities revealed that eight variables coded for each study produced 65 individual effect sizes (Dunn,

Figure I.1
Supervisors' Success Stories

| Name | Position* | State | Type of School** | Academic Gains | Improvement of Attitudes/ Behavior |
|---|---|---|---|---|---|
| Bart Kelliher | D | NY | E, M, S | + | + |
| Dorothy Robertson | O | | | | |
| Richard Quinn | O | | | | |
| Gail Lewis | O | | | | |
| Wanda Dean | PN | MS | E | + | + |
| Sue Ellen Read | PR | OK | U | + | + |
| Penny Todd Claudis | O | LA | E, M, S | + | + |
| June Hodgin | C | TX | E | + | + |
| Larry Howie | T | CA | E | + | + |
| Imogene Carroll | PR | AL | C | + | + |
| Mary Laffey | PN | MO | M | + | + |
| Ann Braio | D | NY | E | + | + |
| Tana Martin | O | TX | E, M, S | + | + |
| Jan Meritt | T | OR | S | + | + |
| Mary Cecilia Giannitti | PN | NY | S | + | + |
| Patricia Lemmon | PN | KS | E | + | + |
| T.Y. Harp | PN | TX | S | + | + |
| Emmett Sawyer | PN | MO | S | + | + |
| Roger Callan | T, D | NY | S | + | + |
| Ilisa Sulner | PN | NY | E, M | + | + |
| Carolyn Brunner | D | NY (I) | E, M, S | + | + |
| Jack Gremli | D | NY | M | + | + |
| Denise Parker | T | MO | M | + | + |
| Bill Leaf | PN | ID | M, S | + | + |
| Dorothy Logan-Alexander | O | MS | M | + | + |

Figure I.1 (continued)

| Name | Position* | State | Type of School** | Academic Gains | Improvement of Attitudes/ Behavior |
|---|---|---|---|---|---|
| Sr. Natalie Lafser | D | MO | E, M, S | + | + |
| Regina White | PN | NY | E | + | + |
| Roland Andrews | PN | NC | E | + | + |
| Gwen Cox | O | OK | E | + | + |
| Dee Ainsworth | T | MO | E | + | + |
| Joan DellaValle | PN | NY | E | + | + |
| Susan Wellman | T | WI | E | + | + |
| Sherrye Dotson | D | TX | S | + | + |
| Julia Kron | D | NC | E, M, S | + | + |
| Denise Stephenson | SA | NC | S | + | + |
| Mary White | SA | AL | M | + | + |

*Notes:*
* PN = Principal; PR = Professor; O = Central Office; D = Director; C = Consultant; T = Teacher; SA = School Administrator.
** E = Elementary School; M = Middle School; S = Secondary School; C = College; U = University; I = International Schools.
*Source:* Chart created by Andrea Honigsfeld and Rita Dunn.

Griggs et al., 1995). The overall, unweighted group effect size value (r) was .384 and the weighted effect size value was .353 with a mean difference (d) of .755. Referring to the standard normal curve, this suggests that students whose learning styles were accommodated could be expected to achieve 75 percent of a standard deviation higher than students who had not had their learning styles accommodated. This indicates that matching students' learning-style preferences with educational interventions compatible with those preferences is beneficial to their academic achievement.

• According to the Center for Research in Education (CRE), the 20-year period of extensive federal funding (1970–1990) produced very few programs that consistently resulted in statistically higher standardized achievement test scores for Special Education students (Alberg et al., 1992). Prominent among those programs that *did* consistently increase standardized achievement tests was the Dunn and Dunn Learning-Style Model.

Contrast these data with those of New York City where, since 1975, the number of Special Education (SPED) students has risen from 35,000 to 167,000—nearly 15 percent of all 1.1 million city students. Worse than the increase in numbers is the fact that most classified SPED students in that— and every other urban center—rarely outgrow that denigrating designation. Fewer than 2 percent are released from the SPED category each year. Conversely, between 97 and 98 percent remain classified. Very clearly, the billions of dollars allocated to the SPED bureaucracy for many years have been ineffective with 98 percent of the students (Edelman, 1998). Compare these data with those of the SPED students in the Buffalo City Schools (Chapter 1).

Thus, this text was written to provide citizens, educators, legislators, parents, and readers from every walk of life with evidence that children need not perform poorly in schools. From rural, mountainous Cascade, Idaho, to metropolitan Buffalo, New York, from the plains of Hutchinson, Kansas, to the bookstores of Oxford, Mississippi, knowledgeable supervisors courageously decided that "when children do not learn the way we teach them, we must teach them the way they learn"!

## ABOUT THE DUNN AND DUNN LEARNING-STYLE MODEL

According to Dunn and Dunn, learning style is the way students begin to concentrate on, process, internalize, and remember new and difficult academic information (Dunn & Dunn, 1992, 1993; Dunn, Dunn, & Perrin, 1994). Thies (1979), Restak (1979), and the Dunns believe that learning style is comprised of both biological and developmental characteristics that make the identical instructional environments, methods, and resources effective for some learners and ineffective for others.

The Dunns describe learning style in terms of individual reactions to 23 elements: (a) the immediate instructional environment (sound, light, temperature, design); (b) emotionality (motivation, persistence, responsibility, structure); (c) sociological preferences (learning alone, with peers, with either a collegial or authoritative adult, and/or in a variety of ways as opposed to patterns or routines); (d) physiological characteristics (auditory, visual, tactual, and/or, kinesthetic preferences, time-of-day energy levels, intake, and mobility needs); and (e) global versus analytic processing determined through correlations among sound, light, design, persistence, sociological preference, and intake (Dunn, Cavanaugh et al., 1982; Dunn, Bruno et al., 1990) (see Figure I.2).

Figure I.2
The Dunn and Dunn Learning-Style Model

## NOTE

St. John's University's Center for the Study of Learning and Teaching Styles conducts an Annual Leadership Certification Institute in New York City during the first week of July. Teachers are taught how to teach students through their learning styles and administrators and supervisors are taught how to administer and supervise such a program. Participants who complete all requirements are certified as Learning Styles Trainers.

## REFERENCES

Alberg, J., Cook, L., Fiore, T., Friend, M., Sano, S. et al. (1992). *Educational approaches and options for integrating students with disabilities: A decision tool.* Triangle Park, NC: Research Triangle Institute.

Dunn, R., Bruno, J., Sklar, R.I., Zenhausern, R., & Beaudry, J. (1990, May/June). Effects of matching and mismatching minority developmental college students' hemispheric preferences on mathematics scores. *Journal of Educational Research, 83*(5), 283–288.

Dunn, R., Cavanaugh, D., Eberle, B., & Zenhausern, R. (1982). Hemispheric preference: The newest element of learning style. *The American Biology Teacher, 44*(5), 291–294.

Dunn, R., & Dunn, K. (1992). *Teaching elementary students through their individual learning styles: Practical approaches for grades 3–6.* Boston: Allyn & Bacon.

Dunn, R., & Dunn, K. (1993). *Teaching secondary students through their individual learning styles: Practical approaches for grades 7–12.* Boston: Allyn & Bacon.

Dunn, R., Dunn, K., & Perrin, J. (1994). *Teaching young children through their individual learning styles.* Boston: Allyn & Bacon.

Dunn, R., Griggs, S.A., Olson, J., Gorman, B., & Beasley, M. (1995). A meta analytic validation of the Dunn and Dunn learning styles model. *Journal of Educational Research, 88*(6), 353–361.

Edelman, S. (1998). Showdown looms as two Rudys vow special-ed revamp. *New York Post*, June 10, p. 6.

*Research on the Dunn & Dunn Learning-Style Model.* (1999). Jamaica, NY: St. John's University's Center for the Study of Learning and Teaching Styles.

Restak, R. (1979). *The brain: The last frontier.* New York: Doubleday.

Thies, A.P. (1979). A brain behavior analysis of learning style. In *Student learning styles: Diagnosing and prescribing programs* (pp. 55–61). Reston, VA: National Association of Secondary School Principals.

# Improved Test Scores, Attitudes, and Behaviors in America's Schools

# Chapter 1

# Bart Kelliher, Dorothy Robertson, Richard Quinn, Gail Lewis, and the Buffalo City Schools: Supervisors Providing a Very Special Education for All Students

*Thomas C. DeBello*

Just imagine:

- A network television crew working for two solid days to finalize a report of spectacular success stories concerned with the *"statistically higher standardized achievement and attitude test scores"* among hundreds of African and Hispanic-American impoverished students in New York State's second-largest urban school district!

- Reversal of underachievement among officially classified Special Education students at all levels—high, middle, and elementary school—within two years of the start of a new program!

- Officially classified Special Education middle and high school students being returned to "regular" classrooms after two years of learning how to teach themselves and each other!

- Officially classified Special Education middle and high school students functioning so well among average students that visiting members of the New York State Board of Regents literally "cannot tell which students are Special Ed and which are Regular Ed!"

- An inclusion program that works for kids who could never before function in a regular classroom!

- A cooperatively developed plan for concerted effort by a small team of seasoned urban teachers and three administrators that actually *worked* and, within a five-year period, changed most of the Special Education program in an entire school system!

- Widespread adoption of an educational "innovation" that worked for many of the most difficult to teach academic underachievers!

   Is that *your* image of one of the largest urban school districts in the United States? One whose student population is comprised of many poverty, minority underachievers? Probably not, but read on to see why its staff and the New York State Department of Education labeled learning styles its "Bridge to Learning!"

## THE BUFFALO SAGA

This story began in 1990 in Buffalo, the second largest urban school district in New York State. The system was experiencing a breakdown in salary negotiations, Teacher Union and Board of Education dissension, few replacements of administrative personnel, and a superintendent of schools who suffered from a debilitating illness that contributed to a lack of leadership.

The district's huge Special Education population was both increasing and failing to make much academic progress—a fairly consistent state of affairs in urban schools. For example, in New York City during the previous 15-year period, the number of Special Education students had risen from 35,000 to 167,000—to become nearly 15 percent of all 1.1 million of the city's students. More debilitating than the increase in numbers was the fact that most classified Special Education students in that—and every other urban center—rarely outgrew that denigrating designation. Fewer than 2 percent were released from Special Education each year; between 97–98 percent remained classified. Very clearly, the billions of dollars allocated to Special Education over many years had been ineffective with 98 percent of the students for whom they had been allocated (Edelman, 1998).

### Two Supervisors Sought to Improve Buffalo's Special Education Program

Bart Kelliher, Buffalo's Director of Pupil Personnel Services, and Dorothy Robertson, one of its staff development trainers, both became interested in exploring the effects of identifying Special Education students' learning styles. In 1990, they designed a Buffalo Learning-Styles Project, through a special funding grant for teams of teachers and administrators, to study various learning-style models and to provide subsequent teacher education and classroom implementation.

### Step One

After studying different models in depth and observing some existing programs, the Buffalo team decided to use the Dunn and Dunn Learning-Style Model (Dunn & Dunn, 1992, 1993; Dunn, Dunn, & Perrin, 1994). As Kelliher reported, "it was the most comprehensive and the best researched." Robertson and the teachers were especially impressed with the "practical approaches that Dunn and Dunn recommended for accommodating students' learning-style preferences." They also were intrigued because the clearly described learning-style strategies differed substantially from what certified Special Education teachers were doing in their classes. As they examined the Dunn and Dunn approaches, the Special Education teachers on the team occasionally said, "No one ever told me that!" or "I've done this, but I did it with all of them. Apparently it only works with this style!"

### Step Two

At just about that time, the Erie I Board of Cooperative Educational Services (BOCES) in Cheektowaga announced a one-week workshop, scheduled for July 1990, specifically on the Dunn and Dunn Learning-Styles Model. Mr. Kelliher, Mrs. Robertson, and five of the Buffalo teachers signed up for that workshop and attended every single session. At the end of that week, those individuals made a commitment to form a Training Team to determine for themselves the effects of learning-style strategies on the Buffalo City Schools' Special Education students.

### Step Three

That team experimented with many of the learning-style strategies they had learned during the BOCES workshop. The more they implemented in the classes of the five participating teachers, the more positive its members became. Dorothy Robertson and Gail Lewis, two members of that Learning-Styles Project, encouraged the teachers by responding to their requests for needed materials or advice, and by actually working with them to (a) identify the students' learning styles, (b) provide students with individual study prescriptions, (c) redesign their classrooms, (d) create tactual and kinesthetic instructional resources, and (e) suggest alternatives if a technique did not work well.

Bart Kelliher provided all the funding he could. He used available monies to equip classrooms with some informal furniture for children who could not sit in conventional wooden, steel, or plastic chairs for any length of time. He allowed Robertson and Lewis to purchase arts and crafts materials so that the team teachers and their students could make kinesthetic floor games for teaching difficult, on-grade-level academic content.

### Step Four

At the end of that first year, student achievement in reading and mathematics increased substantially. Excited, the team shared its findings with then Assistant Superintendent for Instruction Dr. Richard Quinn. Two years later, when introducing a videotape, "The Bridge to Learning," subsequently developed by the Buffalo City Schools and the New York State

Education Department, Dr. Quinn described his first reaction to the team's exuberance for learning-styles-based instruction:

> I'd been around for a long time and there wasn't much that had impressed me. I'd never seen anything as good as what they described as "learning style!" Frankly, I didn't have much faith that the increased scores would continue.

Nevertheless, in response to the students' achievement gains that the team had reported, and partially because the seasoned teachers on the team were so enthusiastic, Dr. Quinn took the next important step. School systems rarely engage in objective evaluation of the programs they adopt. To his credit, Quinn contracted for a team of independent researchers from the State University of Buffalo to design and conduct an evaluation of Buffalo's Learning-Styles Project. The research team was headed by Dr. Renee Parmer, who had impeccable credentials, and whose university administrator had opined that the evaluators "would find little or no gain over the next year."

### Step Five

During summer 1991, staff development became intense and included training conducted by Professors Rita and Ken Dunn, originators of the model, and Carolyn Brunner, then director of the International Learning Styles Center at Erie I BOCES. Dorothy Robertson and Gail Lewis continued conducting teacher-staff development prior to the opening of school in September 1991.

### Achievement Results

Under the supervision of the team of researchers from the State University of Buffalo, classified Learning Disabled (LD) and Emotionally Handicapped (EH) students (K–6) in the Buffalo City Schools were randomly selected and randomly assigned to two groups. The Experimental Group capitalized on individual learning styles; students taught themselves and each other with tactual and kinesthetic resources. The Control Group was taught with conventional lectures, discussions, readings, and writing assignments by their experienced Special Education teachers. Results at the end of two years were conclusive. The Experimental Group had achieved statistically higher test scores than the Control Group in both reading and mathematics on two standardized achievement tests—the *Woodcock Johnson* (WJ) and the *California Tests of Basic Skills* (CTBS). In contrast, the Control Group had evidenced *academic losses* between the pre-test and post-test (Quinn, 1993) (see Table 1.1) (Kyriacou & Dunn, 1993).

Table 1.1
**Results of Standardized Achievement Test Scores in Reading and
Mathematics in Learning-Styles Program (Experimental Group) and Non-
Learning-Styles Program (Control Group)**

| Test Name | Group | Pre-Test | Post-Test | Net Difference |
|---|---|---|---|---|
| WJ* Reading | Experimental | 72.38 | 79.10 | + 6.72 |
| | Control | 76.48 | 71.52 | – 4.96 (loss) |
| WJ Math | Experimental | 69.67 | 84.20 | + 14.53 |
| | Control | 73.52 | 69.09 | – 4.43 |
| CTBS** Reading | Experimental | 18.76 | 31.33 | + 12.57 |
| | Control | 24.83 | 21.25 | – 3.58 |
| CTBS Math | Experimental | 15.83 | 18.61 | + 2.78 |
| | Control | 23.44 | 16.95 | – 6.49 |

*WJ: *Woodcock-Johnson*; **CTBS: *California Tests of Basic Skills.*

Nothing differed between the Experimental and Control groups other
than the learning-styles instruction. Those findings revealed that EL and
EH students who were not provided instruction responsive to their learning
styles achieved significantly less well than LD and EH students who were
provided instruction that complemented their learning styles.

### Attendance Results

Attendance in junior high schools often is seen as a barometer of potential
drop-out rates. With that concern, Dr. Quinn decided to examine student
attendance in the pilot junior high school inclusion program. All Special
Education students formally were placed into academic- and behaviorally
focused self-contained classes and in Resource Rooms for 100 percent of
each day. Two Special Education teachers served as consultant teachers who
worked with students in their regular classrooms. To control for this program focus, all junior high school teachers were trained in learning styles
prior to the start of the 1993 school year and all students were tested to
identify their styles.

At the end of the school year, attendance records of Special Education
students were compared with that same group's attendance during previous
years. Results indicated an average increase in attendance of eight days per
student! Buffalo, New York is well-known for its harsh winters and volu-
minous snowstorms and, according to Gail Lewis, that winter was particularly difficult.

### Attitude Results

In a survey administered to the Special Education students, most reported that their increased achievement had made them want to learn even more! Additionally, they recognized that it was easier to learn when learning through their personal styles—and it was "more fun!" Therefore, students not only responded that they had learned more, but also that they enjoyed school more.

### Expansion Results

That first year, 10 more Special Education teachers were trained. The following year the program expanded to include 24 Special Education self-contained classes. In 1993–1994, 35 self-contained Special Education classes and one pilot junior high school, full-inclusion program was added. At this writing there are more than 120 learning-styles classes—including several at the high school. Buffalo's bilingual Special Education program and a pilot program for gifted students were all using the learning-styles framework at this writing! What was done to develop staff support in spite of economic and morale frustrations? What made this project successful? To whom does the credit belong?

### Answers to Sober Questions

*Question #1: What was done to develop staff support in spite of economic and morale frustrations?*

- The Buffalo teachers had been working without a contract for years. Negotiations between representatives of the Union and the Board of Education were terminated. Morale was low and frustration was high. However, teachers did not turn their backs when offered a chance to choose how to improve instruction for the very students who had been causing them so much distress and with whom they felt the most frustration—Special Education students.

- After exposure to the original one-week, BOCES-sponsored workshop with Dunn, Brunner, and their colleagues, enthusiasm was so high that the team agreed to "give it their all" if administration provided the resources.

- During the first, and ensuing years, Kelliher kept his promise to the team. He wrote proposals, obtained funding, and provided everything he could in the way of support materials to the project. He worked closely with Robertson and Lewis during the first five years and, when they left the system for more lucrative positions in the Frontier School District, continued emotional and financial support to the subsequent trainers.

- After Dr. Quinn had commissioned the research team from Buffalo State University, he waited until they produced their report. When that report reached him, the results showed such statistically solid reading and mathematics gains that he, too, then championed the expansion of learning styles district-wide. At one point, he was promoted to Acting Superintendent of Schools. He retired shortly thereafter to run for public office.

• Buffalo used the Teacher-as-Coach model to support classroom teachers and never wavered from commitments it had made to the teachers. After the State Education Department reported Buffalo's significant gains in achievement, a local school district offered Robertson the position of Director of Special Education and she accepted. One year later, a lucrative position in that same district was offered to Lewis, who also accepted. As these two original trainers left Buffalo, classroom teachers who had been successful with learning styles were "moved up the ladder" and given a chance to "better themselves." This strategy was attractive to classroom teachers whose classrooms were being visited by dignitaries and other professionals on an almost weekly basis because of the successes they had produced.

• Buffalo's substantial Special Education standardized achievement test gains, and the subsequent distribution of the videotape "Learning Styles: The Bridge to Learning," brought recognition and acclaim to the school system and its staff! Self-actualization was evident among teachers, students, and parents. That feeling of accomplishment contributed to the tremendous sense of pride exhibited by all participating teachers to visitors and Board members.

• The training staff members were all teachers on assignment who were provided support while being completely non-evaluative. Additionally, support staff modeled lessons and assisted teachers in making materials that accommodated different learning-style preferences. Classroom teachers were not required to translate theory into practice. Instead, they spent an endless number of hours developing materials and training their LD and EH students to make their own. Although they devoted *many* hours to doing that, it was their choice. They clearly had seen the benefits of teaching their students to create resources that "matched" their strengths.

• Using funding possibilities that were available through state and federal grants made it possible for Kelliher to provide what teachers needed to do a first-rate job! Those materials helped to make the classroom more receptive to varied learners.

• Dorothy Robertson and Gail Lewis were both proud that, as project support staff, they never visited a classroom empty-handed; they always bore learning-styles "gifts" for teachers to use with students.

*Question #2: What made this project successful?*

• Many districts erroneously exclude Special Education populations from standardized achievement tests because their scores lower the district's evaluations. Therefore, no one ever knows how poorly Special Education programs contribute to their students' growth. In effect, despite huge sums of federal and state monies, LD and EH students would be better served in regular classes where *all* students would achieve better if their teachers knew how to capitalize on the youngsters' learning styles. Dr. Quinn had both the good sense and integrity to seek "hard" evidence to verify the degree to which the Learning-Styles Project was effective.

- Both Quinn and Kelliher had the persistence to stay with the successful program and to bring the data to the Board of Education. They also had the courage to confront non-participating Special Education teachers with the results.

- To maintain support, especially after the project had expanded, Gail Lewis invited all teachers to attend after-school workshops once each month. That was when learning-style techniques and strategies were shared. It was also when "make-and-take" workshops and supplies were available for teachers who were interested in joining the project after its success had been made known.

- Four times each year, the *Learning-Styles Trader* was published. That newsletter became an excellent vehicle for sharing teachers' good-practice ideas that had worked in their learning-styles classrooms. Written by the project staff, it included contributions from district-wide "learning-styles teachers" and was chock-full of ideas and information. When anyone wanted to learn what high school teachers were doing to accommodate their students' time-of-day preferences, or needed a tip on where to get the best buy on plastic visors for students with a preference for dim lighting, they would read that widely distributed newsletter. "How can my fourth-graders be taught to make a kinesthetic geography floor game?" Read the newsletter! It's there—and more!

- Buffalo teachers became "connected," motivated, and were supported in their efforts to introduce and maintain learning-styles instruction. They reported feeling more satisfied and more creative than ever before when using this approach to teaching.

- The newsletter, the television program that highlighted the teachers and their students, and the support provided by Kelliher, Lewis, Robertson, and Quinn made teachers feel "respected and appreciated." To their credit, Kelliher and Quinn consistently asked for—and obtained—teachers' feedback.

If time and care were the hallmarks to Buffalo's staff development efforts, the same could be said of its approach with students. Gail Lewis explained that:

> Teachers discussed learning styles with their students at the beginning of every school year. Many of the teachers shared their own learning-style profiles with their students. Teachers then experimented with one or two elements at a time, discussing students' reactions to each new approach.

- Students were told to pay attention to whether they were better able to complete difficult assignments, or to concentrate on and remember what they had learned, as each new approach to style was added.

- Student achievement was monitored during each new period of experimentation to determine whether gains were being evidenced with whichever new strategy was introduced.

- The focus was on students learning how to accommodate their own style preferences when working with new or difficult material. There were "Circle of Strengths" posted in each classroom to remind both students and teachers to address the children's strengths rather than their weaknesses. All students were given a very good understanding of their classmates' strengths and how to help peers who asked for assistance.

- Twice each year, special parent workshops were conducted to familiarize them with the learning-styles approach. Parents were given the opportunity to take an adult learning-styles assessment under the assumption that once parents understood their own learning styles, they would be more sensitive to their children's styles. Parents also were involved in making tactile and kinesthetic materials to help their children with schoolwork.

*Question #3: To whom does the credit belong?*

Clearly, accolades must be directed toward:

- Dorothy Robertson and Bart Kelliher, who had the vision, the energy, and the charisma to implement the system they designed to improve Buffalo's Special Education program;
- Bart Kelliher for selflessly writing proposal after proposal to secure funding to assist the project;
- Dorothy Robertson and Gail Lewis for actively working with teachers in their classroom to assist in the exacting process of change-for-improvement;
- Richard Quinn for pursuing objective evaluations from independent researchers;
- Buffalo's Board of Education members who were sensitive to the needs of everyone involved in the project and supported them to the best of their ability;
- the participating classroom teachers who pioneered instructional change. Unlimited credit must go to those professionals who worked endlessly to change old habits, experiment with new strategies, and to courageously defy colleagues who chided them about the "extra hours and effort" they were devoting to see whether learning styles made important differences in the children's progress;
- the children's parents who accepted involvement in the program and supported it to the community, the Board of Education, and the media; and
- the Special Education students who rallied around their teachers' efforts to help them learn more, more quickly, and more easily. These youngsters proved that learning styles worked better than anything previously had!

## REFERENCES

*Bridge to learning.* (1993). Buffalo, NY: The Buffalo City Schools and the New York State Education Department. Available through St. John's University's Center for the Study of Learning and Teaching Styles, Jamaica, NY 11439.

Dunn, R., & Dunn, K. (1992). *Teaching elementary students through their individual learning styles: Practical approaches for grades 3–6.* Boston: Allyn & Bacon.

Dunn, R., & Dunn, K. (1993). *Teaching secondary students through their individual learning styles: Practical approaches for grades 7–12.* Boston: Allyn & Bacon.

Dunn, R., Dunn, K., & Perrin, J. (1994). *Teaching young children through their individual learning styles.* Boston: Allyn & Bacon.

Edelman, S. (1998). Showdown looms as two Rudys vow special-ed revamp. *New York Post,* June 10, p. 6.

Kyriacou, M., & Dunn, R. (1994). Synthesis of research: Learning styles of students with learning disabilities. *Special Education Journal, 4*(1), 3–9.

Quinn, R. (1993). The New York State compact for learning and learning styles. *Learning Styles Network Newsletter, 15*(1), 1–2.

*Research on the Dunn & Dunn Learning-Style Model.* (1999). Jamaica, NY: St. John's University's Center for the Study of Learning and Teaching Styles.

*Chapter 2*

# Wanda Dean: The Journey of a Blue Ribbon School Supervisor from Oxford, Mississippi to Washington, DC

*Karen Burke and Rita Dunn*

Author! Author! Oxford, Mississippi is home to John Grisham, author of more than nine best sellers, including *The Firm*. Oxford was also the home of Nobel Prize winner William Faulkner and, for 150 years, the site of the University of Mississippi, whose graduate, Greg Iles, is author of the best seller *Mortal Fear*. The university also draws many authors of note who were born Mississippians—Barry Hannah, Willie Morris, and Larry Brown, for example. With these renowned authors and the Ole Miss Rebels, it is hard to say what Oxford is most famous for. However, during October, college football probably puts Faulkner in the shade.

Travel to Oxford, Mississippi and visit a place and a person that it is not famous for—Oxford Elementary School and its administrator, Dr. Wanda Dean. Schoolmarms of days gone by would probably be appalled if they could see the classrooms in the Oxford Elementary School (OES). Seeing students snacking in class, working in various social groups, listening to portable cassette players, learning through huge kinesthetic floor games, and sitting on classroom floors is not uncommon at this school. Under the leadership of Dr. Wanda Dean, OES has embraced this vision of school change. Finding out more about the Learning-Styles Program at Oxford Elementary began with dinner at the "City Grocery on the Square," a favorite eatery of wordsmiths. Dr. Dean spoke of the delicious shrimp and grits with almost the same enthusiasm as when she explained why learning-styles-based instruction is different from other programs that have come into, and fallen out of, favor during the past years. The white cheddar cheese and the paprika seemed to be the key ingredients of the shrimp and grits, but what were the key ingredients of OES's learning-styles program? Wanda Dean enthusiastically explained the beliefs that have become central to the philosophy of OES.

> Most programs advocate one thing—one process, one method of teaching, one set of materials, one new approach that is assumed to be *best* for all students. But the many differences among how children learn evidence that "one size" does not fit all! Different children require different instructional approaches. And although some can adapt to varied approaches, most need instruction to be based on their individual learning styles!

As we walked around The Square in Oxford after dinner, Dr. Dean noted that traffic in the center of town—particularly around the courthouse—could be a problem at times. Being a native of New York City, Karen Burke considered it incredible that anyone could perceive four or five cars passing by simultaneously as causing a "bottleneck"! Nevertheless, she attended to finding out more about how OES students' academic achievement had increased substantially and their behavior problems had decreased since implementation of the school's learning-styles approach to instruction.

Writers Larry Brown and John Grisham often have enjoyed coffee and conversation on the balcony at Square Books. It was while having a cappuccino on that same balcony that Karen realized why the academic results that OES had experienced could keep its staff continually striving toward learning more and more about how to perfect their program.

Many educational theorists have advocated formulas, models, and paradigms that outlined rigid steps toward changing a school. However, it is the translation of a theory into practice that has proven to be an often insurmountable step. The literature in the field has focused on models for effecting change as opposed to concise case studies of prevailing school changes over time. Perhaps that is because there are not many "how-to" books or monographs that succinctly document successful, ongoing school changes. One notable exception was the National Association of Secondary School Principals' guide, *Learning Styles: Quiet Revolution in American Secondary Schools* (Dunn & Griggs, 1988). Using that book as a model, this vignette combines scholarly research, an informative model, statistical data (*hard evidence*), and the real world of a particular school into a description of the implementation process employed by one successful learning-styles supervisor. Thus, this chapter will include both the implementation and diffusion process of a significant change that has been ongoing for nine years—since 1991. It will provide information concerning what was done by the person most responsible for that implementation—the school's principal.

## DEMOGRAPHICS OF OXFORD ELEMENTARY SCHOOL, OXFORD, MISSISSIPPI

Dr. Wanda Dean has been the principal of Oxford Elementary School since 1990. The school is located in a rural area of northern Mississippi. It has a total enrollment of 650 students in grades 3, 4, and 5. The Basic Educational Data System (BEDS) report lists its population as 49 percent Caucasian, 49 percent African American, and 2 percent "Other." When analyzing the school's socioeconomic level, 55 percent of the students were ascertained eligible for either free or reduced lunch.

## DR. DEAN'S BACKGROUND IN LEARNING STYLES

Dr. Dean first became interested in learning styles while involved in coursework for a doctoral degree in Educational Administration. She saw learning styles as a natural complement to the Special Education students for whom she was responsible. Her mentor at the University of Mississippi also had studied learning-styles constructs and agreed to guide Dean's dissertation research. That investigation (Dean, 1982) compared the learning styles of Educable Mentally Retarded (EMR) and Learning Disabled (LD) students with the *Learning Style Inventory* (LSI) (Dunn, Dunn, & Price, 1975–1996). Because the findings revealed that the learning-styles characteristics of the two groups were statistically different from each other, Dean recommended that EMR and LD students be grouped for instruction in accord with their *learning-style strengths* rather than their *handicapping* conditions. Those data inspired Dean to implement a school-wide learning-styles program in which Special Education students would be instructed through their individual strengths, but that dream was delayed until she became an elementary school principal seven years later.

## AN INTERESTING LINK AND A STRANGE COINCIDENCE

In 1989, the University of Mississippi's men's basketball team played St. John's University's (SJU) team in Jamaica, New York in the opening round of the NIT basketball tournament. Most of Oxford's population undoubtedly recognized SJU more for its basketball program under Coach Lou Carneseca than for the significant educational contributions to learning-styles research that its School of Education had been making for more than two decades. SJU is the university where Drs. Rita and Kenneth Dunn's Learning-Style Model was developed during a 32-year period (1967 to the present) by more than 18 faculty and more than 100 graduate candidates. SJU established the first Center for the Study of Learning and Teaching Styles in the United States (1979) and subsequently helped to found 16

additional centers in Alabama, Florida, Michigan, New York, North Carolina, Ohio, South Carolina, Texas, and Virginia and abroad in Bermuda,
Brunei, Finland, New Zealand, and the Philippines. SJU also is the university
that primarily has been responsible for generating extensive research conducted by hundreds of researchers at more than 115 institutions of higher
education (*Research on the Dunn and Dunn Learning-Style Model*, 1999).

Shortly thereafter, Professor Rita Dunn, Director of SJU's Center for the
Study of Learning and Teaching Styles, conducted a seminar for the Mississippi Association for Supervision and Curriculum Development (MASCD)
in Jackson. When an opportunity to raise questions was provided toward
the close of the day, a woman rose and asked, "Dr. Dunn, are you aware
of any programs in which the learning styles of Special Education students
have been identified and responsive instruction then has been provided?"
Without a moment's hesitation, Professor Dunn responded, "Research concerning the learning styles of Special Education students has consistently
revealed the differences that exist among the various categories and between
classified Special Education students and regular students. In fact, one very
fine study was conducted by Wanda Dean right here in Mississippi in 1982."
The woman grinned from ear to ear and Dr. Dunn instantly asked, "Are
*YOU* Wanda Dean?!" As the woman continued grinning from ear to ear,
Dr. Dunn walked toward her, reached out, and the two embraced. They
had never previously met, but when Dean's study had been published in
*Dissertation Abstracts International* years before, Rita Dunn had read it and
written a complimentary note to Dr. Dean!

## OUTGROWTH OF THE COINCIDENCE

Wanda Dean finally implemented her dream of developing a learning-
styles instructional program for the Special Education students in the building where she served as principal and Rita Dunn persuaded her to attend
the SJU Annual Learning-Styles Certification Institute in New York. Dr.
Dean studied the Dunns' Learning-Style Model, became a fully certified
trainer, and seriously applied their research at OES. The staff at OES believe
it is important to examine the work of researchers and innovators like the
Dunns for insights concerning how learning is affected by different variables.
Dr. Dean has spent considerable time and energy under the tutelage of Rita
Dunn and in observing and discussing the applications of this model with
practitioners nationwide. And, in 1997, Wanda Dean served on staff at the
Center's 20th Annual Institute!

### Analyzing the Data

To gather information regarding successful implementation of this program, we sought the perspective of various participants. Information was

obtained through on-site observations, printed questionnaires, and group and individual interviews. The participants for these activities included students, classroom teachers, the school counselor, the principal, and the district superintendent.

## HOW THE PROGRAM BEGAN

The OES program originally began in a single classroom with a teacher who wanted to "try something new." This class served as the pilot group. This one group gradually expanded to a current school-wide program. Expansion occurred only with the support of extensive staff development as well as Principal Dean's guidance and leadership.

## WHEN, WHERE, AND BY WHOM WAS THE TRAINING PROVIDED?

Drs. Rita and Kenneth Dunn provided the initial inservice through an MASCD five-day workshop conducted in Mississippi. Many other staff developers, who were both successful learning-styles teachers or principals and certified learning-styles trainers, also provided training. Staff development sessions were provided at the following sites and were attended by various members of the school staff at different times:

- June 1990: One-day workshop in Jackson, Mississippi.
- July 1991: Five-day workshop in Jackson, Mississippi.
- July 1992, 1993, 1994, 1995, 1996, and 1997: Eight-day workshop at the Learning-Styles Certification Institute in New York.
- May 1993: Two-day workshop in Oxford, Mississippi.
- May 1997: Two-day workshop in Oxford, Mississippi.

Dr. Dean selected well-respected staff to become involved in the initial phases. She believed that their enthusiasm would be contagious and that their successes would be respected. Whenever she assigned a "buddy" (mentoring colleague) to a new or beginning teacher, Dr. Dean always chose a strong learning-styles teacher to provide that support.

Two Parent Teacher Association (PTA) meetings were devoted to learning styles so that the students' parents could become aware of the school's direction. Mr. Roland Andrews, (then) principal of a learning-styles school in North Carolina, conducted the first parent meeting; OES's staff conducted the second. An ongoing program with the local housing authority provides training to all of its staff concerning how learning styles affect their professional and personal interactions with each other and with others. Dr. Dean conducted two learning-styles sessions for a local church that emphasized how both school and home could use learning-styles information to benefit family members. One OES teacher conducted a learning-styles awareness session for the PTA of another school in the district. Sessions also were conducted for the parents of new students before the youngsters began school. Parents were given the opportunity to take the *Productivity Environmental Preference Survey* (PEPS) (Dunn, Dunn, & Price, 1989) to determine their own learning styles. The district's Central Office management has helped by financing part of the training and providing moral support to the principal.

## WHAT WERE THE HELPING AND HINDERING VARIABLES?

Dr. Angela Klavas, Assistant Director of SJU's Center for the Study of Learning and Teaching Styles, visited elementary schools that had implemented the Dunn and Dunn Learning-Style Model in varied geographical locations throughout the United States. Her report (Klavas, 1991) described those factors that both helped and hindered the development of each program. Hindering factors revolved around Central Office mandates and intrusions, supervisors with a different agenda, and lack of financial resources for staff development. Helpful factors revolved around the understandings and insights that both staff and students developed once they became familiar with the learning-styles research and theory concerned with the Dunn and Dunn model and the statistically higher achievement and aptitude standardized test scores that resulted from implementation.

## THE ROLE OF THE STUDENTS

The students at OES also were involved in the planning processes for introducing diverse content, methods, materials, and scheduling. Students did this in cooperation with their teachers and each other. A number of staff members expressed their belief that comments from students indicating the children's high interest in and satisfaction with learning styles provided the incentive for their continuation in the implementation process. These OES students influenced the program's outcomes through their positive opinions.

## THE ROLE OF THE TEACHING STAFF

Most curricular changes directly involve the teachers, and this was true right from the beginning at OES. Many different practices and materials modified teachers' skills. New ideas were disseminated through the distribution of articles, books, and films and interactions created with "outside" consultants. In addition, visits to other teachers who were implementing various aspects of the learning-styles program stimulated further experimentation. Inservice courses were introduced to help teachers consider new content and methods. A program implementation outline was developed and its examination verifies how OES's teachers were placed in the center of its educational reform. Dr. Dean believed that whether or not a learning-styles program will be actualized in any school depends, to a great extent, on the role its teachers play in its adoption and implementation.

## THE ROLE OF THE PRINCIPAL

A new principal who perceived learning styles to be a valuable component of a school's instructional program *introduced* this change, but changes were made based on the expectations and sanctions of the teachers who influenced each other, their students, and the community.

Dr. Dean had never worked at OES prior to being appointed its principal. She was an "outside" innovator who was not interested in merely maintaining the status quo. She had the research background in learning styles and was eager to experiment with its various components. She was aware of the proposition that the major impetus for organizational change is from the outside. The use of consultants, evaluation teams, and professional organizations to stimulate movement toward change made Dr. Dean aware that an organization would be more apt to change in response to an external force than to one that was internal. Presenters, consultants, and researchers were brought in from outside the organization and teachers were sent to outside meetings and seminars to interact with professionals who were experiencing successes with innovative efforts. Dr. Dean was an administrator who advocated a specific change and sought to persuade others to accept her beliefs. Her advocacy was successful to varying degrees with the teachers in her building, but the basis of that success emanated from the personal knowledge, conviction, prestige, competence, and earned authority of this leader and the cooperation and support of her staff.

## A SUCCESS STORY

Oxford Elementary School's success is not a well-kept secret in Mississippi. The United States Department of Education selected OES as a 1996–1997 Blue Ribbon School. The basis of the Blue Ribbon application emphasized a commitment to meeting the needs of a culturally diverse population through learning-styles approaches to instruction. The application included the following statement:

> In 1991, Oxford Elementary School was the first school in Mississippi to implement the learning style model and it now serves as a national resource site for this program. The school's principal is now recognized nationally as an expert in the field and regularly conducts training ses-

sions, as do several faculty members. OES's successful use of learning styles and inclusion can be measured in increased test scores, positive attitude scores, a high attendance rate, and generally appropriate behaviors.

After a rigorous and lengthy application process, Dr. Dean was invited to Washington, DC to accept the well-deserved award. It was a time to celebrate their accomplishments and to reflect on the program that made possible the journey from Oxford, Mississippi to Washington, DC. Some of these accomplishments were revealed in the following statistical data:

- Daily student attendance: 96.6%
- Serious disciplinary incidents: 2.0%
- Daily teacher attendance: 99.0%
- Reading scores: 65th percentile
- Language scores: 71st percentile
- Mathematics scores: 72nd percentile
- Total Battery: 68th percentile

Revised accreditation standards, established by the state of Mississippi, emphasized standardized tests as a measure of school performance. A State Board of Education policy requires all students in grades 4–9 to be tested each October using the *Iowa Test of Basic Skills* (ITBS); prior to 1994 the *Stanford Achievement Test* (SAT) was the required standardized test. Figure 2.1 illustrates one example of the successes that Dr. Dean has celebrated since implementing learning styles as the basic philosophy of OES. The data from 1990 and 1992 represent the time frame *before* learning styles were fully implemented; the data from 1994 and 1996 represent the period *after* learning styles were implemented.

In addition, increased academic success has led to enhanced student self-esteem. Most of the students now understand how they learn and accept learning differences as natural and nothing to cause shame or embarrassment. This acceptance of their own differences has led to an acceptance of differences in others. Dr. Dean commented on how visitors frequently discuss the positive atmosphere they find at OES and the respect evidenced toward students, teachers, and guests. Although she can't quantify this observation, teachers often report that the students appear to be happier than ever before.

## CONCLUSIONS

Dr. Dean's decision to implement learning styles because of her own research and the research of others provided a solid basis for the program. By

**Figure 2.1**
**National Percentile Scores (Grade Four)**

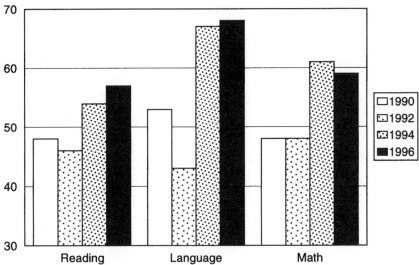

providing inservice opportunities and a plethora of resources for the staff, she hel; .d them introduce learning-style strategies into their classrooms. Her convictions and personal devotion to this relatively complex and ambitious program elicited the wholehearted enthusiasm of OES teachers and students. Her insistence on teacher involvement in both training and decision making appealed to their professionalism. The results support the belief that intrinsic professional rewards are extremely important for motivating teachers. The statistically increased academic achievement test scores supported Dr. Dean's intuitive and research-based convictions. She certainly has proven herself to be a successful supervisor!

## REFERENCES

Dean, W.L. (1982). A comparison of the learning styles of educable mentally retarded students and learning disabled students. (Doctoral dissertation, The University of Mississippi, 1982). *Dissertation Abstracts International, 43,* 1923A.

Dunn, R., Dunn, K., & Price, G.E. (1975–1996). *Learning Style Inventory.* Lawrence, KS: Price Systems.

Dunn, R., & Griggs, S.A. (1988). *Learning styles: Quiet revolution in American secondary schools.* Reston, VA: National Association of Secondary School Principals.

Klavas, A. (1991). Implementation of the Dunn and Dunn Learning-Style Model in United States elementary schools: Principals' and teachers' perceptions of factors that facilitated or impeded the process. (Doctoral dissertation, St. John's University, 1991). *Dissertation Abstracts International, 58*(1A), 88.

*Research on the Dunn & Dunn Learning-Style Model.* (1999). Jamaica, NY: St. John's University's Center for the Study of Learning and Teaching Styles.

*Chapter 3*

# OOOOOOOklahoma, Where Styles Come Sweeping Down the Plain: How Sue Ellen Read Is Helping the State "Do Just Fine"!

*Rita Dunn and Jeannie Ryan*

In the beginning, there are only individuals, acting in isolation and uncertainty, out of necessity or idealism, unaware they are living through
an epoch.

—M.F. Green, *Praying for Sheetrock* (1991)

This quotation easily could describe the learning-styles movement in
Oklahoma and the pioneering journey of Dr. Sue Ellen Read.

## ISOLATION AND UNCERTAINTY LEAD TO PROBING

Dr. Read is a professor of Education at Northeastern State University
(NSU) in Tahlequah, Oklahoma. NSU has an enrollment of approximately
9,000 students on three campuses. Tahlequah is the capital of the Cherokee
Nation of Oklahoma and the NSU's College of Education (COE) prepares
teachers to service the largest population of Native American students in the
United States.

After working with undergraduate students for two years, Dr. Read was
assigned a full-time graduate load and asked to take over the Cognitive
Learning Styles class. To that point, the course had focused solely on hem-
isphericity and Read's departmental chair said simply, "Surely there is more
to learning styles than this. Are you up to it?" Read responded affirmatively
and launched a full-blown effort to determine what learning style really was.

Driven by uncertainty and, at times, discomfort, Sue Ellen began to read
everything on the topic that she got into her hands or onto her computer.
She processed and digested the variety of models that had been classified

under the rubric of learning styles. As her knowledge base gradually expanded, confusion mounted. She waded through models that appeared to be describing differently what appeared to be similar phenomena. She experienced frustration with the efforts of some theorists to cast the brain into a dichotomous mode and she was put off by the lack of experimental research to support the various theories that were being touted commercially. How could she suggest that her students try an approach when there was no evidence to support its efficacy?

Then Dr. Read found one comprehensive, well-researched model that she felt she could offer to her graduate students for examination. The more she read and taught about, and then experimented with the Dunn and Dunn Learning-Styles Model, the more intrigued she became. Its face validity was so apparent to the educational professionals in her classes that they experimented with it eagerly and rapidly brought feedback to class!

## SHORT-TERM IMMEDIATE RESULTS

Before too long, Sue Ellen had to devote part of each class session to her students' reports of the successes they were experiencing when using the information and learning-styles approaches they learned in Dr. Read's class. For example:

- "This child who hasn't sat still for one minute all semester, was so absorbed during the 40-minute period that he did not stop working the Flip Chute math problems during the fire drill gongs! He said he didn't even hear them!"

- "They kept their hands to themselves all the time they were learning the science facts with the Floor Game. I know they were absorbed because all three scored 85 or better on the test!"

- "She stopped crying when she saw me demonstrate the Electroboard and worked steadily with it on the fractions assignment until she had to leave for her next period class."

- "He has never ever paid attention to a lecture before! Today he was glued to his chair! Having him use a Team Learning with peers *first* seems to have set the stage for getting it into his head!"

- "He sat alone during the entire period. After he handed in the assignment, he walked directly over toward his buddies and said, 'Sorry guys! Had to do it by myself!' His friends nodded; they understood."

These comments were from Dr. Read's graduate students—all of whom were classroom teachers experimenting with learning-style strategies with their own pupils (K–12). Often, they invited Dr. Read to visit their schools to observe implementation of the learning-style practices they had learned from her in their class at the university. Gradually, Sue Ellen Read began to hear about and see practitioners who were teaching "brilliantly" emerge all over eastern Oklahoma. Most were elementary school teachers like Cheryl Hallum and Mary Legan in Muskogee. Occasionally, she would see one from the high school, such as mathematics specialist Becky Hoxie in Stillwell. Gradually, many were becoming excellent, confident practitioners who were using learning styles approaches successfully—and were receiving approval from their supervisors and the parents of their students.

## THE WORD SLOWLY SPREAD

Professor Read began receiving an increasing number of invitations to conduct more and more inservice sessions throughout the region. She suspected that most of those "bookings" were coming from solitary, avid teachers who were wearing down their school- or district-staff development committees. She did not anticipate that entire school faculties were interested in embracing learning styles.

## OUT OF NECESSITY AND IDEALISM EMERGED THE FIRST SCHOOL-WIDE PROGRAM

On August 1, 1990, sixth-grade teacher Debbie Garner remained after the final Cognitive Learning Styles class to tell Dr. Read that she had convinced her principal to allow her to use learning styles in her classroom at Berryhill Elementary School. Two weeks later, Garner telephoned to report that she had been asked to become the principal of that school after the unexpected resignation of the prior administrator. She further explained that learning styles made more sense to her than anything she had encountered in her 13 years of teaching. She asked Dr. Read to help her make learning styles a focal point of her entire school. Thus began a partnership that continues to this day.

The partners worked hard to ensure that learning styles permeated the culture of the school. They saw to it that the faculty was well trained, the students were tested to identify their learning styles, and the parents were kept informed of the philosophy and the instructional approaches being introduced. Teacher leaders such as Jan Warner and Susan Cargill began to surface. Both of these teachers enrolled at NSU to pursue master's degrees and Dr. Read began mentoring them directly. Both attended workshops with Professor Rita Dunn and matured into superior learning-styles teachers.

## BERRYHILL ELEMENTARY SCHOOL'S EXPERIENCE WITH LEARNING STYLES

Berryhill is a small, independent school district in Tulsa County that is surrounded by several larger and wealthier urban and suburban school districts. Maybe that is why there was a collective gasp when the 1997 *Iowa*

**Figure 3.1**
**Third-Grade Progression of Students Using Learning Styles**

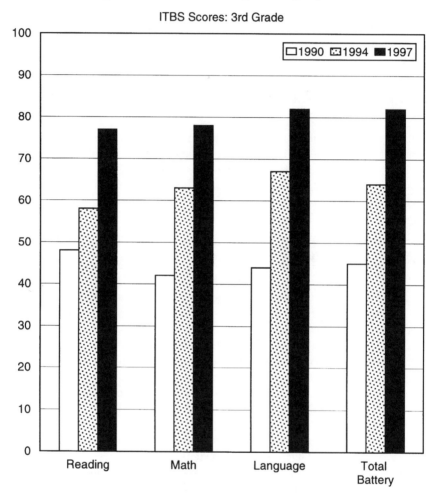

ITBS Scores: 3rd Grade

*Test of Basic Skills* (ITBS) third-grade results were published on the front page of the *Tulsa World* and Berryhill sat at the top the list! Since the inception of its learning-styles philosophy at Berryhill, the national percentile rankings on the ITBS have jumped significantly each year. By 1997: reading scores had advanced from 48 to 77; mathematics scores from 42 to 78; language scores from 44 to 82; and core totals from 45 to 82 (see Figure 3.1). That improvement occurred under the auspices of a new, inexperienced principal and a student population that previously had been poorly achieving. What was changed for those children was the way in which instruction was being delivered to them—through their learning styles!

As word about the learning-style instructional practices at Berryhill began to spread, teachers, principals, and—occasionally—superintendents began to visit the school. Both Principal Garner and Dr. Read told those hoping to reap the rewards of the Berryhill approach to instruction, "You must understand learning styles *conceptually*; it is not a recipe. It is an effective, practical way to individualize teaching and learning.

## EXPANSION OF COURSES AND SERVICES AT THE UNIVERSITY

During the six years in which she was involved with the Berryhill project, Dr. Read became Chair of the Master's of Teaching Program at NSU and the Dunn and Dunn model became the core of that program. She had added both an introductory and an advanced learning-styles class. The Masters of Administration faculty had decided to require that introductory class for all their school administration candidates.

The more educators understood about learning styles, the greater the number of requests there were for Dr. Read's services. She was conducting 30 to 40 faculty-staff development workshops each year and, before long, the College of Education administrators agreed to permit her to provide learning-styles testing services. Soon thousands of *Learning Style Inventories* (LSIs) (Dunn, Dunn, & Price, 1975–1996) and *Productivity Environmental Preference Survey* (PEPS) (Dunn, Dunn, & Price, 1979–1990) were being processed at NSU. To assist with the testing, she was allocated the services of a work-study student for 15 hours each week.

## IMPLICATIONS OF LEARNING STYLES FOR NATIVE AMERICAN STUDENTS

Teachers, both Native American and non–Native American, began questioning the implications of learning styles for the Native American students so prevalent in northeastern Oklahoma schools. Not completely satisfied with the available research, Dr. Read initiated what was to become one of the most extensive studies (n=3,000) ever conducted relevant to the learning styles of Native Americans. Read's investigation also was the only one that ever factored for the impact of blood quantum (Read, 1997).

Certain significant differences did exist between the learning styles of Native American and non–Native American students and by blood quantum. However, Dr. Read's overall analysis agreed with data obtained by researchers Dunn and Griggs (1995). Specifically, all three reported that, despite the small differences that do exist, *within-group* differences were equal to or greater than *between-group* differences. In other words, people are as different from the members of their very own family as their families are different from the families of other cultures. Succinctly, individuals learn very differently from each other and, to be maximally successful, require different approaches, resources, and/or strategies to learn new and difficult academic information. Interestingly, three researchers—Read (1997) and Dunn and Griggs (1995)—all noted that gender was a far greater variable than ethnicity.

## WHERE DID THE PRACTICAL IMPLEMENTATION, RESEARCH, AND TEACHING LEAD DR. READ?

While she was encouraged by the number of elementary school teachers who were beginning to practice learning styles, Dr. Read was not satisfied. She was a former high school teacher and lamented the lack of participation from secondary school educators in the improvement of instruction. And then, into the Master's of Teaching Program walked the "Women from Welch"!

## THE WOMEN FROM WELCH

When they first entered into the Master's of Teaching Program, Pam Benne (Math), Sally Fenska (Science) and Judy Bryan (Language Arts) were teachers at Welch High School. Welch is a rural community that seems very reminiscent of the late 1950s. It encompasses 256 square miles and has an average daily attendance of 370 students pre-kindergarten through twelfth grade. Minorities (mainly Native Americans) comprise 30 percent of the school population; almost half of all students qualify for free or reduced lunch.

After studying about learning styles for just a short period of time, Pam thought she might try it with a student who was failing Algebra I. Gabe was the star quarterback and a gifted kinesthetic learner who definitely was struggling with algebra. Oklahoma has an enforced "no pass/no play" policy and, understandably, the football coach was frantic. Ms. Benne readily agreed to help Gabe after school.

The algebra students had been learning to classify numbers in the real number system through a very abstract and analytical process. Pam developed several Learning Circles with different numbers printed around the periphery of each circle and with the correct symbols hidden on the back. On separate clothespins, she wrote the categories *rational, irrational, integer, whole,* and *natural* and directed Gabe to place each clothespin onto its "matched" correct number.

After several trials, he quickly could classify all the numbers correctly. On the next chapter examination, Gabe was the *only* student in the class who got all the number problems on the test correct. Dramatically, Gabe did play football the following Friday night and the Welch Wildcats did win the game! But the fact that Gabe had performed so well as a result of the learning-style-responsive tactual resource impacted strongly on the three women from Welch!

Having witnessed the impact of this simple hands-on resource on Gabe, the three ladies banded together and totally immersed themselves and their classes into learning-styles strategies. They secured the funds for testing every student in grades 4–12 with the LSI. They then arranged for Dr. Read to visit Welch and explain the identification assessment results to all the students in grades 7–12. The fascinated students caught on immediately and started to explore how this new information might impact on their studying. Although a workshop was available to other faculty members, only Pam, Sally, and Judy really embraced learning styles.

## EFFECTS OF LEARNING-STYLE-RESPONSIVE INSTRUCTION

The differences these three teachers from Welch have made in the lives of their students is palpable. After only one year of using learning-styles strategies, there was a 50 percent increase in enrollment in trigonometry; the female enrollment shot up by 500 percent! In physics, the enrollment rose 125 percent and the female enrollment increased by 400 percent! The eleventh-grade English students were required to take the *Oklahoma Criterion Reference Test* for writing and had a 94 percent pass rate!

## FIGHTING THE ISOLATION TO INITIATE THE EPOCH

### NSU's Summer Camp for Periodic Re-energizing

Because these three women from Welch still work in geographic and professional isolation, they often speak of needing a "fix" from Dr. Read. Liberally translated, a *fix* is a surge of energy derived from discussions and interactions with like-minded mentors who stimulate and energize. Periodically, a *fix* is a necessary component for those who exert continuing pioneering and physically exacting efforts toward a long-range goal. It is because of these teachers and others who voice the same need that Dr. Read and NSU now sponsor a "summer camp" for learning-styles practitioners to unload, reload, and be re-generated!

### Sue Ellen Read's Re-energizing

It began to dawn on Sue Ellen that she, too, needed a *fix*. Because of her isolation, she was uncertain that she was actually teaching the Dunn and Dunn model most advantageously. Although she had read every resource she could locate, and the educators with whom she was working were achieving real success, she was haunted by the concern that she might be neglecting some essential principles.

When Sue Ellen Read was invited to present her research on Native Americans' learning styles at a conference in Dallas, Texas where Professor Rita Dunn was the keynote speaker, she jumped at the chance! Finally, she could hear it from "The Source."

Dr. Read admits that she was not fully prepared for what transpired. She listened to Dr. Dunn's opening address and then immediately proceeded to the break-out session where she was to present her own research. She was facing a crowd of four! Five minutes into her presentation, Dr. Dunn quietly entered the room and took a seat. For a moment, Sue Ellen was once again 10 years old and hearing her mother say, "If you cannot run with the big dogs sister, stay on the porch!"

After the briefest interval, Rita Dunn began peppering Read with questions. At the end of the session, Dr. Dunn said, "You *must* come to New York for training!" Dr. Read did just as she was told.

### Dancing with a Tornado

"Since the day I met her, I have felt like I'm dancing with a tornado," related Sue Ellen. She continued:

> I've never encountered anyone of her stature so willing to give of her time and energy. Yes, it has occurred to me, that she is equally generous with *my* time and energy! Rita Dunn is exacting and demanding. She is also passionate, courageous and, unknown to her, extremely funny. She is the epicenter of the learning-styles movement. This generous genius connected me with others who also worked in isolation and uncertainty. In the past, Rita gave to them as she was now giving to me. I was beginning to understand that I was not alone; I was part of an educational imperative.

### Necessity and Idealism

Attending the Annual Leadership Certification Institute sponsored by the Center for the Study of Learning and Teaching Styles at St. John's University helped Sue Ellen Read begin to fill in the gaps in her knowledge base. Buoyed by the experience, she found it virtually impossible to say "no" to anyone who wanted to know about learning styles. Dr. Read knew that she could not continue to meet the growing training demands, chair a graduate program, teach a full load, and pursue her research interests. She also was committed to joining the ranks of those working worldwide to promote and further investigate the impact of learning styles.

Sue Ellen Read obtained the criteria and application for becoming one of the many centers in the International Learning Styles Network. She began to gather data to support her case for becoming a center director at NSU and for convincing the university's administrators that such a center was needed in northeastern Oklahoma. Even she had been surprised when she began putting the numbers together.

## COMBINING HUMAN RESOURCES TO MAKE THAT CRUCIAL DIFFERENCE TO PEOPLE

In addition to the thousands of LSIs and PEPSs processed at NSU, Dr. Read had provided staff development in learning styles for 62 school districts and 202 different schools. She had instructed the United States Attorney's Office for the Eastern District of Oklahoma on how to use learning styles in the courtroom. A working relationship had been established with the Cherokee County Health Department Child Guidance Center to test clients and train guidance center staff in the use of learning styles.

Dr. Larry Williams, the new president of NSU needed little convincing. He was quick to grasp the need for, and advantages of, establishing a center at NSU. The NSU College of Education had a rich history of leadership in Teacher Education and Dr. Williams was intent on maintaining that role. His approval was granted immediately.

The first person Sue Ellen Read contacted to write one of the required letters of recommendation was State Superintendent of Public Instruction Sandy Garrett, an NSU alumna. Having met Professor Dunn and studied her research, Sandy knew what the creation of a center in Oklahoma could do for learners. Garrett gave her full support.

In July 1998, the International Learning Styles Network Board of Directors approved the application of the NSU Oklahoma Institute for Learning Styles (OIL) to become part of its membership. To provide Dr. Read some additional support, NSU has allocated a graduate assistant to her. In addition, three of Read's former students—Jan Warner, Judy Sherrin, and Dale Lee Woody—currently serve as part-time associates at OIL to help Dr. Read with training and research. NSU also reduced Read's teaching load so that she can devote additional time to OIL.

## WHERE DOES SHE GO FROM HERE?

Sue Ellen is currently working on three new projects:

- The first is a legislative agenda. She is striving to build support among area legislators for OIL. Read is convinced that if the learning-styles movement is to gain epoch proportions, it must have political support.
- Her second effort is to involve more college faculties in the use of learning styles. Dr. Read currently is working with New Mexico Highlands University and Missis-

sippi Valley State University to introduce learning styles into college classrooms and empower students to help themselves.

• The third initiative is the one closest to Sue Ellen's heart. In collaboration with Dale Lee Woody, she is beginning a two-year research project to test the efficacy of using the Dunn and Dunn model with children from violent environments. Based on the work of Bruce Perry, M.D., Ph.D., Woody and Read will test the hypothesis that use of learning styles will significantly reduce anxiety and increase achievement for children who are hypervigilant and easily threatened by conventional classroom environments.

Sue Ellen has her "plate full" and she likes it that way. She says:

> So much of education is based on theory. Although theory has its place, I suspect that we do great harm to teachers and, ultimately to students, with educational Specials of the Week. I often ask my students whether they would give their own child a drug that has been neither tested nor approved by the FDA—one that has not been prescribed specifically for that child. When they answer "No," I ask why they do not demand the same standard for the educational treatments they use with children. I want them to be critical professionals who demand *proof* that each method has an experimental research base and provides specific guidelines for use with individuals. Until they know for whom each method is effective, they need to use and observe it carefully.

Sue Ellen Read's lessons have been impacting instruction in Oklahoma. One of her students summed up her experiences with Dr. Read by stating:

> Dr. Read captivates you with that great humor of hers, appeals to your best teaching instincts, inundates you with a whirlwind of research and activities and, before you know it, it is too late to seek shelter in your old ways of teaching.

Apparently, Oklahoma teachers enjoy dancing with their own special brand of a tornado! Is anyone looking for a partner?

## REFERENCES

Dean, W.L. (1982). A comparison of the learning styles of educable mentally retarded students and learning disabled students. (Doctoral dissertation, The University of Mississippi, 1982). *Dissertation Abstracts International, 43,* 1923A.

Dunn, R., Dunn, K., & Price, G.E. (1975–1996). *Learning Style Inventory.* Lawrence, KS: Price Systems.

Dunn, R., Dunn, K., & Price, G.E. (1979, 1980, 1996). *Productivity Environmental Preference Survey.* Lawrence, KS: Price Systems.

Dunn, R., & Griggs, S.A. (1995). *Multiculturalism and Learning Styles: Teaching and counseling adolescents.* Westport, CT: Greenwood.

Green, M.F. (1991). *Praying for Sheetrock.* New York: Fawcett Columbine.

Klavas, A. (1991). Implementation of the Dunn and Dunn Learning-Style Model in United States elementary schools: Principals' and teachers' perceptions of factors that facilitated or impeded the process. (Doctoral dissertation, St. John's University, 1991). *Dissertation Abstracts International, 58*(1A), 88.

Read, S.E. (1997). Learning styles of Native American students in Northeastern Oklahoma. *Center Review, 6*(11), 40–55.

*Chapter 4*

# Penny Todd Claudis: Curriculum Supervisor and Learning-Styles Coordinator, Shreveport, Louisiana

*Andrea Honigsfeld and Rita Dunn*

Penny Claudis was the heart and soul behind the Learning-Styles Program in the Caddo Parish Schools for four years in the early 1990s. Her dedication and enthusiasm blew you off your feet and, before you noticed, you were soaring high in Penny's world of "matching responsive resources with students' strengths." Her colleagues often were amazed that Penny never ran out of energy when it came to talking and teaching about learning styles to teachers, administrators, community organizations, local colleges, or anyone else who would listen. Penny was ready to go anywhere—anytime: she administered the *Learning Style Inventory* (LSI) (Dunn, Dunn, & Price, 1975–1996) to children, grandchildren, nieces, nephews, and to any interested person—just to spread the word and "win" people's involvement. And for all those years, she was notably successful!

## PERSONAL BACKGROUND

Penny was a teacher long before she became a social studies supervisor in the district. In 1991, she was among the first three staff members from the Caddo Parish Schools to attend St. John's University's Learning-Styles Leadership Certification Institute in New York City. Within a year, Penny became the expert and official coordinator of the Learning-Styles Program in the entire district. Once she was named coordinator, Penny applied for and received Chapter II funding for the program and made it her priority. With generous support from her supervisors at the district level, she delegated her other responsibilities to assistants and focused on planning and implementing the learning-styles model.

## The School District

The Caddo Parish School District is located in Shreveport-Bossier, on the west side of the Red River among the rolling hills of northwest Louisiana. With its 76 schools and more than 51,000 students, it is one of the largest school districts in the state of Louisiana. It employs an excess of 6,600 teachers, administrators, and teaching and non-teaching support staff and, as such, is the third major employer in the region—falling only slightly behind the Barksdale Air Force Base and the state of Louisiana! In light of sheer numbers, it is easy to contemplate the enormous challenge that Penny undertook in providing guidance and support for planning, designing, and implementing what surely must have seemed like a revolutionary approach to teaching and learning.

## In the Beginning

The first three educators from Caddo to receive training in the learning-styles approach were so impressed with the potential it offered for the Caddo Parish Schools that they convinced the Director of Curriculum, Mrs. Wanda Gunn, to establish a local pilot program. All the organization and preparation for that program was delegated to, and coordinated by, Penny. She held parent and community meetings to explain the program and to provide information about the new venture at Caddo to all interested stakeholders in the community. She designed a colorful brochure explaining the concept to parents and invited them to become active participants in the Learning-Styles Program. Another handout in a question-and-answer format addressed all the concerns one might have about the program. Parents volunteered to join faculty study groups to expand their knowledge and skills in the learning-styles approach.

By the school year of 1992–1993, an extensive pilot program based on the Dunn and Dunn Learning-Style Model was ready to take off in nine schools with at least four teachers in each school trained and prepared for this new adventure. In 1993–1994, nine more schools joined the pilot program. Volunteer teachers were trained during intensive local summer institutes and ongoing staff development was coordinated by Penny and offered at different times to meet the participants' time-of-day learning-styles strengths!

With the success that was evidenced in increased student achievement, the district administration became fully supportive of the learning-styles initiative and Professor Rita Dunn was invited to visit Shreveport and conduct an all-day session for selected administrators and designated teachers from each of Caddo's 76 schools. The community was impressed with the enormous body of research Professor Dunn presented, her expertise, and the support and assistance for the program provided by St. John's University's Center for the Study of Learning and Teaching Styles. As a result, Professor Dunn was awarded the "Key to the City" by Shreveport's mayor "in recognition of (her) extensive contribution to education." The planning for that gala celebration began under Penny Todd Claudis's leadership in conjunction with both Caddo's administrators and Shreveport's political representatives.

### Widespread Success

The pilot program was a success among students and teachers alike. Their evaluations demonstrated what a great impact it had on everyone. One high school student commented:

> At first, I thought it wouldn't help too much because I didn't know that anything more was possible than what I was doing to make my grades better. But I was wrong. Learning styles helped me a lot. I went from a C to an A!

Some teachers initially had been skeptical, whereas others were enthused. Although this particular one was unusual, teachers' evaluations typically included laudatory statements like this:

> Learning styles not only made a difference in my students' attitudes, it made a difference in *mine!* I have been teaching for almost 20 years so I guess I was pretty set in my ways. Learning styles brought out the creativity, fun and everything else that I'd had buried inside. I am excited about learning styles and I am excited about teaching again! In other words, learning styles recaptured the spark I lost through the years.

By June 1994, the Learning-Styles Pilot Program had been concluded and the model was available to the entire parish. Penny enabled all teachers new to Caddo to have their own learning styles inventoried and introduced them to learning-styles strategies. *Learning in Style*, the district's own newsletter, kept everyone focused on what was being implemented and how teachers and students reacted. An extensive resource library with books, tapes, sample Contract Activity Packages (CAPs) and Programmed Learning Sequences (PLS) were all at the teachers' disposal. And all of these were obtained and made available through Penny!

Back then, while the learning-styles program was in full swing, a visitor could walk through Caddo schools and see redesigned classrooms that met the environmental preferences of its students. Anyone who looked through the windows would find students working with tactual and kinesthetic resources along with auditory and visual materials—depending on their perceptual preferences. Caddo teachers utilized small-group techniques like Circle of Knowledge or Team Learning with students who learn best by working with their peers. In addition, students might be separated from their classmates as they worked independently near a wall or in a corner or in pairs or teams of three or four. Those students' preference for learning non-traditionally was being accommodated—and it was evident in their improved scores. Finally, had you had the chance to peek into some teachers' closets, you would have found them filled with PLS, CAPs, and Multisensory Instructional Packages that students with different styles were permitted to use to master difficult academic content.

Every classroom did not evolve into a model learning-styles room and every teacher did not became a true believer, but Penny was, and still is, a strong advocate of teaching to students' learning styles. After the fourth year, the program began to lose support because building-level administrators became involved in a new focus of interest and teachers were required to implement that new idea. Gradually, teachers began phasing out the program.

## A SPECIAL EVENT IN PENNY'S CAREER

In 1994, Penny Claudis served on staff at the Learning-Styles Leadership Certification Institute in New York City. She shared her struggles and successes at Caddo Parish Schools in Louisiana with other participants from around the world. Strangely, others decried the pattern that many educational institutions appeared to emulate—that of experimenting with something new for a short period of time; then, regardless of the positive effects, administrators insisting on moving into the next *new* fad!

### Where Is Penny Today?

In 1996, Penny was asked to help form the district's 504/ADA staff. One year later, she became the coordinating specialist for that division in the district's Office of Special Programs. In this federally mandated Office of Civil Rights program, Penny works with children and adults with special needs and with the staff members who serve them. Whenever she has the opportunity, she turns to a trusted tool—learning styles. To this day, she continues to be a resource for the district and for others throughout the state who know of her work.

> My experiences with Rita and Ken Dunn and the wonderful persons I met through St. John's University's Learning-Styles Center changed my professional life! Wherever I go, the Dunns' model is part of me. I have

changed some folks' lives because of what I learned through it. *A part of my being and my heart will always belong to learning styles!*

## REFERENCE

Dunn, R., Dunn, K., & Price, G.E. (1975–1996). *Learning Style Inventory.* Lawrence, KS: Price Systems.

*Chapter 5*

# June Hodgin and the Saga of Alta Vista Elementary School, Abilene, Texas

*Thomas C. DeBello*

Belief in the ability of teachers to assume the professional responsibility of providing practical inservice for their colleagues, team work, and commitment on the part of both staff and administration were the key ingredients of this successful learning-styles program. In 1990, the Abilene Independent School District decided to introduce learning-styles-based instruction across the board to interested teachers. To demonstrate their conviction, administrators initially established two teaching/learning-styles consultant positions. Then the director of Special Education, Mary Island, discussed the concept with the school district staff and encouraged two Special Education teachers, Elesa Oetting and June Hodgin, to attend St. John's University's one-week Annual Learning-Styles Certification Institute to become certified learning-styles trainers. Since that time, both ladies consistently have served the district as consultants. In that capacity, they have conducted staff development sessions and visited schools to provide support for teachers who were interested in hands-on classroom implementation. Gradually, June Hodgin's collaboration with Nell Sims, the principal of Alta Vista Elementary School, and Caren Wooliscroft, a third-grade teacher there, produced remarkable results!

## SCHOOL DEMOGRAPHICS

Abilene is a west Texas town with a school district that serves nearly 20,000 students. Described by Mrs. Hodgin as being a "family-oriented community," Abilene also is home to three universities that contribute substantially to its prevalent ambience of youthful energy and scholarly task orientation. Located in the center of such impressive higher-education resources, the school district has its choice of many well-qualified, recently graduated teachers.

Alta Vista Elementary School's enrollment is approximately 450 students drawn from a community of varied socioeconomic levels and extensive ethnic diversity. As currently occurs in towns and cities throughout the United States, students also vary in terms of their language and emotional development and in their academic achievement.

The staff included 23 classroom teachers with an average class size of approximately 22. Nearly 20 percent of Alta Vista's elementary school population had been classified as Special Education students and included in regular classrooms.

## HOW IT ALL BEGAN

Almost a decade ago, Principal Sims recognized the need for drastic instructional change. Most teachers were teaching as if "one size fit all"—despite the inability of two of every ten children to function at all in traditional classes. Others were functioning, but not very effectively. To their perceptions, they worked "hard," but achieved only minimally. Furthermore, many complained that they felt little satisfaction with their school experiences. And the pattern had continued; teachers taught exactly as they had—whether it worked for the children or not, and children tried to learn exactly as they had—whether it worked for them or not. No one knew of a better way.

Learning styles was one way to individualize instruction and perhaps meet the needs of their diverse student body. To interest staff, June Hodgin gave a short introduction to learning styles prior to the summer vacation, in 1993. Then, during that break, a week-long seminar was offered at the school. Teachers were encouraged to attend and their efforts were supported with a stipend for participating.

From that beginning, June spent half of each day at Alta Vista helping staff as they began to implement learning-style strategies. Through such classroom visits and continuing workshops, teachers gradually developed expertise with various learning-style strategies. Mrs. Sims cited the quality of the on-site training and consultant availability as reasons for the relative ease of the staff's implementation.

Although not unique to Alta Vista, the combination of learning styles and inclusion for Special Education students became highly effective. Kyriacou and Dunn (1994) reported on a decade of research revealing that most students assigned to Special Education were highly tactual and kinesthetic. In addition, they often required extensive mobility and active participation while learning. Despite those clearly documented personal traits, tactual and kinesthetic children invariably had been taught through lectures accompanied by questioning and readings. These were *auditory* and *visual* instructional strategies that required consistent, day-by-day and hour-by-hour adaptations by essentially tactual and kinesthetic learners. Having to concentrate by constantly adapting to someone else's teaching style caused many children emotional and physiological stress. In turn, that stress manifested itself in "inappropriate" school behaviors.

In addition to having to master new and difficult information by listening and reading rather than by manipulating and experiencing, tactual and/or kinesthetic school children often were required to "sit still, listen, and pay attention." These school behaviors also require adaptations of their natural learning styles for youngsters who need frequent (if not ongoing) movement and involvement. Nevertheless, documentation that such youngsters *can* learn, but in a different style, was evidenced as special needs students became relatively successful when provided kinesthetic floor games, hands-on instructional resources—such as Flip Chutes, Electroboards, multipart Task Cards, and Pic-A-Holes—in classrooms that made formal seating available and permitted mobility. These latter alternatives were provided with the stipulation that no student with a different learning style in that class was to be distracted by how another individual learned. Furthermore, each student whose learning style *benefited* from non-traditional resources was required to achieve higher test grades each week than he/she had before (Dunn, 1996). Although many other schools have helped such students make the breakthrough to academic success, Abilene's model was so comprehensive that it is worth examining!

## PLANNING FOR INCLUSION WITH STYLE

What have the results of this collaboration been? Like Scott Thomson (1982), Principal Sims believes that learning style provides educators with an exciting tool for individualizing instruction. She confirmed that it met the needs of Alta Vista's Special Education students. In many ways, it also broadened the curriculum so that students could maximize their opportunities. Teachers once reluctant to have inclusion students in the past now say that they do not want any of their students to be "pulled out" for special help, for example, "I would never want my students in a pull-out program again . . . I need them in my room!"

Initially, Special Education students did not take the Texas statewide academic tests (TAAS). Today, 90 percent of Alta Vista's Special Education students participate in the state-standardized achievement testing with impressive results! Eighty percent of the third-grade Special Education students in inclusion learning-styles classes passed the exam, whereas only 74 percent and 62 percent of the two non-learning-styles classes passed!

Caaren Wooliscroft charted her classes' TAAS reading results over a three-year period. She documented an increase in the percentage of both her regular and Special Education students passing each year. Since using the learning-styles approach, 100 percent of her regular education students have passed the statewide reading examinations, and better than 74 percent of her Special Education students also have passed—an unusual outcome!

Success bred success, and, in the 1996–1997 school year, Alta Vista Elementary School won an Inclusion Grant from the Region XIV Educational Service Center because of the progress that had been made by teachers in responding to the learning styles of their students. This grant went a long way toward providing additional materials and training. Indeed, the grant provided increased technology for student use in their classrooms!

Second-grade students in classes at Alta Vista were compared with their counterparts in another school in the district in which teachers had not been trained in learning styles. Over a two-year period, students were administered the *Kaufman Test of Educational Achievement.* The scores of those classes in which teachers had used learning-styles-responsive strategies, on average, had reduced the number of students falling below grade level by 30 percent, in contrast with the classes where the number of students failing nearly doubled!

Increased achievement encouraged others in the district to implement learning-styles programs also. Elesa Oetting reported similar results in another school with which she had collaborated. Fourth-grade students also had increased their reading levels as measured by the *Kaufman Test of Educational Achievement.* In grade four, 64 percent of the students had gained from 1 to 1.9 years' growth and 24 percent had gained from 2 to 2.9 years; 6 percent had gained from 3 to 3.9 years' growth! Fifth-graders in that same school had performed equally well; 36 percent had gained 1 to 1.9 years; 21 percent had gained 2 to 2.9 years; 29 percent had gained 3 to 3.9 years; and 7 percent gained 4 to 4.9 years!

Abilene teachers have presented these results to various groups, such as their Parent-Teacher Association and a local television channel. The latter spotlighted learning styles as one of its educational segments.

Learning styles has become an excellent tool for counseling parents who became highly supportive of teachers' suggestions for making studying and homework easier for their children. Parents appreciated the non-judgmental aspects of learning styles. Learning-styles consultants Hodgin and Oetting also have used the homework and teaching information based on learning styles to increase the expertise of many Teacher Education students attending their area's three universities.

Nell Sims offered colleagues eight ways to determine that their staff was moving effectively into learning-styles-based instruction. The following items had to be observable:

1. more individualized instruction such as students using different instructional resources to master the same objectives;

2. more requests for construction materials for teachers and students to make instructional games;

3. more small-group activities for peer-oriented students and those who enjoyed variety (learning in several ways);

4. change in the appearance of the classroom, for example, informal seating for some, brighter and dimmer sections, some opportunities for mobility for those whose style required periodic activity;

5. requests for book tapes associated with the Carbo Recorded Book Method;

6. more interest in creating centers to provide supervised mobility and kinesthetic learning;

7. differences in teachers' attitudes toward children who learned differently; and

8. an increased belief that all children can learn.

Clearly, Abilene's learning-styles program was the result of a successful collaborative effort. By combining a practical inclusion model with learning styles, Nell Sims and June Hodgin designed a formula for success for Alta Vista Elementary School. For another successful inclusion model based on learning styles, see Chapter 1, which describes the successes of the Buffalo City Schools.

## REFERENCES

Dunn, R. (1996). *How to implement and supervise a learning-style program.* Alexandria, VA: Association for Supervision and Curriculum Development.

Kryriacou, M., & Dunn, R. (1994). Synthesis of research: Learning styles of students with learning disabilities. *Special Education Journal, 4*(1), 3–9.

Thomson, S.D. (1982). Next steps. In *Students' learning styles and brain behavior: Programs, instrumentation, research* (pp. 217–223). Reston, VA: National Association of Secondary School Principals (NASSP).

*Chapter 6*

# The Most Profound Gift a Teacher Can Share: Larry Howie and the Chico Unified School District, California

*Roger J. Callan and Rita Dunn*

Imagine a giant of a man—six-foot-six at least, standing erect like an army officer but smiling from ear to ear. Add a hardy handshake combined with a shock of grey hair, a dash of ebullience, and a pinch of laughter and you have the beginnings of this energetic dynamo from Chico, California. His background is extensive and includes six years of, teaching in overseas American schools, and experiences as a private restaurateur and an Alaskan fisherman! For the past 22 years, he's been a teacher at two sites—the John A. McManus and the Emma Wilson Elementary Schools—both of which have felt the impact of his leadership and expertise. He used to think that good schooling was dependent on the personality and dedication of the teacher, but knowledge of learning-style strategies has changed his mind. In 1997, he told an audience at the Marriott Marquis Hotel in New York that, although he'd always had a hands-on approach to teaching and had treated all his students sensitively, he had never previously helped each child learn with specific instructional strategies based on how that individual learned best.

## WHERE IT ALL BEGAN

One hundred miles to the north of Sacramento, the capital of the state of California, lies the town of Chico. It seems to be a microcosm of the United States—an unlikely mixture of occupations and people, ranging from a campus of the state university to active farms, and from a Caucasian majority to a Hmong minority. Its school district has housed between 7,000 and 10,000 students drawn from mixed socioeconomic backgrounds. Class size is about 20 in K–3 as mandated by state law, approximately 30 in grades 4–6.

In 1992, the John A. McManus Elementary School reflected the more challenged sections of this small society. It housed a low-achieving student population and an unenviable reputation in the school district. Most of the teachers at McManus were veterans, with the norm being more than 24 years of service each. One of them, a six-foot-six man with a shock of grey hair, Larry Howie, attended a one-day workshop focused on learning styles with two colleagues, in Sacramento in 1992. They had seen the workshop advertised as claiming to enable teachers to teach their students according to their individual learning styles. At the workshop, they heard about the effects this approach had had in various schools and the rapid achievement of students following the introduction of learning-styles instruction. This experience had a profound effect on Mr. Howie, who said, at the time, "If the research reported to us is even half true, this is the most important opportunity we can have to really help our students."

Indeed, Mr. Howie was so impressed that the next day he arranged to attend the weeklong summer institute in learning styles offered each year by St. John's University in New York City. After listening to his description of the learning-styles workshop and realizing how it coincided with her own beliefs about individual learners, Larry's wife, Cathy, decided to go with him! Later they described this new approach to teaching and learning as "earth-shattering."

When they returned home, Larry and his two colleagues decided to experiment with learning-styles techniques in their classrooms during the 1992–1993 academic year. They became a cadre within their school and; as a team, were eager to present staff development on learning styles to interested colleagues. The effects of their efforts were seen in the positive and excited attitudes of the McManus teachers. That, in turn, made a convert of their principal to the extent that he traveled to Texas in April 1993 to attend a three-day learning-styles seminar. Hence, the first stage of the McManus learning-styles experience was based on enthusiasm, attitudinal change, eagerness, goodwill, and a deep-down feeling that this approach was, after all, sensible. As Larry says, "People and educators understand learning styles from a gut level. Learning styles makes sense."

> Frankie was a hearing-impaired student with low self-esteem and a non-chalant attitude about school. He rarely completed assignments and basically didn't care much about himself or learning. Frankie was academically behind! He was not doing—or at least not turning in—his homework. I asked him where he did his homework and Frankie replied: "My folks make me sit at the table with that big light on it." I then asked him to show me his Learning-Style Profile. Of course it showed that he needed informal seating and low light!

I encouraged Frankie to talk with his mom about an informal design and low light. He did, and she agreed to try it. His homework was never a problem again. Last year, Frankie received the school award for being the "most improved sixth-grade student." This was an astounding growth in academic success and self-esteem!

## IN THE BEGINNING

That remarkable first year of implementing learning styles at McManus consisted of a few teachers doing a few basic, easily administered approaches that produced dividends out of all proportion to their effort while implementing them. Teachers prepared students by giving them the *Learning Style Inventory* (LSI) (Dunn, Dunn, & Price, 1975–1996). This provided a solid foundation on which to prescribe individual instructional programs for each student. Breaking with the usual pattern of implementation of a learning-styles program, the teachers began to redesign their classrooms to adapt to the students' learning needs, which made their new approach instantly noticeable in the school.

Parents were informed of the gradual implementation from the beginning of the school year in September. Larry addressed the PTA to explain learning styles and recruited parents to help construct tactual materials. Their children's profiles also were explained and, as Larry reported, parents were "totally shocked and impressed that I could know their children so accurately and precisely. Some parents even began to see their own children in the new light of learning styles and it made sense to them." As Larry frequently found, before understanding the learning-styles concept, parents and teachers often judged that there was only one effective way to teach children—as they had been taught! Larry found that "Parents tend to seek the educational experiences they had—and assume that their learning style was the same as their children's. At times, that belief system "caused problems for children who learned differently from their parents and who then could not perform well in school. It also caused terrible home tensions for both the child and the parent."

Larry found that "Parents during conference time were very impressed with the specific information I shared with them from their own child's LSI. I think it helped separate family issues that may have been affecting the success of their child. Parents often said, "Oh, I see that now. I wouldn't have thought of that," or "I wouldn't have allowed my child to do her homework that way because that's not how I was taught. But now I understand why she wants to!"

Larry also found that teachers tend to teach the way they were taught, although those strategies may not have been optimal for them. He suspects that the uninspired result of such an approach over the years might well be that familiar and sad sight, the "burned-out teacher."

Gradually, the learning-styles approach took root in this and in other schools in the area. Larry acknowledged that "Several . . . teachers told me that they were just about burned out from teaching. When they began using learning styles, they were rejuvenated by teaching and understanding the complexity of their students."

Best of all, students—as well as teachers—appreciated the new approach! Larry's school had been one with a preponderance of underachieving students. Test scores for many usually had been below grade level, with students described by their teachers as "average to low achievers." During that pioneering year, students were prepared for the administration of the LSI by hearing specially prepared stories about how most people are capable of learning identical material, but in different ways. It was explained to them that although one person might simply sit down and read about a new idea, another might need to experience an activity related to that idea or, as his students said, "walk through it." Another person might want to "feel his way through to understanding the idea" by using his hands as a learning tool. Some write, some draw, some build, some take notes while listening to another explain, and some need manipulatives like Task Cards or Electroboards (Dunn & Dunn, 1992, 1993; Dunn, Dunn, & Perrin, 1994). Still another might want to hear about the new idea. Each learns the same information, but through a different strategy.

The children understood and accepted this explanation, and they then answered the 100 LSI questions. Learning-styles folders were created to enable students to begin thinking about learning in a new way—through their unique learning-styles strengths. Students' perceptual strengths, as revealed by the LSI, were printed onto a card—with the strongest modality placed at the top and the second strongest modality following the first. The card was taped to each child's desk top as a constant reminder of that youngster's best way to learn something first—and the best way to reinforce that learning—that child's second step. Larry prepared tactual materials ahead of time, before the learning-styles sequence of concentration was started. Very quickly, students were creating their own resources to respond to how they needed to begin and reinforce learning.

Students were encouraged to follow their own learning styles each day, every day. "The more they used their learning-styles strengths, the better they became—with very few exceptions. Students were more comfortable than they had ever been before during lessons and study times. Many loved to learn through Team Learning experiences (Dunn & Dunn, 1992, 1993) before the class officially began a new curriculum. And, of importance, Larry believes that students thoroughly enjoyed learning about the similarities and differences among them and their classmates—and their teachers—and their parents' learning styles. How each person learned became the center of their conversations for weeks!

Phil was a student of mine two years ago. Recently I bumped into his mother. Phil was complaining to her about his first semester grades at junior high school. He was upset; he had gotten one B+; all other grades were As. Two years before, Phil had been described as having "fourth-grade ability in fifth grade"—but we had found that 15 learning-style preferences affected how he needed to study.

## ENGULFED IN THE PROCESS

As the new techniques began to take root, Larry noticed something intriguing. Once teachers began to address the learning styles of their students with LSI-prescribed activities, a transformation began. The new ways of teaching and learning created an extremely participative and interactive class. What occurred validated what they were trying, and made the teachers increasingly aware of the importance of learning styles. The test scores for their entire school, as compared with those of other schools in the district, were dramatically improving! One year later, in 1993, that school population improved more than any other in their district. With the reputation and population that school had previously had, the test gains caused more than a few eyes in their district to turn their way.

Larry theoretically questioned, "What's different at my school compared with other schools in our district? Learning styles! After two years of implementation, the school's mathematics scores were elevated 18 points on the standardized achievement test used by the district. So shocked were the Central Office personnel that each teacher was asked if students had been permitted to use calculators on the test—which had been forbidden. Of course, they had not. What *had* happened was that teachers had been teaching their students to use their learning-styles strengths to get the most out of them—and had succeeded! And that had happened on a school-wide basis because, by then, most teachers had begun to adapt the new approach.

> My students learn to do their personal best. Their level of confidence is continually increasing, which allows them to set higher goals for themselves. They are less frustrated by setbacks; instead, they think about what they can do to remember better than previously. They focus on how they begin to learn new and difficult information and how they reinforce it. They are more tolerant of each other and more supportive of each others' efforts and personal achievement.
>
> As soon as students begin earning higher grades, they become impressed and delighted with themselves! Those at the lowest end of the spectrum usually took a little longer to show growth, but their eventual smile of victory is my reward! In addition, my colleagues at John A. McManus named me "Teacher of the Year"!

## ADMINISTRATIVE AND PARENTAL SUPPORT

Administrative support was an important element in Larry's story. Although he was the instrument of change and actually provided the instructional leadership in the school during the first year, the principal quickly realized the efficacy of this new approach and became both proficient and a strong supporter himself. When he left for a better position, the next principal was uncomfortable with the degree of student involvement that the learning-styles program required and had to be convinced that it was what had caused the increased test gains. Thus, the program "went on hold" and received only scant financial and professional support immediately after the first principal left. For example, all inservice programs were deleted from the school schedule. However, once parents have been exposed to the learning-styles theory, they almost always become great fans of the process. Larry exclaimed that "The personal gains are so inspiring that many parents from other teachers' rooms seek information about how learning styles works."

As a result, the PTA organized a three-part series on learning styles and urged community members to attend. Parents took the *Productivity Environmental Preference Survey* (PEPS) (Dunn, Dunn, & Price, 1980), the adult learning-styles identification instrument. The PTA then sponsored an evening for interpretation of parents' learning-styles printouts and requested more information about other elements of the Dunn and Dunn model. The last evening focused on how parents could help their children by using learning-styles strategies and resources to help them study at home.

## EXCITING OUTCOMES

There were other, less obvious improvements in the school environment. Parents commented on how their children did not want to miss a day of school and would insist on attending even when not feeling well. In the past, many of those students would have stayed home. Many of these students had developed a special connection and involvement in their learning-styles environment. Larry's experience led him to believe that, when students are fully involved in instructional choices and decisions, and are held accountable for their achievements, they perform at levels beyond what most adults expect. He is convinced that students want to be involved in the whole experience of a learning-styles classroom.

> One day, while in the staff room, I was preparing a Group Analysis— another learning-styles approach intended for peer-oriented students. A colleague asked me about it, and I invited her to observe. When the lesson was over, I gave her the materials I had just used, and she decided to try that same lesson with her second-grade class. She later reported

that she had received the best writing that she ever had with the Group Analysis from those students. I was not at all surprised. That's exactly what had happened with mine!

The good news spread because the message was accurate and became the topic of many teachers' conversations. Larry soon received invitations to visit other schools and tell them the secret of his success. He addressed teachers and parents throughout the area—as far south as the public library in San Francisco where he spoke with a group sponsored by the Parent Education Resource Center. At one school, an inservice was held after school for both teachers and students. Having diagnosed the students' and their teachers' strongest perceptual strengths from their learning-styles profiles, Larry explained learning styles to each of them through their primary strength. In other words, he created four presentations, each concentrating on one of the four perceptual modalities—auditory, visual, tactual, and kinesthetic— and directed each participant to the presentation that was most likely to respond to how he/she would learn best.

Larry's initial success occurred simply by colleagues seeing what he and the other pioneering teachers were doing in their classroom in the weeks following the Sacramento workshop. Larry and his co-teachers' infectious enthusiasm about the ideas and approaches that the learning-styles concept embodied won initial attention. The training that Larry, Cathy, and their colleagues provided increased the pace at which other teachers became involved in this movement.

As Larry said at the time: "Students' attitudes have changed from a lost and unrelated view of their own education, to a take-charge type of empowerment that radiates smiles of success. Many students who probably would have begrudgingly gone through school with a minimum of success have now become self-directed learners." Larry Howie became the first certified learning-styles trainer in California. He then began to teach colleagues throughout the school district and in near-by districts some of the learning-styles approaches that had worked for him. Several other inservice workshops followed and, eventually, Larry and Bruce Luchessa, a colleague and friend, began their own consulting firm—Learning in Style.

He enthusiastically indicates that what made this approach to teaching so exciting for him was the fact that it enabled him to teach each student individually. That is what he has seen teachers respond to—and what made good teachers become better teachers. Again, here is what Larry reported:

> I used to think that good schooling lay in the hands of the teacher who was required to provide good quality education. I believed that if teachers taught well, their students would learn. How wrong I was! Even though I always used a lot of "hands-on" approaches to teaching, and tried to treat all my students individually, I was not specifically helping

each student to learn in the way that best suited to him. I'm sure I was always helpful to my students, but now I can accurately design resources for, and help my students to design their own methods so that they learn in ways that are advantageous to them as unique individuals.

The main change in my mind concerning what is "good" schooling actually is in having a reliable and valid instrument to measure my students' styles. I also now understand a great deal more about global and analytic processing, and how I can adjust my teaching, and my students' study habits, to accommodate any of their critical learning-style elements.

Also, providing students with tactual and kinesthetic materials and using small-group strategies for introducing and reviewing curriculum units makes a tremendous difference for some of the youngsters. I've also learned that no single way of teaching is effective with all students! And finally, the subtle and not-so-obvious new perspective for me is that all students, from any ethnic or background, can learn and blossom in a learning-styles environment.

## OUTCOMES OVER TIME

Larry has been using learning-styles strategies with his classes since 1992. He even has seen elementary school graduates return from their junior high schools and ask, "Does this class like Circle of Knowledge as much as we did?" When invited to see for themselves, the returning students joined in a cooperative reinforcement technique with his (then) present class. Larry described that "wonderful experience" with distinct pleasure.

Finally, seventh-graders shared their success stories of how well learning styles had helped them. Larry obviously was invigorated by those students' experiences as they gained insight into how they learned. One youngster described it as when "the light went on"; another said that he inadvertently had grasped an idea in a totally different way and now used that approach all the time. For most teachers, such moments are the best justification for being in the education profession. Larry says: "Student growth through learning is what education is all about. Seeing students bored or frustrated, giving up, or dropping out is a nightmare to a good teacher!"

Larry Howie has discovered an approach that grapples with these teacher horrors, and has come out on top. Students learn where previously they could not. They now enjoy learning where once they would have been baffled or angry. They work in an environment that is uniquely their own because Larry has been brave enough to do the unthinkable—transform his classroom into a learning environment that accommodates 30 individual learning styles. Teachers who claim this is impossible while, at the same time, stating how desirable such a goal is, should take heart; it can be done. As Larry Howie says, "The experience that best validated the importance of learning styles to me occurs all the time in my classroom. I am still constantly astounded to see my fifth- and sixth-grade students totally absorbed in learning. I am delighted as an educator to see my students working in a productive and supportive atmosphere. Visitors always comment on the high level of quality the students' work demonstrates. Students are extremely comfortable in a learning-styles classroom."

What more is there to say, except *floreat Larry!*

## REFERENCES

Dunn, R., & Dunn, K. (1995). *Teaching elementary students through their individual learning styles: Practical approaches for grades 3–6.* Boston: Allyn & Bacon.

Dunn, R., & Dunn, K. (1993). *Teaching secondary students through their individual learning styles: Practical approaches for grades 7–12.* Boston: Allyn & Bacon.

Dunn, R., Dunn, K., & Perrin, J. (1994). *Teaching young children through their individual learning styles.* Boston: Allyn & Bacon.

Dunn, R., Dunn, K., & Price, G.E. (1975–1996). *Learning Style Inventory.* Lawrence, KS: Price Systems.

Dunn, R., Dunn, K., & Price, G.E. (1979, 1980, 1996). *Productivity Environmental Preference Survey.* Lawrence, KS: Price Systems.

# Chapter 7

# Imogene Carroll Teaches Teachers to Teach Themselves: Stillman College, Tuscaloosa, Alabama

*Maryann Kiely Lovelace and Rita Dunn*

Since 1987, Dr. Imogene Carroll has been introducing the concept of learning styles to her Teacher Education students at Stillman College because she believes that future teachers need to understand themselves as learners. Once they have knowledge of their own styles, they have a better understanding of how children learn and how to teach them effectively.

Dr. Carroll chose to use the Dunn and Dunn Learning-Styles Model with her students because "it makes more sense than any other learning-styles model I've examined. It is practical for teachers and easy for them to use because they can implement it gradually, over time." She has found that components of the model are extremely helpful because they provide: specific instructional methods to complement students' unique styles; extensive research documenting its effectiveness; directions for making and using instructional resources; assessment inventories; and student profiles that "tell exactly what you have to do to teach this person!"

## THE BACKGROUND

Stillman College is a 120-year-old institution that is supported by the Presbyterian Church. It houses more than 1,000 students, 99 percent of whom are of African-American descent. Dr. Carroll originally introduced identification of students' learning styles into the Teacher Education program in the fall of 1987. It now has expanded to include all incoming freshmen who are administered the *Productivity Environmental Preference Survey* (PEPS) (Dunn, Dunn, & Price, 1996) as part of the college's diagnostic orientation procedures. Approximately one-fourth of the students who attend Stillman College are enrolled in Teacher Education; a majority of them plan to become elementary school teachers. Dr. Carroll wants to be certain that these future teachers "are knowledgeable about learning-styles and the many responsive approaches that can be incorporated into instruction for children from diverse backgrounds."

Dr. Carroll has changed her own classroom practices since she attended St. John's University's Learning-Styles Certification Institute in New York in July 1987.

> I am much more aware of my college students' needs and individual differences. When the students know my style, they understand me better as an instructor. *Best* of all, they understand, and are much more accepting of, each other.

In Dr. Carroll's course, all students take the *Productivity Environmental Preference Survey* (PEPS) (Dunn, Dunn, & Price, 1996) during the first week of classes. That information is summarized, interpreted, and discussed. Everyone makes a Learning-Styles Badge (see Figure 7.1) to describe his/her individual style. Then they discuss their learning-style strengths with classmates, display their badges, and suggest ways in which each can study and do homework in ways that complement their unique strengths.

Students then make smaller versions of their "badges" and wear them in class for several sessions so that they become aware of each others' learning-style strengths. They develop instructional resources to teach identical information through alternative resources to permit individuals to learn the identical material differently. Dr. Carroll believes that "This visual display of each student's style and the cooperative effort to develop alternative ways of teaching helps them all understand—and respond to—the differences between and among learners."

Dr. Carroll has made some interesting observations about her students by summarizing the information obtained in their PEPS learning-styles profiles. Since 1987, she has found that her Teacher Education students—who are "Alabama's teachers of tomorrow"—are mostly auditory learners who prefer structure and an authority figure present while learning. In addition, more than 60 percent of the students are afternoon or evening learners. Knowledge of these elements has helped Dr. Carroll understand her students as well as plan appropriate classroom activities for them.

After they are made aware of their own learning-style preferences, students learn to make and use learning-style-responsive materials and resources. For example, students create tactual materials such as Flip Chutes, Electroboards, and Task Cards to use with people who remember new and difficult information most easily when learning with hands-on materials.

In Dr. Carroll's science methods course, the next step involves advanced applications of these strategies. "Each student designs a learning-styles Learning Center with an elementary school science topic as its focus." Dr.

**Figure 7.1**

**Identification Badge Created by Dr. Imogene Carroll as a Device for Developing Students' Awareness of Their Own and Their Classmates' Learning-Style Strengths**

NAME_____

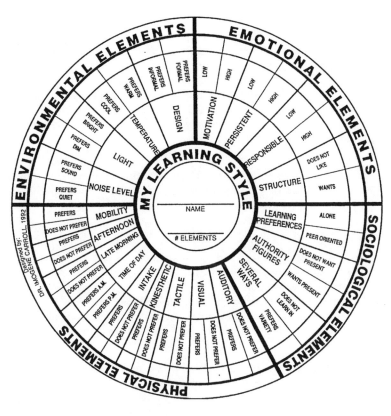

Carroll has accumulated videotapes and color photographs of learning-styles centers that have been developed and used by her students during the past decade. After making the center's and other learning-styles materials, these future teachers must learn to use these materials in the classroom. "All materials are used in their clinical experiences and student teaching."

Students in Dr. Carroll's classes also "learn about and participate in small group techniques," recommended by Dunn and Dunn (1992, 1993) and Dunn, Dunn, and Perrin (1994). Students participate in Team Learning for introducing new and difficult material, Circle of Knowledge for reinforcing information, and Brainstorming as a problem-solving activity. Then they design their own small group activities for use with the classes they teach.

As Dr. Carroll's students become advanced, they are taught to design Contract Activity Packages (CAPs). They also administer the *Learning Style Inventory* (LSI) (Dunn, Dunn, & Price, 1996) to elementary school students. Many students accompany Dr. Carroll to workshops and inservice sessions in nearby schools. They therefore learn first through applications to themselves and each other, and then observe that knowledge being used with youngsters in local classrooms.

According to Dr. Carroll:

> This learning-styles program has a pronounced effect on students as they become teachers. Our students become increasingly aware of individual differences and the fact that children don't all learn at the same rate or in the same way. Also, they recognize how their personal learning style affects their teaching style. I see them make every possible effort to accommodate children's styles once they become aware of their own learning and teaching styles.

Student-teachers' enthusiasm about learning styles also makes them desirable to employers. One recruiter told Dr. Carroll how one of her students had responded to his inquiry about learning styles. He said:

> Her eyes lit up, she began telling about the class, and explained how knowledge of her own and the children's styles had helped her plan and introduce lessons. She even described how the children had used their styles to demonstrate what they had learned and how even that had helped her to evaluate the outcomes. She opened her portfolio and showed photographs of resources she had made and lesson plans she had developed to include learning-styles-based instructional methods.

The recruiter also admitted that he had never seen such a rich variety of resources and so much positive excitement generated by both excellent results and creative work! Dr. Carroll admits, "I'm sold on learning styles. I believe in the concept and have seen the results of what happens when students become aware of learning styles. They are much more understanding of each other—and of the children they teach."

## REFERENCES

Dunn, R., & Dunn, K. (1992). *Teaching elementary students through their individual learning styles: Practical approaches for grades 3–6*. Boston: Allyn & Bacon.

Dunn, R., & Dunn, K. (1993). *Teaching secondary students through their individual learning styles: Practical approaches for grades 7–12*. Boston: Allyn & Bacon.

Dunn, R., Dunn, K. & Perrin, J. (1994). *Teaching young children through their individual learning styles*. Boston: Allyn & Bacon.

Dunn, R., Dunn, K., & Price, G.E. (1975–1996). *Learning Style Inventory*. Lawrence, KS: Price Systems.

Dunn, R., Dunn, K., & Price, G.E. (1979, 1980, 1996). *Productivity Environmental Preference Survey*. Lawrence, KS: Price Systems.

*Chapter 8*

# Mary Laffey: Missouri's "Principal of the Year"

*Andrea Honigsfeld and Rita Dunn*

Come take a trip to Columbia, Missouri—the location *Money Magazine* constantly ranks among the "best places to live in the nation" in its annual survey of the 300 largest cities of the United States! Columbia is right in the center of Missouri—between St. Louis and Kansas City. If you've come this far, you must meet an outstanding educator—recipient of the Metropolitan Life/National Association of Secondary School Principals' (NASSP) 1995 award for "best principal in the state of Missouri"—Dr. Mary A. Laffey! This petite, charming, erudite woman will welcome you at Oakland Junior High School, a lovely building on a peaceful, tree-lined neighborhood in Columbia.

## PERSONAL BACKGROUND

Mary Laffey has been the principal of Oakland Junior High School for almost a decade and a half. Prior to that, she served as assistant principal in that very same building. Under her tutelage, Oakland Junior High School was recognized twice as an outstanding junior high school in Missouri. Dr. Laffey has seen Columbia, her "favorite place in the Midwest," more than double, from a small town of 35,000, and develop into what has been described as one of the most highly recommended environments in which to live and rear children in the nation!

Dr. Laffey is a dedicated educator with an extensive background at the middle school level. Her expertise includes such diverse foci as reading remediation, learning styles, individualized instruction, and teaming teachers for an integrated curriculum approach.

Mary Laffey appears ready to consistently assume leadership roles—inside and outside the school district. Concurrently, she served as president of the Missouri Association for Supervision and Curriculum Development (MASCD), middle-level representative for the Missouri Association of Secondary School Principals (MASSP), and on the state committee of the North Central Association that accredits schools in that region!

## THE SCHOOL DISTRICT

The young people attending Oakland Junior High School also have seen many changes in the past few years—a period of intensive restructuring. Oakland Junior High School's student population has steadily increased but, at the same time, there has been extensive teacher turnover. Nevertheless, these students have been fortunate. Their school is located in one of the top 16 model districts in the nation, as recognized by the National Governors' Association. Their school also was acclaimed a Nationally Recognized School for Excellence in Drug-Free Education and received recognition as one of the nation's "outstanding junior high schools." Directly related to these accomplishments, students are aware that their principal has been recognized as one of the best principals in the state of Missouri!

This growing district serves nearly 16,000 culturally diverse students in 28 schools, and accounts for an annual student population growth of 300 to 400. In that regard, Columbia students represent more than 25 different nations throughout the world.

Another way in which the Columbia School District excels is in the number of its graduates who continue their education into college. During the past few years, more than 75 percent of graduating seniors have been accepted into higher education; the state's average is approximately 55 percent!

## IN THE BEGINNING

Oakland Junior High School, like any public school you might walk into, has its share of students who do not achieve as well as the majority. These youngsters frequently become increasingly frustrated because of their academic failures and desperately need their teachers' personalized attention and assistance. As a result of Mary Laffey's personal interest in and concern for these adolescents, she specifically instituted a program designed to identify *how* these students could learn new and difficult information—she identified their learning styles. Then she provided extensive staff programs to develop Oakland's teachers' ability to teach with instructional approaches that complemented the poorly achieving students' styles.

Toward that end, she originally enrolled for training with both the *Gregorc Learning Style Delineator* and then McCarthy's 4MAT model. However, it was not until she participated in St. John's University's Annual Learning-Styles Leadership Institute in New York City (1988) that she felt she had found a valid and reliable tool to address the needs of the poor readers in her school. That Institute provided training in the use of the Dunn and Dunn Learning-Style Model. Dr. Laffey found this model to be "practitioner-oriented; it provided sensible *how-to* applications for both teachers and students."

In 1989, when Oakland Junior High School administrators evaluated and then critically analyzed the school's reading program, they recognized that the approaches being used had not enabled sufficient academic progress by poorly reading youngsters. The reading specialist at that time, Denise Parker, was eager to know what she could do to help the struggling seventh-, eighth-, and ninth-grade readers. Because Principal Laffey had just returned from St. John's University's Learning-Styles Leadership Institute, she was eager to address the special needs of Oakland's students and decided to target the neediest students first—those in the reading program.

Dr. Laffey first shared the Dunn and Dunn Learning-Style Model's diagnostic and prescriptive approaches with Denise Parker. The pair then jointly implemented that model with one of Ms. Parker's reading classes. They witnessed immediate successes! Dr. Laffey reported: "From that initial inservice, we revised our entire reading program on the basis of that learning-style model. As the success of that program spread across the school, we gradually expanded the school focus on learning styles."

Three years later, the national journal *Teaching K–8* (Elliot, 1991) featured Oakland Junior High School as an exemplary learning-styles program because of the documented successes it had evidenced when using the Dunn and Dunn Learning-Style Model as the basis of its reading program.

## SUCCESSES

The seventh-, eighth-, and ninth-graders in Denise Parker's reading program experienced instantaneous breakthroughs. For the first time in their lives, they had been taught through their learning-style strengths rather than through their weaknesses. Most of those below-reading-level students were revealed as being tactual and/or kinesthetic learners, and Ms. Parker had all the tools necessary to respond to their uniqueness—and all the support she could wish for from her principal. Very quickly, Task Cards, Electroboards, Pic-A-Holes, and Flip Chutes replaced traditional lectures, readings, and materials. Classrooms were re-designed to permit comfortable seating and lighting. Students were encouraged to work in school and to study at home based on their sociological preferences—alone, in pairs, or in small groups. Achievement and aptitude test scores rose steadily right from the beginning. Once the learning-styles approach was in place, poor readers evidenced academic gains that never had occurred before!

## ANALYSIS

How did the success of one principal and one reading teacher in a single classroom, re-named *The Reading Place*, eventually serve students in remedial reading throughout the entire building? Mary Laffey's answer was in the particular brand of instructional leadership she exercised, combined with the soundness of the Dunn and Dunn Learning-Style Model. She explained:

> Beginning a learning-styles program is cost-effective. It is far more expensive to save or redirect disenfranchised learners than to prevent their failure. It actually costs more *not* to meet the needs of students because of the ultimate costs of retention and the increased special education services that become necessary when remediating students' deficiencies.

Gradually, the learning-styles program at Oakland Junior High School was expanded.

- All incoming seventh-graders were administered the *Learning Style Inventory* (LSI) (Dunn, Dunn, & Price, 1975–1996).

- Students were shown how to use their learning-style strengths when studying difficult information.

- Teachers were provided ongoing staff development in learning-style-responsive strategies.

- Some of Denise Parker's colleagues started using those approaches in mathematics and social studies as well as reading. When they, too, saw students' immediately increased scores, Dr. Laffey felt the need to educate everybody about the effects of learning-styles-based teaching.

- Parents and business owners in the community were extended invitations to learn about the school's learning-styles approaches during short information sessions. Parents responded most positively. They recognized the individuality of their own children and applauded the school for endeavoring to help them improve.

- The Superintendent of Schools and the Board of Education had been introduced to the concept prior to any implementation efforts and had been supportive of the program from the beginning. They also were appreciative of Dr. Laffey's "front-line leadership," the teachers' willingness to experiment, and the extensive parental support.

During the past decade, Mary Laffey has remained a dedicated leader of learning styles. In 1991, after providing initial inservice for her teachers, she gained full support from the School Board, which financed a team of Oakland's teachers to attend the Annual Learning-Styles Leadership Institute in New York. A few years later, Professor Rita Dunn personally provided advanced inservice training in the Columbia Public School District. By 1995, that school district offered a three-hour college course in learning styles and a five-day summer institute on-site for its staff. Teachers trained and certified by St. John's University's Center for the Study of Learning and Teaching Styles teach these classes.

During the past few years, Oakland Junior High School has been restructured to best meet the needs of its changing student population. At the same time, the growing number of young, inexperienced teachers on staff resulted in a refocus on the learning-styles program. Mary Laffey believes that her role as a supervisor is to help new teachers build a strong instructional base with tools and strategies that respond to the needs of the youngsters they are required to educate. Learning styles is one of the strategies that all new staff members are required to master from the very beginning of their careers in that school!

## SUMMARY

What are Dr. Mary Laffey's personal beliefs? She remains convinced that learning styles have benefited her enormously as an educator and instructional leader. Through that process, she found the key to unlock the door to learning for those students who had not succeeded without it. She also recognized that awareness of her own learning and teaching styles improved her leadership ability and permitted her to reach more of her staff more effectively.

A final word of advice to colleagues from Mary Laffey:

> Begin with teachers who are interested. Help them become aware of their own learning and teaching styles and the power of helping youngsters take charge of their own learning. Students and their parents become your strongest advocates! That and their improved grades become the driving force that wins everyone else!

## REFERENCES

Dunn, R., Dunn, K., & Price, G.E. (1975–1996). *Learning Style Inventory.* Lawrence, KS: Price Systems.

Elliot, I. (1991, November/December). The reading place. *Teaching K-8, 21*(3), 30–34.

*Chapter 9*

# Ann Braio: Big-City Director of Special Education

*Andrea Honigsfeld and Rita Dunn*

Yonkers, a school district with more than 3,000 Special Education (SPED) students, can be seen as a challenging undertaking for any administrator. However, Dr. Ann C. Braio is certainly not just any administrator. This diversified urban setting, just north of New York City, is the fourth largest city in the state. Because of the many divergent cultures and ethnic groups that have relocated to Yonkers, this city has changed extensively during the past years.

Yonkers' projected revitalization program for its downtown waterfront area, coupled with federal and state initiatives to improve the education of all students, should yield positive outcomes for its citizens. These changes also should impact positively on its SPED population. Dr. Braio, an extraordinary professional, takes on Yonkers' challenges with ease, zest, and a passion for helping all students under her tutelage.

This energetic, five-foot-one woman, with a consistent smile, exudes enthusiasm toward everyone. Her unpretentious manner puts any visitor at ease immediately. Perhaps Dr. Braio, director of SPED for the past two years, can attribute her success to the fact that she rose from within the ranks of the Yonkers Public Schools. This is a woman who grew up and flourished within the system during a two-decade period.

## PERSONAL BACKGROUND

"Annie" is a "born" educator—the teacher who consistently wants to better herself and the lives of all the children with whom she interacts. She began her professional career as a young General Education teacher of second-graders in a small Catholic school in 1970. During the eight years she worked at Holy Cross School, parents of her most needy students constantly turned to her for advice and guidance concerning how to help their children achieve better. At about that time, during the 1970s, SPED was an upcoming field in response to the federal regulations known as Public Law 94–142. That law mandated the provision of SPED services for eligible students, and Ann Braio was among the first educators to become deeply involved with translating the spirit of the federal legislation into practical classroom strategies to improve education for children who found it difficult to cope with traditional schooling. Dr. Braio wanted to be part of that movement because she strongly believed in addressing the special needs of underachievers scientifically—and it seemed to her that PL 94–142 was leading in that direction. That law required that educators identify poorly performing students and analyze *why* they had become underachievers. The next step was to develop an individualized educational plan for each so that every teacher with whom they came into contact would know the most appropriate resources and instructional strategies to use to teach each youngster, based on a team of experts' planning.

After earning a master's degree in SPED, Ann worked with neurologically impaired elementary school students for seven years. Her intelligent insights and never-ending effort and dedication were acknowledged with the Jenkins Award, an annual recognition allocated to the "best teacher of the year."

Dr. Braio never ceased seeking new and better information. She yearned to expand her own knowledge base and returned to higher education for a second master's degree in School Administration and Supervision. Gradually, she completed a professional diploma in Instructional Leadership and kept being promoted from one position to another. These included assignments as a SPED chairperson, teacher trainer, SPED coordinator, principal and, in 1997, the district-wide SPED director of the Yonkers City Public Schools.

Responsibility for overseeing the academic, social, and emotional development of more than 3,000 "special needs youngsters" under the guidance and instruction of approximately 200 Special Educators was exactly what Ann felt ready to handle. A graduate of St. John's University, Ann was confident that she had received the best preparation possible for this challenging new position. She had earned both a professional diploma and doctorate examining and researching the construct of individual learning styles (Dunn & Dunn, 1992, 1993; Dunn, Dunn, & Perrin, 1994). Her studies under the direct mentorship of Professor Rita Dunn, whom she considers a friend and inspiration, had helped her realize that learning-style-responsive instruction was the way to reach all her underachieving students, regardless of their official labels in either general education (GENED) or SPED. The combination of Dr. Braio's excellent educational and experiential background, plus her in-depth research on learning styles, had suggested that children who were not performing well in conventional schools were those who needed different environments and approaches than most teachers had been taught to provide.

## THE SCHOOL DISTRICT

Yonkers is the largest public school district in Westchester County. It contains more than 23,000 students who speak 41 languages. Their parents are immigrants from approximately 100 nations and the children are being taught by more than 3,500 teachers. Students attend one of 38 neighborhood schools surrounded by historic sites, museums of local and American history, and a wildlife sanctuary overlooking the magnificent Hudson River.

The school district takes pride in being characterized as innovative. Its leadership believes in teamwork and considers it a key element in producing effective schooling. Innovative magnet programs, specific curriculum activities, and a wide range of extracurricular programs have been offered to students of all ability levels because of the district belief that centers around providing high-quality SPED services for all who would benefit from them.

## IN THE BEGINNING

As a doctoral student at St. John's University, Ann immersed herself in the study of learning styles. She experimented by responding to the various identified learning-style preferences of her own SPED students. For example, one year, she had a group of youngsters who did not seem to be responding to the multitude of visual and tactual resources that Ann had provided for them. After administering the *Learning Style Inventory* (Dunn, Dunn, & Price, 1994), she found that most of her students were highly auditory and global children who attended better to stories and anecdotes than to factual information. She suddenly understood and, therefore, could respond to the needs of, these auditory youngsters who so liked listening to stories. She then authored a book, *Mission from No-Style: Wonder and Joy Meet the Space Children* (Braio, 1988) to explain the concept of learning styles to the children through a storybook so that they could understand how they each learned. This book has been translated into several languages and has been used by hundreds of educators throughout the world since its inception.

## THE SUCCESSES

Over time, the focus of education in Yonkers was re-directed. Rather than SPED or Resource Room classes in which poorly achieving students were isolated for segments of the school day, a strong move toward inclusion was launched by the New York State Education Department. Inclusion required that SPED students be maintained in GENED classrooms and receive instruction from specialists within their regular classes—rather than apart. Ann's doctoral thesis focused on researching a system in which both SPED and GENED students gradually were introduced to selected learning-styles approaches as part of the instruction provided for both. While teaching a variety of grammar units, the teachers under Ann's supervision incrementally introduced strategies for responding to students' varied environmental and perceptual preferences (Braio, Beasley, Dunn, Quinn, & Buchanan, 1997). Those strategies not only statistically increased students' achievement, but also successfully facilitated the integration of the two groups.

As a result of that successful 10-week research study, Ann revealed the effectiveness of learning-styles-based instruction for SPED students. In addition, although that research was completed in 1994, the teachers whom Ann taught to develop—and have their students create—tactual/kinesthetic resources continue to use those materials because of the gains their charges made.

## TEACHER TRAINER

The New York State–supported SPED and Training and Resource Center (SETRC) of Yonkers consistently has conducted inservice courses on learning styles. The intent was to motivate and encourage teachers to create learning-styles classrooms replete with instructional materials for highly tactual, kinesthetic, or global students—who comprise the largest percentage of SPED students. Parents also were encouraged to use learning-styles approaches at home with their children when working on new and difficult academic assignments. Ann has been a pivotal leader in providing many of these workshops for SETRC and multiple other agencies.

In addition, Ann also has been teaching learning-styles undergraduate education courses at Manhattan College. She capitalizes on her adult students' learning-style preferences to demonstrate the relative effectiveness of learning difficult information through individuals' unique strengths. Finally, she frequently serves as a guest speaker at St. John's University's Annual Leadership Certification Institute in New York City and has served on several students' doctoral dissertation committees.

## SUMMARY

Dr. Ann Braio has been on her own mission for learning styles for decades. She is an outspoken advocate of using learning styles to individualize instruction. She considers one of her life calls to be teaching others about learning styles and to share the various strategies that relate to it with colleagues, so that the next generation of educators also can benefit from it.

Ann believes that one of the luckiest experiences she has had was to be exposed to the extensive research and responsive strategies of learning-styles approaches during her doctoral studies. Once she became aware of how she learned best, she understood how to use her personal strengths and learning-style preferences to her advantage. She then was able to apply what she had learned to her own growth and success. This is the knowledge she is committed to sharing with as many people as possible through her work as a SPED director and college teacher.

## REFERENCES

Braio, A. (1988). *Mission from no-style: Wonder and Joy meet the Space Children.* Jamaica, NY: St. John's University's Center for the Study of Learning and Teaching Styles.

Braio, A., Dunn, R., Beasley, M.T., Quinn, P., & Buchanan, K. (1997). Incremental implementation of learning-style strategies among urban low achievers. *Journal of Educational Research, 91,* 15–25.

Dunn, R., & Dunn, K. (1992). *Teaching elementary students through their individual learning styles: Practical approaches for grades 3–6.* Boston: Allyn & Bacon.

Dunn, R., & Dunn, K. (1993). *Teaching secondary students through their individual learning styles: Practical approaches for grades 7–12.* Boston: Allyn & Bacon.

Dunn, R., Dunn, K., & Perrin, J. (1994). *Teaching young children through their individual learning styles.* Boston: Allyn & Bacon.

Dunn, R., Dunn, K., & Price, G.E. (1975–1996). *Learning Style Inventory.* Lawrence, KS: Price Systems.

*Chapter 10*

# Tana Martin Finds That Learning Styles Add Up in El Campo, Texas

*Maryann Kiely Lovelace and Rita Dunn*

What can you do if your district's standardized test scores need improvement? Tana Martin, the Mathematics K-12 Supervisor in the El Campo Independent School District in Texas had to find a way to reach students who had not successfully mastered the mathematics portion of the state's exit examination, the *Texas Assessment of Academic Skills* (TAAS). Her response was to implement a learning-styles program.

El Campo is a culturally diverse, rural district with students of mixed socioeconomic levels. Tana described both the community and the educators as "closely knit and concerned with the education of *all* students within the district." The El Campo High School staff was described as "both mature and experienced."

Learning styles were introduced to teachers in staff development sessions provided by Brenda Spiess, mathematics consultant for Quality Education Systems in Richardson, Texas. Tana indicated that the Dunn and Dunn model was chosen because it:

- has a strong research base;
- helps teachers understand why many global, tactile, and/or kinesthetic learners struggle when learning math; and
- includes strategies that validate global or right-brained intelligence patterns by showing how to produce learning successes.

The inservice session began with a full day of teacher training that focused on global learners and demonstrated strategies responsive to each modality preference. That initial training was followed by two more visits that encouraged the creation of materials to be used in classroom instruction. The end result was that each mathematics teacher developed a set of learning-styles manipulatives for each targeted mathematics objective.

The first learning-styles materials developed by these teachers were selected "to target student modality preferences—with particular emphasis on resources for teaching tactile and kinesthetic learners." At first, tactual materials were created to reinforce targeted mathematics concepts with hands-on manipulatives such as Learning Circles, Pick-an-Answer Cards, "Home-Light" Cards (single-question Electroboards), Match-Mate Card Strips, folders, and posters. The next set of materials was focused on helping kinesthetic learners. Teachers designed kinesthetic activities to motivate and engage students through games and competitions.

The program was a success! According to Tana, "The learning-styles program certainly helped us improve students' TAAS scores!" She and her colleagues did not believe that it was the sole reason for the success, but it certainly played a huge part! Although many changes subsequently were made, the learning-styles program provided a beginning vehicle for communicating the curriculum to students in ways they enjoyed learning, and it enabled them to master the objectives.

Academic gains were documented. Previously, in grades five through eight, only 60 percent or less of the students had passed mathematics. After the learning-styles program was implemented in 1996–1997 during their sophomore year, more than 80 percent of the students passed mathematics. This was a dramatic increase in student performance!

Caucasian students tended to outperform their economically disadvantaged African-American and Hispanic counterparts. However, after learning-styles instruction, all cultural groups performed better than previous classes in the same school. In addition, African-American students evidenced the most dramatic increases. Historically, no more than 30 percent of these students had passed mathematics. After the learning-styles program had been implemented, more than 70 percent passed.

Hispanic students increased from less than 50 percent who were passing to more than 70 percent passing. Caucasian students increased from approximately 80 percent to 100 percent passing—remarkable by anyone's standards! Economically disadvantaged students improved from no more than 45 percent passing to more than 60 percent passing mathematics.

These increases convinced Tana that all students could succeed. "I have always believed that all children could learn—and would, if the materials were presented in a way that worked for them. No one expects all students to learn at the same speed or produce the same quality of work, but they *can* learn!"

As a result of these successes, Ms. Martin planned to expand the program to more mathematics classes, such as Algebra I, Algebra II, and Geometry, and to eventually revise the entire district into a total learning-styles program. She looked "forward to expanding what we currently are doing."

Ms. Martin has been a firsthand witness to how learning styles completely changed the attitudes of an entire staff. "I personally have seen a whole group of teachers become extremely motivated toward teaching math in my own department at El Campo High School! Their attitudes have become totally positive because of their successes—with both their innovative learning-styles instruction and their students' improved grades." She is certain that the initial training the teachers experienced was crucial to their success and that the major components that contributed to their successful learning-styles math program included:

- having basic training with follow-up sessions;
- a presenter who conducted the training who also was teaching and using learning styles in her own classroom on a daily basis;
- access to sturdy, high-quality manipulative materials that made the individualization of instruction quick and easy;
- time to create needed resources; and
- teaming with other math teachers who also shared the same curriculum and pressures.

Tana Martin concluded with the following advice for supervisors interested in implementing learning styles successfully.

> Be patient! Having educators attend learning-styles inservice will not insure that they use it in their daily teaching. It takes time and their colleagues' success stories to get them thinking in terms of changing what they do. Even then, all teachers will not "buy into" any single thing, but watching the teachers who are having success with the program usually is all it takes!

*Chapter 11*

# Jan Meritt Sees Merit in Using Learning Styles with All Students in Klamath Falls, Oregon

*Maryann Kiely Lovelace and Rita Dunn*

What do you do when your daughter's second-grade teacher tells you that your child belongs in Special Education and you *know* that she's wrong; worse, you know that Special Education is not the answer for your child?

Mrs. Meritt attended her first learning-styles workshop in the hope of finding ways to help her daughter Emily, who was experiencing many problems in school. By Jan's own admission, she "never dreamed" she would use learning-style methods with her secondary science students! However, as she worked with the Dunn and Dunn Learning-Style Model with her daughter, she found that it "*made sense* and should work for *all* kids!"

It has been almost a decade since Jan first was exposed to learning-style strategies but, since that first year, she has been beginning her chemistry classes each September by "commenting about learning-style things that happen in class." For example, she will say, "That was a global answer. Can you be more specific?" or "It's OK; you're just not auditory. Write it into your notebook and illustrate it so that you'll remember!" Jan assures her students that, in her class, they will "find out how they learn so that each can get the most value out of the time they spend studying." She emphasizes that she will show students how they can raise their grades *without* increasing the amount of time they study. By the time Jan introduces the Dunn and Dunn Learning-Style Model and discusses its extensive research base, her students are ready to "SEE, HEAR and TOUCH learning styles!" When Ms. Meritt discusses the differences among how people learn, she uses examples from her own family as well as from past and present students. She also stresses that "no learning style is better than any other; just different!"

The highly successful learning-styles program in Klamath Falls began when the district sent a team of interested teachers to the one-week Annual

Learning-Styles Certification Institute in New York City. The teachers who went to New York for training were referred to as the "Learning-Styles Cadre." That trip for the training obligated each of them to provide staff development for other interested district staff. Ms. Meritt believes that the personal characteristics of the teachers involved in that initial program contributed substantially to the program's success, for they were open to change, well respected in the community, and able to communicate easily with their peers.

She recalls that "The cadre met once a month as a support group. In the beginning, that mutual support made a big difference. Any problem that, at the moment, seemed overwhelming, quickly was put into proper perspective at those meetings." She strongly feels that anyone trying to implement a learning-styles program should have a similar group of colleagues on whom to lean.

Parents and community leaders were informed about learning styles to solicit their enthusiasm and involvement. A full-page story explaining the program appeared in the local newspaper. Whenever a local learning-styles workshop was presented, parents and community members were invited to participate.

Elementary teachers planned evening presentations at which they introduced the learning-style model to parents and advised them of what to anticipate in terms of their children's reports about classroom activities. In her high school, Jan set up a display about learning styles for Parent Conference Night. She noticed that many parents of students who were not enrolled in her classes came to speak with her about learning styles. She also noted that "Parents really were impressed with the Electroboards the students were using to learn science!"

Jan noticed two problems in the implementation of the Klamath Falls Learning-Styles Program and suggested solutions for them. First, her district did not require its administrators to attend the same training as its teachers. She believes that "for a program to be successful, administrators and teachers need to have the same understandings and talk the same language. Not requiring administrators to attend the workshop hindered the pace at which the program was implemented and, ultimately, its continuation over time as new administrators replaced former ones."

The second problem occurred when students began discussing learning styles in their other classes. Jan noted that, "Some teachers wanted more information and have since adopted parts of the program. Other teachers deeply resented being told that they were not allowing for their students' learning-style differences—although they weren't." She believes that "staff support comes when other teachers see positive results; then they buy in."

In Jan's chemistry classroom, all students take the LSI and receive an analysis of their results with a personalized prescription for how to do their homework. "Students then are introduced to each chapter in the book with their perceptual strength and are reinforced through their next two strengths. Once students know their strengths and how to introduce material to themselves, their potential begins to bloom!"

The overall academic gains at Klamath Union High School have not been very dramatic because prior to the introduction of learning styles, students already were performing at an average to above-average level. However, Jan pointed out, "individual academic turnarounds really stand out!" She described a "bright, but unmotivated" student named Chris who had failed every test until he started using a Flip Chute to help him study. Jan enthusiastically reported that, after using that tactual resource, "Chris earned the highest grade in the class on the next test! He certainly used the Flip Chute a lot after that and it's hard to describe what those top science test scores did for his newly emerged confidence!"

Jan Meritt assured us that the attitudinal gains that learning styles produced were "the greatest part about the program. Learning-style strategies reduce the number of problems teachers face, so we can get on with the business of teaching." Support for this statement came from a district substitute teacher who was concerned about the reactions of several male students she previously had sent to the office for poor behavior. She told Jan that when she entered her informal classroom, noted the leisure of its seating, and recognized those boys from the previous class sitting in Jan's classroom, she was certain that she was "in for it!" To her amazement, the young men she feared were well behaved and worked during the entire period. The substitute reported that she "became a believer," and has since taken workshops on learning styles to better prepare her for working with problem students.

The resources Ms. Meritt found to be indispensable for learning-styles successes included administering the *Learning Style Inventory* (LSI) (Dunn, Dunn, & Price, 1990) to identify students' styles, an easy-to-follow learning-styles how-to textbook, the St. John's University homework disc that yields students' prescriptions, and "periodic workshops to revitalize tired teachers!" She also recommends that supervisors lend their support, provide inservice time for learning-styles development, and act as the coach and cheering squad.

Students in Jan's classes have been greatly affected by the implementation of learning styles in their classroom.

- Bonnie Davis told how she personally "figured out how to do an assignment differently so I could learn what I was doing better!"
- Juan Barajas recalled how "My grades and concentration improved and I felt less anxious while studying."
- Trish Williamson noted that "Learning styles has changed how I study because now I know how I learn and can do so faster than before."
- Bethany Sonerholm insisted that "Learning in a learning-styles classroom is easier!"

Jan Meritt believes that "learning styles produces better behaved students who are more eager to learn. A learning-styles classroom requires active involvement and builds students' self-esteem. It shows each student how to succeed!"

**REFERENCE**

Dunn, R., Dunn, K., & Price, G.E. (1995–1996). *Learning Style Inventory*. Lawrence KS: Price Systems.

*Chapter 12*

# Mary Cecilia Giannitti: Guiding Angel of Hempstead's Sacred Heart

*Thomas C. DeBello and Rita Dunn*

> The day our little school closed was a very sad day for me, our teachers and our students. We were doing so much good for so many young people!
>
> —Sr. Mary Cecilia Giannitti

Indeed they were—as verified by many published articles and a chapter in a book describing "a quiet revolution" in successful secondary schools in the United States (Dunn & Griggs, 1988, 1989a, b). Sacred Heart Seminary in Hempstead, New York adopted a learning-styles approach to instruction in 1979; diocesan financial issues required it to close 15 years later. During that decade and a half, students experienced the wisdom and guidance of a real-life angel who taught them how to teach themselves, and each other, through their individual learning styles!

## HOW THE PROGRAM EMERGED

Before adopting learning styles, students at Sacred Heart were taught with traditional whole-class methods exclusively. According to Dr. Giannitti, achievement levels were "average" and discipline was not what it should have been. It became apparent to her that changes were needed.

Through doctoral studies at St. John's University, she became aware of the learning-styles approach. She was "intrigued with the Dunn and Dunn model's accurate diagnoses of how students learn and how to teach them based on their strengths."

As principal of the school, she began by encouraging her teachers to "just try" a few individualized activities based on their students' interests and abilities. She explained the concept to members of the school's executive board, won their support, and decided to launch a program school-wide. From that simple beginning grew an exemplary model school that attracted national and international visitors and spawned many replication projects.

What were the first steps Sr. Mary took?

- At least one year before launching the learning-styles program, she introduced the entire teaching staff to basic learning-styles instructional strategies.
- She explained with which students each method was likely to be effective and challenged them to see whether her predictions were accurate.
- She encouraged classroom experimentation with learning-styles strategies and asked for feedback.
- When teachers used the new methods with their classes, she asked them to share the results briefly at faculty meetings.
- When some teachers resisted, she explained the research that showed the significantly increased achievement test scores in schools capitalizing on students' learning styles.
- She insisted that the techniques were "good for children and we owe it to them to help them learn in any way they can!"
- In two cases where teachers remained recalcitrant, she suggested they find employment elsewhere.
- She involved parents in the dream she had to build "the best school in the diocese," and taught them to create instructional resources for the students who were unable to produce their own.
- She taught students to create their own instructional materials and to teach themselves and their classmates.
- She elevated academic expectations for everyone.
- She inspired children to find "better ways of learning and teaching each other" and tolerated no failure. When students did not succeed with one method, she insisted, "Let's try another way!"
- She got the entire faculty to work together making instructional resources and helped them develop new forms of classroom management to complement the new procedures.
- Through all this, she remained unassuming, but persistent. She had established a utopian goal and it was going to have "a fair chance!"
- At each faculty meeting and on professional days, staff continued to learn more and more about learning styles.
- One at a time, she went into each classroom to demonstrate how the new strategies worked.
- In 1979, custodians, parents, and some of the older students helped to re-design the entire school to facilitate the new approach—with little or no additional monies. The excitement and enthusiasm that evolved "won everyone's support!"

Even with an energized staff eager to change, staff development and support were critical factors. Continuing on-the-job training was always part of the process. In time, Sr. Mary recognized that her efforts had paid off. Because of this program, she spent less time on discipline and more time on supporting teachers in their classrooms.

Dr. Mary Cecilia Giannitti learned not to "give teachers too much at once" and overwhelm them with information. On occasion, she gave them "a shot of adrenaline" by bringing in consultants from the Center for the Study of Learning and Teaching Styles. However, *she* personally supported faculty on an almost daily basis throughout the process. Her only regret was that, during those early days, there were no learning-style schools her teachers could visit to see what the program should have looked like. "It's always easier to improve on what somebody else has done than to create a perfect model from scratch!"

## WHAT WAS SACRED HEART AND ITS STUDENTS LIKE?

Visitors' initial reactions to Sacred Heart Seminary often centered around the picturesque facility and the ideal number of students per class—each impeccably dressed in slate-gray trousers or a skirt and a blue blouse. It was difficult to persuade them that a learning environment that seemed "just right for individualizing instruction" had not always been that way. Indeed, visitors often believed that Sacred Heart was a school for children from well-to-do families.

Actually, adolescents attending this grade 6–8 school were bussed in from 34 different school districts and often were the offspring of mobile military personnel and transient professionals. Many of the students previously had failed in their schools. In an era before societal recognition of child abuse, many of these youngsters had been subjected to military-type discipline meted out by fathers used to living in an essentially autocratic adult environment. Many of the students came from divorced or separated families where both parents worked. More often than not, they lived in a single-parent environment barely above the national poverty level (Dunn & Griggs, 1989).

> Some parents had registered their offspring in Sacred Heart Seminary as a last resort; the children had either failed in, or "hated" their previous schools. Initially, those students exemplified the typical frustrations of at-risk or dropout populations. They were either aggressive or withdrawn, boisterous or non-communicative, conforming or non-conforming. Dr./Sister Mary Cecilia Giannitti (began) each youngster's schooling by testing for learning style and explaining how he or she (was) most likely to succeed academically. (Dunn & Griggs, 1989a, p. 56)

Because instruction was based on what that learning-styles diagnostic test revealed, the results quickly became apparent. Within weeks, parents were telephoning the school to express their appreciation for the changes they saw in their children's attitudes and behaviors.

## WHAT CHANGES WERE MADE?

Before introducing learning styles, general meetings of parents and students were held. At those meetings, both groups were informed of the changes that would enable students to have options for learning in terms of their perceptual modalities and environmental preferences. Other changes accompanied different modifications. For example:

- Small-group strategies like Team Learning, Circle of Knowledge, Brainstorming, and Case Studies were adopted to permit students to study alone, in a pair, in a small group of three or four, or directly with the teacher.
- Classroom management included new wall charts to direct students to use their strongest modality first when learning. They then were guided toward using their second strongest modality for reinforcing.
- Re-designed classrooms included both formal and informal seating, areas for discussion and interaction, and other areas for quiet contemplation and focusing while concentrating.
- New reporting procedures for parent conferences in which students were invited to participate!

Parents were delighted with the reports of their children working on new and exciting individualized and group activities. In fact, many parents offered to assist in any way possible. These are the changes that were made to directly affect instruction:

- Every attempt was made to accommodate students' preferred time of day through flexible scheduling and rotation of classes by cycle so that all courses were taught at some time during students' peak energy periods. Eighth-graders were permitted to take their standardized achievement tests during the preferred time of day of the largest cluster of students.
- Every classroom included both traditional seating and an informal carpeted area where students could work without tension. Dr. Giannitti reported that this transformation of a totally conventional school into one that at least partially suggested permissiveness to visitors was not easy for her personally. Had the research on children's need to be relaxed while concentrating not been so strong, she might not have experimented with this particular aspect of learning styles. As it worked out, this was one of the most effective strategies incorporated!
- When small group instructional strategies were introduced in 1980, both the principal and teachers anticipated the worst, for many of their students had consistently

been admonished for not sitting erectly, quietly, or attentively. Gradually, as the teachers' repertoire of style-responsive strategies expanded to include student-centered techniques for cooperatively learning and reinforcing new and difficult academic information, the faculty became aware of how much better their adolescent population was learning. As a result, teachers kept adding more and more peer-oriented approaches. Eventually, prospective faculty were indoctrinated in those strategies as a condition of their employment!

• Teachers taught all students to introduce new and difficult academic material through their strongest perceptual modality and to reinforce that same material through their second strongest modality (Dunn & Griggs, 1989b). Then, for homework, each student was required to *use* the new information learned that day in a *creative* way by developing a new resource. The next time the class met, 10 minutes were spent by the students in *sharing* with one, two, or three classmates the resource each had made for homework. After they corrected each others' resources, those were mounted on classroom walls for others to share during "free" moments.

• Every student became cognizant of his/her learning-style strengths and could verbalize what he/she was learning, how, and why to anyone who questioned. That also was accurate for Sacred Heart Seminary's elementary school component as well!


## WHAT WERE THE RESULTS?

In 1986–1987, the *Iowa Test of Basic Skills* was administered to all Sacred Heart students in their best time frames—early morning or afternoon. Eighty-five percent of the middle school students achieved at the middle of the tenth-grade level (10.5) at a time when other diocesan students' overall scores were *decreasing!*

Students' achievement and attitudes toward school improved greatly, and word of the school's successes spread. One parent wrote:

> Within weeks, we saw remarkable changes in attitude(s) and behavior(s), and an increase in self-esteem. . . . In an era when the dropout rate is rising, and boredom, apathy and poor behavior have become the norm. . . . Sacred Heart's students are orderly, well behaved, and most important, succeeding academically.

Because its entire staff had become totally committed to this program, visitors observed learning styles in action throughout the day at every grade level. In addition, Sacred Heart Seminary received awards for its excellence. However, it was evident that, to Sr. Mary, the best accolades came from her students. Students consistently recognized the benefit of the learning-styles program to them personally. The following accounts were typical of *students' evaluations of the program*:

- I really learned so much since I started this school. I learned to teach myself!
- In this school, I learned how to learn information!
- It is better to take the test at your best time of day. You can do better (Dunn & Griggs, 1989b).
- This is the best school I ever attended!
- Everyone should go to a school like this!

Implementation of the learning-styles-based program did not come without some expense, but Sr. Mary explained that, through a redeployment of funds formerly used for workbooks and other conventional supplements to textbook programs, some money became available. Additionally, the parental support that had been promised materialized, and much of it came in the form of making hands-on resources for students' classroom use.

## A DECADE LATER

What advice would Sr. Mary Cecilia Giannitti offer supervisors just starting to introduce a learning-styles program? After identifying learning styles and discussing them with students, she believed that "creating an environment that can provide for those differences" was crucial. In addition, sustaining staff commitment over 15 years was no easy accomplishment. She recommended that supervisors "stay on top of" the current research and share it with teachers and parents on a continuing basis. And, whenever possible, teachers should visit other schools that are using learning styles to exchange ideas and keep their own strategies fresh and energizing.

Sacred Heart Seminary had a strong impact on its former students, teachers, and the profession itself. Although the school is no longer operative, Mary Cecilia Giannitti knows the good it has done and the lasting contribution it has made. She continues to support learning styles through adjunct teaching at Dowling College in Oakdale, New York—and elsewhere.

## REFERENCES

Dunn, R., & Griggs, S.A. (1988). *Learning styles: Quiet revolution in American secondary schools.* Reston, VA: National Association of Secondary School Principals.

Dunn, R., & Griggs, S.A. (1989a). A quiet revolution in Hempstead. *Teaching K–8, 18*(5), 54–57.

Dunn, R., & Griggs, S.A. (1989b). Learning styles: Quiet revolution in American secondary schools. *Momentum, 63*(1), 40–42.

*Chapter 13*

# Patricia Lemmon: A Delicious Kansas Lemmon-Aid!

*Jeannie Ryan and Rita Dunn*

Fate often is capricious! In 1990, the Hutchinson, Kansas School District elected to send two administrators to St. John's University's Annual Learning-Styles Institute in New York City. The male principal who had been enrolled suddenly decided to transfer to another district. The assistant superintendent then elected to send a replacement—Ms. Patricia Sue Lemmon, principal of Hutchinson's Roosevelt Elementary School. What we vividly remember was the telephone call received shortly before the Institute: "We're sending a replacement—a very conservative principal. We don't expect much change, but no other principal can attend on such short notice!"

When Ms. Lemmon first walked into the introductory session, she certainly appeared to be conservative by New York standards—in clothing, decorum, hair-do, and lack of cosmetics. During that entire week, she maintained an elegant poise indicative of a stereotypical school teacher; her manner, somber speech, dark-toned clothing, and pensive mood apparently did not contribute to much gaiety. However, that same Ms. Lemmon who initially expressed only minimal sympathy for the principles or practices of learning styles internalized everything she heard and gradually brought a vivid new form of schooling to rural Kansas. And she positively affected the lives of many young children.

## IN THE BEGINNING

One week of exposure to practitioners who had been using learning styles intrigued Ms. Lemmon. She thought it was a "common-sense approach to instruction that not only tells you what to do but also how to do it." Principally, however, she was interested in the research indicating that "easy-to-do strategies actually increased achievement!"

Ms. Lemmon returned to the Roosevelt Elementary School and gave an adult learning-styles identification instrument, the *Productivity Environmental Preference Survey* (PEPS) (Dunn, Dunn, & Price, 1979, 1980), to her staff. Knowledge of their own styles intrigued many of them. She then provided introductory training for teachers and introduced the concept to some of the other school personnel—secretaries, the school nurse and librarian, and the custodian. One year was spent on introducing learning-style practices into the school. Eventually, Ms. Lemmon "knew it was working" when she noticed that more and more classrooms were being re-designed to accommodate diverse styles and the staff became talkative about the changes they observed in students.

Ms. Lemmon also overviewed learning style for Roosevelt's PTA, assessed the participants' learning styles, and rode the wave of their excitement. Because of the PTA's enthusiasm, she was advised that she could count on parental financial support. Subsequently, the PTA paid for the annual assessment of students' styles and for selected materials and equipment.

## RESULTS OF THE LEARNING-STYLES PROGRAM

It was no wonder that the PTA was supportive. Roosevelt Elementary School's *Iowa Tests of Basic Skills* (ITBS) scores were compared with those of other schools in the same district. The scores for African-American, Hispanic American, Euro-American, and free or reduced-lunch students were not significantly different from each other. In addition, their ITBS scores were higher for Ms. Lemmon's school. She called that "a landmark discovery!" Furthermore, Roosevelt's Special Education students also had benefited from the learning-styles instruction.

After the use of learning styles, Roosevelt Elementary School had only 2 or 3 percent of its population identified as Learning Disabled (LD). Ms. Lemmon explained the reason behind the low number. "Teachers recognized our students' differences and addressed those differences through their learning styles." One observer noted how quiet the halls always were at Roosevelt and Ms. Lemmon explained that "when students are actively engaged in learning, they do not have time to be disruptive."

## RESULTS OF *IOWA TESTS OF BASIC SKILLS* IN READING AND MATHEMATICS

The ITBS offered another look at a remarkable testing situation. After reading about time-of-day preferences, Ms. Lemmon wondered why schools did not administer standardized achievement tests at students' highest energy levels. Therefore, she decided to see whether taking a test at a student's "best time of day" influenced his/her test results. Based on their LSI results, some students were tested in the early morning, others in the late morning, and others in the afternoon. In addition, the principal decided to allow students to take the test in the style that best suited them—in bright or dim light, at a desk or on a carpet, and while munching on a snack, if they so chose. Ms. Lemmon was amazed at the results. Significant gains in both reading and mathematics were evidenced, as well as an increase in the overall composite scores for both subjects (Lemmon, 1985)!

## ALWAYS LEARNING NEW IDEAS AND PRACTICES

One year after Ms. Lemmon introduced learning-style strategies into Roosevelt Elementary School, the National Association of Secondary School Principals and St. John's University co-sponsored the first National Conference on Learning Styles and Brain Behavior, in 1982. At one of the regular PTA meetings, Ms. Lemmon shared with parents her excitement about the new information that was emerging on the brain and the part it played in learning. One of the parents asked her whether she planned to attend that conference, to which Ms. Lemmon responded "No." He asked her why, and she explained that she had used up her travel allowance for the year at the Annual Learning-Styles Institute in New York.

Just before she turned off the light in her home that same night, Ms. Lemmon's telephone rang. It was one of the children's parents. "Pat," the father said, "You are going to that conference on the brain! A group of us have decided that it is too important for you to miss, and we have agreed to pay your travel expenses. And we want you to go!" And she did!

## THE PRINCIPAL'S PERCEPTIONS

Students, parents, and teachers were pleased with the impressive test results. But Ms. Lemmon added:

> The results of our learning-styles program were more than increased test scores. Students were more comfortable in school than they had ever been before. Parents appreciated their child being accepted on the basis of how he/she actually learned. Learning styles allowed every youngster to be perceived as an individual. And the staff was thrilled to see reluctant learners suddenly eager to do well in this new environment. It wasn't hard and it was very gratifying! Most teachers said that they would never go back to their "old way" of teaching.

Ms. Lemmon was quick to offer advice for anyone interested in using learning styles as the basis for school instruction—as she did in 1980. "Be enthusiastic, provide help, offer suggestions, and go into the classroom."

She stressed the need to establish goals and avoid moving too quickly, and she warned against introducing the concept and then expecting others to translate it into everyday classroom practice. She explained that, to gain staff commitment, training needs to be provided over a period of time. The program must be continuous and supportive. If it is not, do not anticipate huge gains. "Principals have to assume leadership."

Although she has retired, Ms. Lemmon still assumes a leadership role in the Hutchinson Public Schools. The new principal invited her to continue staff development so that new teachers were equally well prepared to use the learning-styles approach. Ms. Lemmon stressed the need to offer many types of support. She believes in reinforcing ideas with articles, research, success stories, and training from those who are knowledgeable.

## INTERESTING TRUE STORIES

*The Case of the Reluctant Piano Practitioner.* Ms. Lemmon is full of anecdotes that stress the power of change. She remembers a parent who sought guidance for her daughter. The young girl never wanted to practice the piano. Lemmon quickly looked up the student's time-of-day preference, which was morning. Although the mother was reluctant to permit early morning piano practice, Ms. Lemmon convinced her that avoiding the confrontations would be worth the hassle. From the first day of morning practice sessions, the daughter practiced without an argument and the piano lessons thereafter were changed to Saturday mornings.

*The Case of the Recalcitrant Homework Do-er.* Another mother stopped by Principal Lemmon's office and explained that she had a problem with her daughter doing her homework. The mother had insisted that her daughter study right after school, but the daughter's LSI printout had indicated that her preference was early morning. Given the option of *when* to study, the youngster elected to awake an hour earlier each morning and did homework without argument.

*The Case of the Midnight-Oil Burner.* Another parent discovered her child reading a book in bed at night with a flashlight. She told Ms. Lemmon that she was "disappointed that the school would encourage a child to do such a thing." When confronted with the child's reading problems in the past, the mother admitted that it was good that the child *wanted to, and was reading voluntarily.* Nevertheless, she was reluctant to allow the child to continue reading at night. When Ms. Lemmon asked whether she was more concerned about the child's improved reading scores or the extra hour she remained awake at night because she wanted to read, the mother smiled and answered, "The proof is in the pudding! Her reading has improved a great deal, so I guess letting her read at night worked!"

*The Case of the Visual Learner.* During a two-year period, Peter was frequently in trouble both in school and at home. He often was hyperactive, failed to follow directions, and had a resentful attitude. The LSI revealed that Peter was a *visual* learner. He could not listen for any length of time and, when he did pause to hear what was being said to him, he could not remember much of what he had been told. His teacher began writing his assignments and placing them on the corner of his desk. She advised his parents to leave his list of chores on the refrigerator and to try drawing pictures that reflected what they wanted him to do. The very first day she tried it, Peter's mother returned from work to find that he had done everything she had *written* on her list. Delighted with the results, she hugged him and asked Peter why he had done everything she'd asked him to do that day. He quickly responded, "Because you TOLD me to!"

*The Case of the Praying Sinner.* Two first-graders had been sent to the principal's office because they'd been fooling around in class instead of completing their assignment. Their former first-grade teacher, who happened to be there, told them that Ms. Lemmon was on duty in the lunchroom but would be back soon. She suggested that they sit quietly and wait for her to return. One of the youngsters sheepishly asked, "Do you know if Ms. Lemmon has a paddle?" The teacher hid her smile, thought for a moment, and then answered, "I suspect she has one." The same young man then asked, "Do you think it would help if we prayed?" The teacher nodded and replied, "It certainly can't hurt to pray!" Then, as she walked away, she could hear one boy praying, "Now I lay me down to sleep . . .".

## A DECADE LATER

Ms. Patti Sue Lemmon has taught a lot of people about learning styles. She has trained many teachers and administrators and has graciously greeted many visitors who cared to visit Roosevelt Elementary School. Although retired, she continues to offer her Lemmon-aid to all those smart enough to ask for it!

## REFERENCES

Dunn, R., Dunn, K., & Price, G.E. (1979, 1980, 1996). *Productivity Environmental Preference Survey.* Lawrence, KS: Price Systems.

Lemmon, P. (1985). A school where learning styles make a difference. *Principal,* 64(4), 26–29.

# Chapter 14

# A 100 Percent Pass Rate on the Statewide Exam for Graduation: T.Y. Harp Made it Happen!

*Nancy Montgomery and Rita Dunn*

Dr. T.Y. Harp has been a coach, high school teacher, and high school principal in both Louisiana and Texas over a 40-year period. He also has been an outstanding "practice-what-you-preach" leader in learning styles! He spins a "mean yarn" in ordinary, everyday conversation and holds the attention of everyone present—young and old. The magnetism is not his charisma—although the man is charismatic. The magnetism exudes from his earnest, down-to-earth wisdom and blatant honesty! For example, he told us this about a senior staff member in his school in Corsicana, Texas:

> A teacher once told me that when she re-designed her classroom to respond to her students' learning styles, she had a problem with students sitting outside her line of vision. She also didn't much like them lying on the floor when they did their assignments. I told her, "Then get them off the floor and in front of you!"
>
> She replied, "But T.Y., they learn better that way!" I said, "OK, then you can choose to have a greater teacher comfort level or increased student achievement." [He smiles boyishly.] I knew which she would pick!

Of course he knew "which one she would pick!" T.Y. knew his faculty well! And when he decided to change Corsican High School in Corsicana, Texas from a traditional to a learning-styles school, he knew exactly what to say to the members of his staff so that they'd "*do what's right for kids!*"

## EXPLAINING LIFE THROUGH DOWN-TO-EARTH ANALOGIES

Dr. Harp always has a story; they emanate from 40 years of educational leadership and almost 20 years of experience with learning-styles implementation with high school students and staff. For example:

> A student told me that he felt more comfortable in the learning-style classes than in the traditional classes. However, every time I'd notice him, there he was, sitting upright in a standard plastic student desk. When I asked him, "Wouldn't you rather position yourself less formally in one of those beanbag chairs, for instance?", he told me, "Dr. Harp, being comfortable for learning is not so much about where your body is or just how you're sitting. It's more about what feels right to you inside."

Had you been lucky enough to hear that story firsthand, you would have noticed how T.Y.'s silver head slowly nodded in affirmation of the boy's insight. You also would have noticed how his eyes twinkled and how his smile lit up his entire face!

Dr. Harp often reflects on many meaningful moments in the history of Corsicana High School's learning-styles successes (Dunn & Griggs, 1988). Among the many letters of appreciation he has received from parents over four decades, he clearly remembers what one mother wrote:

> For the first time in 11 years, our son told us that he actually likes school and no longer is fearful of going to math classes. He explained that, since learning styles, school has been an "emotionally safe place to be" while learning. That means a lot to us. Thank you!

## FROM RACE RIOTS TO PERSONAL COMMITMENT

In the small southern town of Corsicana, Texas, its high school experienced race riots in the building during the mid-1970s. Several years later, after learning-styles instruction had been put into place and was flourishing, Dr. Harp addressed Corsicana's high school faculty and softly reported:

> I no longer believe that we need to assign administrators and teachers to supervise the cafeteria and other common areas. Instead, I think it would serve us all better to work with the kids to build trust and to establish guidelines for appropriate social behavior.

An audible gasp passed among all in attendance at the meeting. That gasp was followed by the expected usual objections, such as, "But I was here during the riots!" and "This won't work!" However, during the past few years, the school atmosphere had changed. That change had been particularly noticeable since the inception of learning styles.

Students had played an integral part in transforming the school environment. It—and they—had changed from requiring adult control to demonstrating self-commitment to responsible behavior. Because much of his time had been spent walking through the school's corridors and classrooms, Dr. Harp had intuited that students seemed to be concerned with maintaining the autonomy the new instructional system had provided. They also were enjoying the academic success most of them were experiencing.

Despite some faculty insecurity about "leaving the kids unsupervised" in certain areas of the building, rules were established, agreed upon, and widely disseminated and discussed. A couple of months later, when Dr. Harp perceived that the kids—and the teachers—were ready to test the new system, it was adopted. Not surprising to people with conviction about learning styles, there was a smooth transition toward the newly established "Honor System."

Dr. Harp, of course, had been correct. He is a strong "people person." Before most faculty had realized it, he had sensed that the entire educational community had changed. Suddenly, everyone connected with the high school seemed to glow with a positive self-image. Students were interacting maturely and sympathetically with each other—and everyone else on campus. For example:

- many high achievers had become aware of, and concerned for, classmates who were struggling to improve their grades. Dr. Harp had observed classes in which students who understood the content voluntarily were helping others;

- low achievers were expressing their admiration for high achievers and accepting assistance;

- athletes were becoming interested in academics and, simultaneously, interest in academics had blossomed throughout the school; and

- imperceptibly, race relations continued to improve dramatically.

## HOW THIS GREAT MAN'S BELIEF IN STUDENTS EVOLVED INTO HIS PHILOSOPHY, CONVICTIONS, AND COMMITMENT

What was it about learning styles and Dr. Harp's own evolution that persuaded him to become a learning-styles specialist? How did he develop the traits that made him an outstanding principal? Dr. Harp says that as far back as 1952, he was uncomfortable with "the way things were." He questioned many things. For example:

- Why doesn't anyone ever explain to students how important it is to work hard every day in school?

- Why is there a grading scale that each teacher is permitted to apply differently?
- Why don't the kids who fail ever do any better the next time around?
- What prevents teachers from reaching these youngsters?

In addition, T.Y. Harp was aware of the toll that failure wrought on adolescents' self-esteem. He clearly remembers poorly achieving math students who thought "smart kids are good in school because they're smart." They actually believed that the teacher didn't matter and that they were predestined to math failure.

When contemplating the difference between "good" and "bad" students, T.Y. decided that it was their attitudes toward themselves that mattered most. Those who had failed in previous math classes were defeated before they even started the new semester. That knowledge haunted him until the early 1980s when his wife, Marylou, a Special Education trainer, returned from the National Association of Secondary School Principals' (NASSP) national convention "on fire about a speaker whose session she had attended." She told him, "You have to go see Dr. Rita Dunn!"—and he was ready.

## A DIVERSE, MIDSIZED, SUBURBAN SOUTHERN HIGH SCHOOL

Located in the suburbs of Dallas, Texas, the Corsicana Independent School District had a total student population of approximately 5,000. The high school had a population of 1,300 students, a class size of 32.5, and was economically varied. Sixty percent of its students were of European-American descent, 30 percent were African American, and 10 percent were Latino. The pupil-teacher ratio was 15 to 1 with a support staff of 14 and a faculty of 87.

Demographic information provides little more than a superficial picture of what is possible. Corsicana High School (grades 9–12) had two extremely important advantages: (1) its principal, T.Y. Harp, truly was concerned about young people and was intent on delivering to them the best quality education possible; and (2) with the introduction of learning styles, Corsicana boasted "a staff that would go to any length to help its students!"

### The Early Years

Dr. Harp attended the NASSP convention the following year and the year after that. He spent time in Professor Rita Dunn's sessions, read the publications she distributed, and then attended St. John's University's Annual Learning-Styles Institute "to see whether the whole picture held together!" He decided that he wanted Dr. Dunn personally to address his faculty at Corsicana High School. T.Y. believed that her enthusiastic conviction and extensive research would persuade some of his faculty to invest time and energy into introducing at least some learning-styles approaches to their students. In his words, he wanted her to help him "get the ball rolling."

Thus, after three years of sober contemplation and planning, T.Y. brought Dr. Dunn to Corsicana to visit the school. He asked her to help faculty formulate its learning-styles philosophy. The following year, Dr. Harp revisited the Learning-Styles Institute in New York, a bit wary and "waiting for the other shoe to drop." Since many other advocates of learning theories seemed to move from one program to another, he wondered if Dr. Dunn would be "whistling a different tune" after those four years. However, what he discovered was additional new research to support St. John's University's learning-styles approach. By that time, he thoroughly believed in the possibility of increased achievement through the Dunn and Dunn Learning-Style Model. Indeed, at the Learning-Styles Institute in New York, he had met other principals from various parts of the nation whose schools had experienced statistically higher achievement with it (Dunn & Griggs, 1988). Therefore, Dr. Harp returned to Corsicana and began a formal program.

## HOW DID CORSICANA TEACHERS START THEIR PROGRAM?

First, teachers tested the incoming freshmen with the LSI. They continued that process until, four years later, all students in the school had learning-style profiles and prescriptions for studying and doing homework based on their strengths. After he talked with the faculty, 30 of the 87 volunteered to begin implementing learning styles right away. Although they continued exploring the concept at subsequent meetings, only 12 of the original 30 actually became fully involved with the program that year.

The following summer, Dr. Harp returned to the Institute with two of his most committed teachers. At the following year's meetings, he had these teachers share their knowledge and experience with the entire faculty. They inspired most of their colleagues to begin to make changes by using learning-styles approaches. Apparently, learning how well the program had worked for these teachers motivated others to join in.

## THE IMPACT OF LEARNING STYLES ON STUDENT CHARACTER

Perhaps the most remarkable feat achieved by the teachers who decided to experiment with learning-styles-based instruction at Corsicana High School occurred during the third year of implementation—even before the school reached critical mass with implementation. To be graduated with a secondary school diploma in Texas, all seniors were required to pass the Texas Assessment of Academic Skills (TAAS). In preparation for creating an environment to accommodate their students' needs, counselors carefully tested for time-of-day energy levels and administered the examination accordingly. Thirty-two students who previously had failed the test were now re-tested at their "best" time of day.

Another 27 students—who had barely passed Algebra I and were currently failing Algebra II with averages below the fiftieth percentile—were placed into a total learning-styles classroom environment with teachers who believed in the concept. There they were (a) allowed choices of how and where to learn in the re-designed classroom, and (b) taught to *begin* learning through their strongest perceptual modality and then to *reinforce* learning, through their secondary perceptual strength. At that point, the supervising teachers had attended the Learning-Styles Institute in New York City.

The students involved in that class were trying to catch up on all the algebra they had missed over the past three years so that they could pass the TAAS math examination. Their first accomplishment was that they all passed the Mathematics Department's examination. However, the state of Texas would deny them the high school diploma if they did not pass the TAAS statewide tests. Therefore, the 32 who had failed Algebra II and the remainder of the senior class all were administered the TAAS test at the same time.

After a wait of several weeks, the statewide results finally came in. The entire school had become interested in learning styles and everyone was anxious to hear the results of the TAAS. When Dr. Harp's voice on the PA system called for everyone's attention, a blanket of silence overtook every classroom, office, and hallway. Pupils, staff, faculty, and administrators had cooperated diligently and worked tirelessly for this moment.

The principal paused as everybody held his/her breath. When Dr. Harp announced that, *for the first time in the school's history,* and in an amazing rarity for any Texas high school, 100 percent of the senior class had passed the TAAS test, every classroom erupted in thunderous, ecstatic shouting and applause! Thinking back over those 40 years, and considering his present position as a consultant emeritus for the Corsicana School District during this decade, Dr. Harp identified that single moment as perhaps his most rewarding!

## TOTAL IMMERSION

After the third year's tremendous success of a 100 percent pass rate on the statewide TAAS examination, Dr. Harp was disappointed that more teachers were not involved and that the program was not advancing rapidly enough to suit him. It was at this point that he thought to himself, "If I die today, learning styles probably won't be here on Monday morning."

However, he continued (1) regular staff development meetings on learning styles, (2) sharing literature from the Learning Styles Network with faculty, (3) daily support and involvement, and (4) administrative assistance from all supervisors. Then, suddenly, implementation reached a pinnacle during the fourth year! Walking through the corridors one day, the principal realized that every single classroom had gradually progressed in room design; not one traditional arrangement remained. Whereas some teachers had done more than others, he knew that it was "a slow process getting everyone on board." However, every effort had made a difference.

## EFFECTS OF LEARNING-STYLE-RESPONSIVE INSTRUCTION ON SCHOOL DISCIPLINE

Before students' learning styles were acknowledged in Corsicana High School, most teachers regularly had sent Dr. Harp at least 10 referrals each for discipline problems every semester. During the autumn of the fourth year, he received only one! During that entire year, he received only three referrals for discipline school-wide! Dr. Harp believes that most classroom management problems evolve either from students not wanting to be made to feel stupid or not wanting to be told that they cannot learn.

> If students think, "Miss Jones doesn't like me," they feel stigmatized; so they go ahead and cause trouble and then get kicked out. Teachers get sucked into this cycle thinking that there is a "personality conflict" between them and their disgruntled students. But that is not what is really happening.

Dr. Harp parallels the situation to that of a criminal who has nothing left to lose and no longer cares if he gets caught. With many pupils' great need for mobility, being cramped in hard little desk chairs is a problem that "wastes a lot of pencils": going to the sharpener being the only acceptable reason to get up. Once students at Corsicana were permitted to learn in informal settings and given the freedom to move, a lot of the discipline problem was resolved.

A marked decrease in graffiti and vandalism also resulted. Even in reporting what little vandalism that remained, students were cooperative with school officials. It was clear that they had a vested interest in their school and had participated in making the new philosophy a reality. Average daily attendance increased 5 percent. Even salespeople visiting the school to sell textbooks and supplies remarked to the principal that "This is the nicest bunch of kids!" Youngsters expressed pride in their building and their classrooms; they reported being happy to come to school.

## THE PRINCIPAL'S PERCEPTIONS OF WHAT MADE LEARNING STYLES WORK

When asked how he got his school community to embrace the learning-styles philosophy, Dr. Harp outlined the following steps.

### Step One

He administered two critical instruments to the teaching staff: the (1) *Productivity Environmental Preference Survey* (Dunn, Dunn, & Price, 1980) to identify how each teacher preferred to learn new and difficult academic information, and (2) *Teaching Style Inventory* (Dunn & Dunn, 1993) to identify how each teacher preferred to teach. He then helped his staff to understand their own learning and teaching styles so that they could analyze their innate preferences and make conscious choices when addressing their students' learning styles.

### Step Two

Dr. Harp initially worked with 15 volunteer teachers who each selected two high- and two low-achieving students to test with the LSI. Those students' learning styles were shared at a faculty staff meeting that everyone attended. It showed all the teachers why certain students performed well—whereas others could not—based on the degree to which their teachers coincidentally used strategies that responded to the students' styles. Even teachers who had not volunteered for the program became interested in the learning styles of specific students because those youngsters were in many of their classes too—not just in those of the volunteer teachers!

### Step Three

After students' learning styles had been identified with the LSI, Dr. Harp and the volunteer teachers found that they could work with anyone who had complained about a student who either had—or caused—a problem. The student's LSI profile often explained why the problem had occurred. Better than that, the student's LSI proposed a solution!

### Step Four

Reinforcing what worked for other successful supervisors in this book, Dr. Harp initially invited both students and teachers to present specific examples of their successes with learning-styles approaches at faculty meetings. Teachers described problems that had been solved because of their emerging knowledge of students' learning styles and students talked about why and how learning styles had impacted their attitudes and achievement.

Collegiality and collaboration improved as teachers shared their narratives. T.Y. encouraged staff to experiment with just one activity of their choice that they were willing to try—and then to report what happened. He believes that both he and his co-workers "became more talented, loving, caring people and educators" as a result.

### Step Five

Dr. Harp and the teachers who gradually were becoming successful with learning styles provided ongoing staff development for interested teachers. If teachers were not able to attend one meeting, they were encouraged to attend the next one and learn a different strategy—that the principal then encouraged them to try. When the strategy worked, he encouraged the teacher to share what had happened with it at the next staff meeting.

### Step Six

Dr. Harp suggested that everyone who provided staff development in learning styles actually use the method that was being taught to teach that method. Thus, if a Circle of Knowledge to reinforce information was the inservice topic for that day, it was introduced through a Circle of Knowledge so that everyone attending actually experienced the strategy. "If learning styles have value, you can convince your faculty by using it to help them learn to become better teachers."

## A DECADE AND A HALF LATER

Dr. Harp no longer worries about learning styles becoming an integral part of the Corsicana High School program. He retired in 1990, but is gratified to see that the program is still firmly in place. Indeed, more than a decade later, Dr. Harp continues to offer district-wide inservice in learning styles! The feedback he receives is that both teachers and students feel positive about themselves, their work, and their relationships with their school community. Tangible academic successes continue.

Teachers report that they go to work believing they can reach their goals. Students report that their learning-style prescriptions for studying and classroom accommodations make them feel worthwhile and confident. They report new successes and appear optimistic and ambitious about meeting greater challenges. Corsicana has bought the legacy of learning styles into this area of Texas.

Always impatient with the seemingly painstaking process of implementation, Dr. Harp reminds us that success occurs through a series of steps that lead forward and backward and forward again. Then, all of a sudden, "evidence kicks in that the approach is taking hold!" He urges other supervisors to be patient and persistent; the results will be worth the wait. "It's not how hard you push, but how *consistent* the efforts. You can't do it all the first week or the first year. After 10 years, there are still things we need to do!"

He insists that learning-styles based instruction is no more expensive than traditional methods. He also asserts that, in regard to teachers' greatest fear—losing control at the high school level—the incontestable fact is that *classroom control will improve.*

The evidence of T.Y. Harp's 40 years as an educator tells us that when kids get caught up in learning-styles classes, they are "swept away! They learn and achieve; there is just no cause for behavior problems anymore." In his words, learning styles "guarantees success!"

## REFERENCES

Dunn, R., & Dunn, K. (1993). *Teaching secondary students through their individual learning styles: Practical approaches for grades 7–12.* Boston: Allyn & Bacon.

Dunn, R., Dunn, K., & Price, G.E. (1975–1996). *Learning Style Inventory.* Lawrence, KS: Price Systems.

Dunn, R., Dunn, K., & Price, G.E. (1979, 1980). *Productivity Environmental Preference Survey.* Lawrence, KS: Price Systems.

Dunn, R., & Griggs, S.A. (1988). *Learning styles: Quiet revolution in American secondary schools.* Reston, VA: National Association of Secondary School Principals.

*Chapter 15*

# Emmett Sawyer: Leveling the Playing Field at Glendale High School in Springfield, Missouri

*Jeannie Ryan and Rita Dunn*

When youngsters watch sporting events, they often imagine playing sports professionally one day, or representing their nation in the Olympic games. Perhaps they dream of becoming a superstar. Eventually, reality hits! Very few get to play professional sports. Those who do spend hours training to become stronger, faster, and tougher. Some just are not born with the right genetic material; they are too slow, too weak, too small, or too tall for that particular sport. However, the rules are clear. Athletes know what it takes to succeed!

Schools, however, do not always have clear rules. Schools also are not in the business of denying opportunity to anyone. Emmett Sawyer, former principal of Glendale High School in Springfield, Missouri, saw the implementation of learning styles as a way to "level the playing field that is the public school." For years, Dr. Sawyer has stressed to students that it is fine to be different. For more than a decade, he used the *Learning Style Inventory* (LSI) (Dunn, Dunn, & Price, 1975–1996) to provide adolescents with interesting information about themselves and their personal learning strengths. When questioned, he explains that "the field becomes level when students and teachers realize that everyone—not just auditory, analytic, formal-design learners—can be successful academically."

## IN THE BEGINNING

Emmett Sawyer's relationship with learning styles began more than a decade ago when he was principal of Logan-Rogersville High School in a small town in Missouri. He attended a St. John's University's Learning-Styles Workshop conducted in Missouri and, eventually, the Learning-Styles

Leadership Certification Institute in New York. Emmett experimented with many of the strategies suggested for the tactual and kinesthetic learners in his school and was pleased with the results. He shared that know-how with teachers and became further impressed with the ease with which some of them implemented learning-style-responsive strategies with seniors and juniors who had not been performing as well as they might have. He was particularly impressed when one of his own children's grades increased substantially after being taught about personal learning-style strengths! Before long, Dr. Sawyer was invited by the various school districts and the Missouri National Association of Secondary School Principals (MNASSP) to describe at their conferences the successes that Logan-Rogersville students were having with learning-style strategies.

## A MOVE TO SPRINGFIELD, MISSOURI

After several years, Mr. Sawyer was invited to apply for the principal's vacancy at Glendale High School in Springfield, Missouri. Many of Glendale's students were high academic performers and college-bound. Seventy-eight percent of its graduates went on to college in 1997, based on the number of seniors who took the ACT/SAT. Nevertheless, the faculty and administration were not comfortable resting on those accomplishments. The staff of Glendale recognized that an increasing number of students were exhibiting at-risk characteristics. In response to the mission of the school, a Learning Center was created. Then a transition class, called Falcons Actively Committed to Success (FACTS) was created for ninth-grade students based on an analysis of research that suggested that students who make a transition from one building to another often need extra help. School personnel suspected that the students selected to work in this ninth-grade class would benefit from learning-style-centered academic and social support during their first year in high school. Therefore, an important component of this class is that all ninth-graders take the *Learning Style Inventory* (LSI) (Dunn, Dunn, & Price. 1975–1996).

Step 1 was to administer the LSI. The Dunn and Dunn model was selected because it was supported by award-winning research and was easy for parents, students, and teachers to understand and for schools to implement. In addition, Emmett Sawyer had witnessed the positive effects that model had produced for many students in his previous school. He also was aware of the strong support network available for practitioners at the Center for the Study of Learning and Teaching Styles at St. John's University in New York City.

Dr. Sawyer was aware that one of the reasons he had been appointed as Glendale High School's new principal was that he had successfully implemented learning-styles instruction at his previous high school (Dunn, 1996,

p. 42). Therefore, he immediately introduced Central Administration and the Board of Education to the concept and some of its practices.

He was fortunate to have been appointed to a school in transition. The Glendale faculty had been discussing the need for change for several years. Teachers had been coupling Sawyer's enthusiasm for the Dunn and Dunn approach with readings on developing a nurturing and disciplined learning environment for high school students. Gradually, the school adopted a 4-by-4 block schedule that required several instructional strategies to be employed during each 90-minute class period to maintain student attention and active participation. Learning-style strategies in which students could master difficult information through their personal strengths fit the bill perfectly! Dr. Sawyer noted that:

> We needed an information base on our students that would help us diagnose how they learned best and then prescribe instructional strategies that matched individuals' learning-style preferences. As faculty recognized the diversity of styles among their students, discussions about responsive instruction gradually emerged. We wanted students to have a chance at being successful!

Teachers slowly adjusted their relationships with students to allow for some informality and varied study modes. Students became aware of codes of acceptable behavior and regulations for conducting themselves like ladies and gentlemen in response to faculty acceptance of their unique style traits.

## REACHING OUT TO PARENTS

Emmett Sawyer understood the need for parental involvement. In Logan-Rogersville High School where he previously had been principal, he had held many individual meetings with parents whose adolescents were completing the LSI. However, at Glendale High School, he inserviced the parents of ninth-graders as a group. He found the opportunity on the night of the ninth-grade mixer dance. While those youngsters were attending the dance with the Student Council, Dr. Sawyer met for an hour and a half with their parents. He explained that the LSI was being administered to every incoming ninth-grader and that each would receive suggestions for how to study and do homework through his/her personal learning-style strengths. He also explained the need to move slowly so that faculty could feel comfortable with this new process.

## REACHING OUT TO TEACHERS

Simultaneously, Sawyer encouraged teachers to dabble with learning-styles strategies at their own rate and based on their personal choices.

When one teacher wanted to experiment with room re-design for students who found it difficult to sit still for lengthy periods, that was encouraged. When another teacher was concerned with kinesthetic learners who needed mobility and was willing to try Floor Games, I encouraged that effort and volunteered to visit the class and help implement the new strategy. When another teacher wished to incorporate Contract Activity Packages for independent students, that effort was applauded. As teachers gained confidence, they implemented more and more of the program.

Sawyer believed that inherent in a successful innovative program is the belief that teachers should be permitted choices in the implementation process. He observed that "Some teachers cautiously want to wait and observe what is being done in other classrooms. Most teachers want to be certain that an innovation will benefit them and their students. This is not uncommon in the change process and should be addressed before individuals are urged to move forward."

Teaching is a complicated activity that can be physically and emotionally draining. Principal Sawyer never seemed to lose sight of the effort it takes to alter "the way we've always done this" as he tried to build a strong foundation for the learning-styles-based high school. Dr. Sawyer also understood that he could not be a silent supporter of this new endeavor at Glendale. "It is important for a leader to be knowledgeable and experienced." Dr. Sawyer encouraged faculty on a regular basis and he established support groups for the teachers who were trying new methods. However, he cautioned that teachers were not the only ones in need of support.

Network with other administrators who are implementing learning-styles programs. Learning styles will change the look of a school. The building will be different, and that very difference threatens some people. That can make leading a school through the change process very lonely—even when the change increases achievement and improves both students' attitudes and behaviors! Administrators and supervisors also will need support and encouragement from whomever is leading the movement.

Perhaps the key to Sawyer's success can be seen in an exercise he did at his former school. He asked his teachers to describe the characteristics of students who had the best chance of becoming academically successful in their school. Teachers responded that successful students must be auditory—able to remember at least three-quarters of what they hear in a 40- to 50-minute lecture. Successful students also must be analytic—able to learn in a brightly lit, quiet classroom in conventional, formal seating, and without taking breaks or eating until either the assignment has been completed or the time is over. Such students also must be highly motivated, conforming, and authority-oriented. Teachers quickly realized that few students in that school had either all or many of those characteristics. The clarity and frustration that emerged during that exercise was the key to future changes in that school. Teachers understood how discriminatory past practices had been and how they had favored one small group of students by requiring that everyone else emulate them and fit that same pattern. One teacher suggested that such students were "so unique that they could not even be normal."

## A SPECIAL CASE

One student, Sheila, had been diagnosed as Learning Disabled (LD) and assigned to a Resource Room for special assistance. Dr. Sawyer was advised that Sheila would not graduate; although a senior, she lacked one unit of social studies credit. In sympathy for the youngster, Emmett offered to work with Sheila independently and began teaching her the required material traditionally. After several months, Sheila had made little progress and it became evident that she would not complete the unit in time for graduation.

As a last resort, Dr. Sawyer examined Sheila's LSI. He realized that he should have converted the required information into a Programmed Learning Sequence (PLS). Sheila required a great deal of structure, needed to learn information in small doses, and should have been introduced to the content visually but reinforced tactually. He did that and, suddenly, Sheila began to complete material faster than he could convert the textbook into the PLS format. In short, Sheila completed the course, graduated, and gained enough confidence to decide that she would continue her education by going to college.

Because of his earlier experiences at Logan-Rogersville High School, Dr. Sawyer is convinced of the impact that learning-styles-based teaching can have on students. He is a firm believer and advocates teaching to students' learning styles whenever he is questioned about this approach. However, before he could fully implement learning styles in the new high school, he was promoted and now serves as Assistant Superintendent for Curriculum and Instruction in the Springfield Public Schools. Dr. Sawyer appreciates the recognition that the promotion suggests. However, had he remained Glendale High School's principal, he would have sought the development of a "more mature" learning-styles program than was possible during the first few years of:

- moving and relocating his family in a new area;
- developing rapport with an existing senior faculty;
- coping with the establishment of a previously designed, imposed alternative program;
- dealing with a changing school population that became a target for gang activity;

- administering a large high school;
- responding to school and community crises;
- completing a doctorate; and
- co-authoring a book (Della Valle & Sawyer, 1998).

Emmett Sawyer continues to be somewhat of a construction worker. His mission is to "dig up the playing field. It may be a bit messy. It certainly will be different from other playing fields. But eventually, it will be level and fair for all students." And that is what he believes education should be!

## REFERENCES

DellaValle, J., & Sawyer, E. (1998). *Teacher Career Starter*. New York: Learning Express.

Dunn, R. (1996). *Everything you need to know to successfully implement a learning-styles instructional program*. New Wilmington, PA: Association for the Advancement of International Education, p. 42.

Dunn, R., Dunn, K., & Price, G.E. (1975–1996). *Learning Style Inventory*. Lawrence, KS: Price Systems.

*Chapter 16*

# A Learning-Styles High School Grows in Brooklyn: Roger Callan Creates a Demonstration Model Through Faith

*Nancy Montgomery and Rita Dunn*

In the summer of 1998, the International Learning Styles Network Board voted Bishop Kearney High School (a Catholic girls' school in Bensonhurst) provisional status as a Learning-Styles Center under the direction of Dr. Roger Callan. This is the first time ever that a Center will be created in a high school![1] The institution plans to gradually become a demonstration secondary-level model for other schools whose teachers and administrators want to observe a learning-styles program in action.

## IN THE BEGINNING

More than a decade ago, in 1988, Dr. Callan attended his first Institute for "Teaching Students Through Their Individual Learning Styles" (the Institute) led by Drs. Kenneth and Rita Dunn. At the time the upper-school principal of Holy Child School (K–12) on Long Island, Roger Callan (not a Dr. then) knew nothing of learning styles and was fed up with educators touting the latest fads and gimmicks. Although the lower-school principal asked him to participate in the Institute, Dr. Callan thought he had seen and tried it all already. Cynical and blasé after experimenting with theories and models proposed by such presenters as Madeline Hunter and Bernice McCarthy, he was tired of impractical or unwieldy new methods of instruction. Frankly, he described his attitude toward Rita Dunn's opening talk as, "OK, lady, impress me!"

What took place during the training, and Dr. Callan's experiences during the next 10 years, to bring him to the directorship of a Learning-Styles Center in a high school—often considered the most challenging for teachers who wished to implement innovation? How did this chairperson of the religious studies department single-handedly and single-mindedly transform his building into a model for others to observe? Dr. Callan refers to himself as "just a teacher," and wonders why his story would even be included among those of curriculum supervisors, principals, and superintendents profiled in this book. Let's find out why an educator of values and morality would give up a principalship and choose to return to the classroom as his venue for practice and research in learning styles.

## IMMERSION IN AND PREPARATION FOR LEARNING STYLES

Back at the opening session of the Institute more than a decade ago, what immediately captured Dr. Callan's interest was that, for the first time during a seminar or workshop introducing an innovative learning theory or method, *teachers* themselves stood up extemporaneously to tell their stories of success with this approach. He says emphatically to this day, "I have never heard teachers talk that enthusiastically, that committed, to a model of instruction, before." These educators had attended the Institute previously, returned to their schools, applied what they had learned in New York to their classrooms, and had come back for more!

The following year, Dr. Callan made two decisions: he would apply to enroll in the doctoral program to specialize in learning styles at St. John's University, Queens, and he would begin to implement the Dunn and Dunn model in his own high school—traditionally the most difficult educational level at which to make inroads. The mostly Catholic girls who attend this parochial school in Brooklyn essentially were from a lower-middle-class or upper-working-class, Italian-American background, with a minority of pupils representing other ethnicities. Some newer technologies and strategies were already in place to build upon—computers with programs selected for adolescent learners and cooperative-learning groups that Dr. Callan indicates were effective with many—but not all—of his students.

## FIRST STAGES OF IMPLEMENTATION

Although he knew studying for his doctorate while implementing learning styles would "make or break" him and, although at times he thought he might "go berserk," he immediately found learning-styles instructional strategies rewarding and liberating for himself and his students. He began by presenting his students with choices of how they might demonstrate their mastery of newly learned content. Teachers and administrators visiting his class were highly impressed with the essays, projects, videotapes, videocassettes, art work, computer demonstrations, and group presentations youngsters created.

Although four more teachers accompanied Dr. Callan to the Institute the following summer, and their administrators were either "sympathetic" or laissez faire (which most are not, he is sorry to say), he was disappointed that there was little follow-up. He knew instinctively that the institution needed a "cadre for change," a structure for inservice training, and strong administrative support for sharing ideas and developing materials. Despite the fact that he could not effect much of this on his own, he plunged ahead.

The following year, Roger Callan implemented the first stage of change in his position as head of the small religion department. He had the full cooperation of the three other religion teachers who had read his classroom study of the effects of his effort with one phase of learning styles—homework prescriptions based on individual students' "strengths," which had been published in *The Bulletin*, the official journal of the National Association of Secondary School Principals (Callan, 1996). Having observed the success and excitement engendered in Dr. Callan's classes, the three teachers chose to try that approach with their students. In addition, having informally talked with Dr. Callan and observed his classes as his learning-styles program progressed, they saw the sense of it and picked up several strategies on their own. In that respect, it was important that his colleagues participated in the decision making and did not require mandates imposed by their administrator.

Together, during the first two months of the term, the four teachers formally tested the entire freshman class by administrating the *Learning Style Inventory* (LSI) (Dunn, Dunn, & Price, 1975–1996) after explaining to students the why and how-to of the model. All four teachers, who would teach the whole freshman class all year long, had agreed to use this approach for teaching the religion curriculum. Afterward, all freshmen took their turn in the computer lab getting their homework and how-to-study-based-on-their-individual-learning-style-prescriptions. The teachers explained how students could identify their perceptual strengths and time-of-day energy levels, and how re-designing the traditional classroom could help them to better respond to their individual preferences. The after-school program also became part of their direct demonstration to students of how they individually could study and learn according to their LSI profiles. Dr. Callan stresses the need, especially during this initial phase, for well-informed, committed counselors and faculty to take plenty of time to talk with pupils in depth, showing them the practicality and benefits of capitalizing on their profiles.

## RATIONALE AND MISSION OF THE DEPARTMENT AND SCHOOL

Dr. Callan describes the philosophy of the Religion Department as one that acknowledges that all students have gifts that God has bestowed upon them. In an atmosphere of openness and acceptance, with a conscious effort not to be narrow in their focus, the teachers launched the new freshman religion course entitled "Personhood," an exploration of how we, as human beings, learn and grow with God's guidance. The department and the school's spiritual framework is that people have natural talents that can be developed into skills, which they then are called upon, as children of God, to use to achieve what He wants for them—leading to their vocational choices.

To help us become the people God wants us to become, the learning-styles approach helps us identify the gifts of our strengths and strip away any obstacles that stand between us and our highest ability to learn. In other words, the learning-styles model helps us to clear the path so that adolescent learners are less prone to fail and, thus, to feel and exhibit anger and frustration. Particularly for entering high school students, the Department wants to emphasize teaching youngsters how to deal with obstacles to learning on their own in the course. Gradually, the students' learning skills will become applicable to their other subjects.

Dr. Callan, knowing the importance of gradual implementation with consistent, thorough follow-up at each stage, had secured a commitment from Department members and the freshman class to see the plan through for that entire school year. The next step was to work with the freshmen and their teachers across disciplines to identify each student's most difficult subjects and also to work with guidance counselors to adapt counseling strategies.

The results were most encouraging. At the end of only one year, a careful survey revealed that all the freshmen's grades and standardized test scores had risen dramatically. That increase occurred even in math, which had been very difficult for many of the pupils when they had been taught with traditional methods, prior to the beginning of the learning-styles program.

Dr. Callan notes that the program has been in effect for three years now, with that class of freshmen now entering their senior year. This is the point where he is planning to implement the model throughout the entire building. He is still waiting for permission to more thoroughly construct real learning-styles classrooms, with attention toward a detailed re-design that offers students diverse environments to accommodate all kinds of preferences.

## A MODEL FOR IMPLEMENTATION

Dr. Callan's advice to others who aspire to become learning-styles supervisors is to keep thorough records of what they learn, what they implement, and what ongoing evaluations imply. He recommends that educators visit many learning-styles schools and classrooms to see what implementation of the model looks like in action.

He emphasizes the importance of the guidance staff being closely involved. He is concerned about the overall transformation, as well as the daily support of pupils as they begin to understand themselves as learners and apply new techniques. He wants them to use knowledge of their personal strengths in all their subjects—with a special focus on their most challenging areas. The guidance staff needs to have access to all student records relating to learning styles. Because they see students daily, they need to know about the learning-styles model and believe in the rationale or philosophy behind it. If the teachers have worked together to create a mission or goal statement that incorporates learning styles, students should be made aware of it. The power of self-knowledge and their newly gained skills will help them understand themselves, their classmates, their teachers, and their parents better than ever before.

Dr. Callan plans to invite the guidance counselors to the next Annual Learning-Styles Certification Institute in New York and to include them in further implementation meetings and activities. In his opinion, they need to be fully trained in the model.

Beginning with a basic commonsense approach is important. Application of theory must be practical. Dr. Callan urges others to keep track of ideas brainstormed and experimented with by the faculty and staff—and then to select manageable starting points. High school teachers, he believes, often are more conservative than elementary and middle school educators and so can be more reluctant to change. Traditionally, they go into their classrooms—the kingdom where they are sovereign—and feel captive to the curriculum that must "be covered." As a result, high school teachers need to be exposed to classes that model learning-styles success and become aware of the benefits of collegial cooperation.

With 800 to 1,000 adolescents coming through their doors each day, it is difficult for secondary instructors to envision individual attention to the learning preferences of each student. That is why Dr. Callan was moved to research and write the article for the NASSP—to demonstrate with hard evidence that a learning-styles approach could be effectively implemented and would produce empirical results—increased achievement at the high school level. He refers to his first sentence in that article, "High school teachers traditionally are reticent to adopt learning-style teaching techniques" (66). It is that reticence of teachers that can be the most challenging for supervisors who hope to lead a school toward change.

## RECIPE FOR SUCCESS

It is especially critical to prepare carefully at the high school level because teachers don't have the same room and the same students all day as teachers do at the elementary level. One cannot create a learning-styles classroom without the understanding and cooperation of other teachers who share the same room. If other teachers don't know or support what the learning-styles instructor is doing, they often complain.

Necessary, too, is the support of the administration, which can influence teachers to adopt learning-styles strategies. Dr. Callan cannot stress enough the importance of a regular structure for the implementation of the model through inservice training in which a cadre of mentors takes beginners through a step-by-step process. He suggests that the atmosphere of meetings should be open and experimental with an emphasis on teachers talking to teachers about accommodating learning-styles needs in their classrooms. He remembers the impact on him of first hearing at the Annual Learning-Styles Institute in New York in 1988, how the teachers who were present had tried the learning-styles approach and were eager to share their success stories.

It is important, too, that teachers be provided with the resources and materials they need. The freedom to experiment with a little re-designing of the classroom, as well as to obtain some casual furniture, equipment, supplies, and the LSI, are important.

Dr. Callan urges other doctoral students studying learning styles to submit articles for publication in journals such as *Educational Leadership, Bulletin*, and *The Clearing House*. Having never thought of himself as a potential published scholar, Dr. Callan was encouraged to write and submit his manuscripts by Professor Rita Dunn. He found that to be integral to his credibility at Bishop Kearney as he initiated the program, which led to his current directorship of the Learning-Styles Center. As for continuing to broaden his credentials as a learning-styles leader, he completed his studies with experimental research concerned with the effects of time-of-day energy levels (Callan, 1998). He completed his Learning-Styles Certification in three years and is now a key staff member of the Annual Leadership Certification Institute in New York. He also continues to conduct research and write extensively (Callan, 1995, 1996, 1997). He also has taught adjunct classes in learning styles at St. John's University.

## A TEACHER LEADS THE WAY

Ten years ago, a totally uninformed Roger Callan walked into the opening session of the Annual Leadership Certification Institute highly skeptical of being told about yet another new pedagogical fad without documented results or practical application. When Professor Dunn took the floor, he said to himself, "All right, convince me." In the fall of 1998, Dr. Callan became the director of the very first High School Learning-Styles Demonstration Center. Bishop Kearney in Brooklyn, New York will be the prototype for demonstrating improvements in achievement, attitudes, and behavior through the Dunn and Dunn Learning-Styles Model in secondary education.

What did he do—armed with only a smattering of knowledge in the beginning and a growing interest in the approach—to lead his peers and administrators toward national recognition as a Board-Certified Learning-Styles High School? He modestly credits his achievement to the following—conviction, demonstration, suggestions, and an evidence-based argument.

A learning-styles supervisor needs to immerse himself in the tradition of research and literature, and go through as much formal training as possible. This should lead naturally to the conviction that learning styles works. Thus, when teachers implement the approach in their own classes, their students demonstrate for other teachers the excitement and success they experience while learning. Dr. Callan has been careful not to preach or be pedantic; instead, he merely spends a lot of time in discussion with his peers, *suggesting*, but not lecturing or recruiting. And finally, he urges them to debate the difficulties of implementation with adolescents and allow them to assume more and more authority and responsibility for their own learning. Implementation takes time and cooperative effort on the part of everyone in the institutional environment.

Dr. Callan reminds us that the Dunn and Dunn Learning-Styles Model is about educators learning how to teach to the strengths of their young charges. It also focuses on instructing students to teach themselves through their own strengths. It encompasses human relations and motivational psychology. It is about the common mission of all educators, in both Catholic and public schools, to help young people fulfill their God-given potential and make their greatest contributions to society. Dr. Callan has shown himself to be a model of teaching by example—teaching himself, his students, his peers, and his administrators. He did not understand why he had been selected for inclusion in this book about leading educators and learning-styles specialists. But Dr. Callan's story belies his reflection on his career to date: There is no such thing as "just a teacher."

## THE WORDS OF STUDENTS

Dr. Callan repeatedly refers to the words of his students in order to explain the impact of learning styles at Bishop Kearney High School. Let us close remembering their voices:

- After I learned the basics visually, I reinforced them tactually. When I went into class the next day, for the first time, I knew what was going on. . . . When I took the "trig" test, I felt confident; I knew the material and scored a 92! I rarely ever score that high in math!

- The biology teacher taught us mitosis. As teachers usually do, she talked about it. On the test later that week, I was shocked to get a 91. I realized that what made it happen was because I read about the topic (visual) *before* the lecture and then reinforced the information by listening (auditory). That helped me get such a great grade!

- Because my strongest perceptual strengths were auditory and kinesthetic—which means that I learn best by listening and being active, for science, I taped myself reading my notes on my hardest subject out loud *before* the test, and then listened to the tape as I ran outside for 40 minutes. Learning while moving and listening turned out to be such a positive act that, on the test, my usual grade of 70 went up to an 88!

- After learning through my strengths, the thing that surprised me was I could raise my hand proudly with the answer, and when the biology teacher called on me, I was ready! I was happy to know that all that studying had paid off. It was worth it!

## NOTE

1. Twenty university and corporate Learning-Styles Centers currently exist throughout the United States and Finland, New Zealand, and the Philippines. Applications are pending for Bermuda and Brunei (see Apendix A).

## REFERENCES

Callan, R.J. (1995). The early-morning challenge: The potential effects of chrono-biology on taking the Scholastic Aptitude Test. *The Clearing House, 68*(3), 174–176.

Callan, R.J. (1996). Learning styles in high school: A novel approach. *Bulletin of the National Association of Secondary School Principals, 80*(577), 66–71.

Callan, R.J. (1997). Giving students the (right) time of day. *Educational Leadership, 55*(4), 84–87.

Callan, R.J. (1998). An experimental investigation of the relationship(s) among the time-of-day preferences of students taking a comprehensive test in sequential mathematics and achievement in the test. (Doctoral dissertation, St. John's University, New York).

Dunn, R., & Dunn, K. (1993). *Teaching secondary students through their individual learning styles: Practical approaches for grades 7–12.* Boston: Allyn & Bacon.

Dunn, R., Dunn, K., & Price, G.E. (1975–1996). *Learning Style Inventory.* Lawrence, KS: Price Systems.

*Chapter 17*

# Ilisa Sulner Sets the Stage for Special Education Successes in New York

*Nancy Montgomery and Rita Dunn*

Ilisa Sulner knows the frustration of trying her best—and still failing. She remembers "that feeling in your throat that doesn't go away" when you believe that you are stupid in school. Tied for the highest reading achievement score in the whole sixth grade, Ilisa was failing math miserably. Her parents couldn't understand why their daughter's teacher—"dynamite" with traditional methods of instruction—wasn't getting through to her. Ilisa's mother and father fared no better when they tried to tutor her at home. Somehow, Ilisa's mother knew that her daughter *needed a different kind of help* to learn math. Fortunately, the college-student tutor her parents hired used manipulative games—similar to the tactual and kinesthetic resources that learning-styles advocates recommend for many youngsters today (Dunn & Dunn, 1992, 1993; Dunn, Dunn, & Perrin, 1994). Those games helped Ilisa score in the 90s in math and pass the difficult Regents examination required by the state of New York.

Later, after 20 years of teaching and administrative experience in New York City's Special Education class and buildings, Ms. Sulner reinterpreted that past failure:

> I wasn't "bad" in math. I had the wrong math teacher—*for me*. I could succeed when I was taught in a way that I could *understand!* That experience made clear the desperation people feel when they really do try, but just cannot understand what their teacher is trying to teach them.

In the past, when Special Education students in her school reacted to the frustration they felt by throwing a chair or striking out at their teacher, Ms.

Sulner immediately recalled that strangulating feeling in her throat from trying—but failing.

> I was a child who could control my actions, but my challenged students don't have the needed internal mechanism to control certain behaviors. By luck, I was paired with a tutor who accommodated my learning style. These kids haven't had that luck!

Now, years later—not through luck, but through rigorous academic preparation, planning, and determined implementation—she and her staff have adopted and are continuing to perfect a research-based mission and philosophy. Ilisa Sulner has led her school faculty into bringing about unprecedented improvement in their students' achievement, attitudes, and behavior by incorporating learning styles into how they teach.

## EARLY RECOGNITION OF THE NEED FOR A DIFFERENT WAY OF TEACHING SPECIAL EDUCATION STUDENTS

As a classroom teacher of Special Education students during the late 1970s, Ms. Sulner realized that:

> Special Education students cannot learn by sitting still and listening, because they cannot sit still and they cannot remember much by listening. Neither can they stay on task for long periods of time. Instead, they require several different short assignments and multisensory resources so that they hear, see, feel, and use new information to make knowledge meaningful to their lives. These students learn through active involvement (kinesthetically) and with hands-on activities (tactually). Most also need to move about frequently.

Instead, Ilisa Sulner, the teacher, experimented with puzzles and games to teach functional skills. She borrowed an adding machine from her mother's office and developed simple addition and subtraction problems on it. Then her students were able to practice through active manipulation of the machine to solve problems based on their lives.

## INTRODUCTION OF LEARNING STYLES INTO SPECIAL EDUCATION

During the 1990s, the Special Education student classification known as emotionally disturbed increased tremendously and encompassed the full range of human cognitive ability. By then Ms. Sulner had become a principal who was dismayed to find the "same old thing happening in most classrooms." Students still were being told to sit quietly in their rows of chairs as their teachers stood at the front of the room and either lectured or asked simple recall questions that required one-word answers. This scenario had failed throughout the nation for many regular education students (including herself back in sixth-grade mathematics!). How could it be expected to elicit enthusiasm and interest, and enhance achievement among Special Education, emotionally disturbed high school students?

By happenstance, she saw a poster advertising a presentation by Professor Rita Dunn, director of the Center for the Study of Learning and Teaching Styles at St. John's University in Queens, New York. Ilisa Sulner sat in the audience at a Barnes and Noble bookstore to hear about how to rear children to become gifted. She was inspired by both Dr. Dunn's presentation and the thorough grounding of her research over the course of 30 years. Ms. Sulner reported having a "revelation"—a realization of what she somehow sensed had been missing in SPED classrooms and in the training of teachers.

She decided that if she could immerse herself in learning about the Dunn and Dunn Learning-Style Model and apply it in her building, she might decrease teachers' burn-out, demoralization, and self-blame when their students did not achieve. She also hoped that by using learning-styles strategies, her teachers could make a real difference in the lives of their students.

## PROFILE OF ONE URBAN SPECIAL EDUCATION HIGH SCHOOL

Ms. Sulner is the principal of a self-contained Special Education school that provides programs for students with handicapping conditions from the ages of 4.9 to 21. The school is located in an economically diverse, crime-ridden community in New York City; its population is largely African American and Hispanic. Ninety-five percent of the student body receives free lunches under Title I. Typical of Special Education schools in New York City, it has a population of about 300. Its demographics are representative of the full range of New York City's five boroughs.

In addition to its African-American and Hispanic populations, the student body is comprised of numerous ethnicities and races; a small minority is Caucasian. Ilisa Sulner reports that a significant number of students are from one-parent families; many live with grandmothers or are reared in foster care. Of 100 typical students, only 10 are girls. The ratio of boys increases when students are grouped by severe handicaps and emotional disabilities.

Although federal law mandates that students return to regular education classrooms as soon as possible, the vast majority who enter into Special Education remain in self-contained classes throughout their school careers and do not graduate. Many drop out. Almost 14 percent of the city's total student body in Special Education accounts for 25 percent of New York City's entire education budget.

## RESEARCH ON LEARNING STYLES AND SPECIAL EDUCATION

Other practitioners who had used the Dunn and Dunn learning-styles approach had reported statistically higher standardized achievement and aptitude test scores among poorly achieving and Special Education students within one year. That occurred at every academic level in urban as well as in suburban and rural schools (Brunner & Majewski, 1990; Klavas, 1993; Kyriacou & Dunn, 1994; Perrin, 1990; Stone, 1992; Quinn, 1993).

A meta-analysis of 42 experimental studies conducted with this model between 1980 and 1990, at 13 different universities, revealed that eight variables coded for each study produced 65 individual effect sizes (Dunn, Griggs, Olson et al., 1995). The overall, unweighted group effect size value (r) was .384 and the weighted effect size value was .353 with a mean difference (d) of .755. Referring to the standard normal curve, these data indicated that students whose learning styles were accommodated could be expected to achieve 75 percent of a standard deviation higher than students who had not had their learning styles accommodated. This indicated that matching students' learning-style preferences with educational interventions compatible with those preferences was beneficial to their academic achievement.

Federal researchers at the Center for Research in Education who studied the 20-year period (1970–1990) found very few programs resulted in statistically higher standardized achievement test scores for Special Education students (Alberg, Cook, Fiore, Friend, Sano et al., 1992). Prominent among those programs that *did* consistently increase students' standardized achievement test scores was the Dunn and Dunn Learning-Styles Model.

Contrast these data with those of New York City where, since 1975, the number of Special Education students has risen from 35,000 to 167,000— nearly 15 percent of all 1.1 million city students. Worse than the increase in numbers is the fact that most classified Special Education students in that—and every other urban center—rarely outgrow that denigrating designation. Fewer than 2 percent were dropped from the Special Education category each year. Conversely, between 97 and 98 percent remained classified. Very clearly, the billions of dollars allocated to the Special Education bureaucracy for decades have been ineffective with 98 percent of the students (Edelman, 1998).

Extensive funding, the special training of Special Education teachers, reduced class size, and years of exclusive education have not succeeded in improving the performance of 98 percent of New York's Special Education students. Very clearly, that system does not work (Dunn & Griggs, 1999). In addition to its high cost, it is impossible to estimate the damage that Special Education has done to both teachers' and students' emotional health and confidence. Ms. Sulner strongly believes that it is crucial that all Special

Education teachers are taught to implement the Dunn and Dunn Learning-Style Model.

## STAFF DEVELOPMENT TO IMPLEMENT CHANGE

Ms. Sulner knew the value of having teachers experience learning through their own style before asking them to use specific strategies with their students. She appreciated the importance of teacher-made materials, but she wanted to motivate her staff to spend the time required to develop manipulatives for tactual learners and to construct games and organize realistic activities for high school kinesthetic learners. Teachers often are wary of additional demands on their time and pocketbooks, and impatient with impractical research and inapplicable statistics. Ilisa is in a district with high teacher turnover due to the challenges of teaching Special Education populations. When she approached her staff, some of the teachers were eager to learn how to improve behavior management in their classrooms.

Her staff often included arts and crafts projects when teaching. They also had some experience with re-arranging their rooms and occasionally used small group instruction. Although they had used some commercial manipulatives, they were unfamiliar with the tactual and kinesthetic resources suggested for responding to underachievers' "strengths." Furthermore, none of the teachers had been exposed to the components of Programmed Learning Sequences (PLS), Contract Activity Packages (CAPs), or Multisensory Instructional Packages (MIPs) (Dunn & Dunn, 1993). Ms. Sulner's instincts told her that with her:

- teachers, it would be wise to begin with concrete, practical applications rather than with a philosophical or research base; and
- students, it would be wise to begin with instructional strategies that allowed them (1) some mobility while learning and (2) to be at least partially independent of both their teacher and their peers.

   *Step one.* First, she and her curriculum coordinator led workshops in which teachers could attend, look, touch, manipulate, and try out materials such as Electroboards, Flip Chutes, Task Cards, and kinesthetic Floor Games (Dunn & Dunn, 1993). She wanted the staff to experience how it felt to learn through perceptual modalities other than the visual and auditory.

Ms. Sulner constructed an MIP on scuba diving and used that package to demonstrate how teachers could use manipulatives to reach new goals for higher standards and improved literacy. Many of the New York City students had little, if any, contact with scuba diving. However, she showed her teachers how their students could learn an entirely new set of vocabulary words and concepts through that novel subject. After sampling several MIPs, a few teachers agreed to try one with their students. They quickly acknowledged the achievement, attitude, and behavior gains that they observed! Unanimously, they reported the results at the next staff meeting and, suddenly, many teachers were committed to learning about the research and rationale that would help them understand why the Dunn and Dunn Learning-Style Model worked.

At that point, Ms. Sulner made available articles, books, and manuals from the Learning-Styles Center at St. John's University to answer each teacher's questions and concerns. By then, many of the teachers were "hooked!"

## IMPACT OF LEARNING STYLES ON THESE SPECIAL EDUCATION STUDENTS

Students became responsive to the school's new emphasis on learning styles. They got together and made an immense chart of the 21 elements that comprise each learner's style. That chart remains mounted in the entrance to the building and is the first thing that greets visitors. It is so beautifully wrought, outsiders would think that teachers had made it. Ms. Sulner attributes the care that went into its construction to the enthusiasm of the youngsters, who, for the first time in their lives, were learning about themselves.

## OBSERVABLE IMPROVEMENTS

After the first year of study and planning, the atmosphere in the building became positive and upbeat, with staff, teachers, and administrators united in a common new mission. During the second year, adaptations were made for global and analytic processors and time-of-day energy levels were accommodated as much as possible given the constraints of busing and cafeteria schedules. Students also were shown how to learn in ways they *could!*

## PLANS FOR THE FUTURE

In an overwhelming show of support for their belief in the importance of learning styles, the teachers and staff voted that a high percentage of the financial resources for faculty development be allotted to further training in learning styles. Ms. Sulner is impressed that, rather than her having to impose these methods of instruction, teachers are asking for them because they have seen the results. The superintendent of the district for Special Education and the chancellor continue to be extremely supportive of the district's efforts to integrate learning styles into the curriculum.

Ms. Sulner was awarded grants in conjunction with the school's Goals 2000 proposal and its Comprehensive Educational Plan. Funding was readily provided for materials, staff development, and especially for workshops for the high school team because the principal and the School Board Committee had identified mediocre practices and explicitly described incremental steps to elevate achievement and attitudes. In addition, money was provided for the participation of 15 teachers and administrators in the 1998 Learning-Styles Certification Institute, held each summer in New York City.

Since Special Education students in New York City are not required to participate in standardized, formal testing, most are granted testing modifications. During the third year of the program, Principal Sulner and her team will review goals for the mastery of skills and students' Individualized Educational Plans and will gather hard data and see what remains to be accomplished.

Some long-time teachers remain resistant to change and some new hires are nervous about classroom control and deviating from traditional methods they learned in the education courses they took. Therefore, it is planned that the teachers who attended the Learning-Styles Institute will mentor the uninitiated by modeling, regular discussions, and some team teaching.

## REFLECTING ON EFFECTIVE PRINCIPALS

Ilisa Sulner believes that "the principal should be the best teacher in the school," and she is consciously moving toward that goal. She can talk from firsthand experience about the impact of learning styles on her teachers' attitudes and careers, and on her students' learning and lives. She asserts that "the principal's *real job* is to help teachers provide the best instructional program possible for children."

## REFERENCES

Alberg, J., Cook, L., Fiore, T., Friend, M., Sano, S. et al. (1992). *Educational approaches and options for integrating students with disabilities: A decision tool.* Triangle Park, NC: Research Triangle Institute.

Brunner, C., & Majewski, W. (1990, October). Mildly-handicapped students can succeed with learning styles. *Educational Leadership, 48*(2), 21–23.

Dunn, R., & Dunn, K. (1992). *Teaching elementary students through their individual learning styles: Practical approaches for grades 3–6.* Boston: Allyn & Bacon.

Dunn, R., & Dunn, K. (1993). *Teaching secondary students through their individual learning styles: Practical approaches for grades 7–12.* Boston: Allyn & Bacon.

Dunn, R., Dunn, K., & Perrin, J. (1994). *Teaching young children through their individual learning styles.* Boston: Allyn & Bacon.

Dunn, R., & Griggs, S.A. (1998–1999). Epilogue—It grows too late too early: Facts speak for themselves. In R. Dunn & S.A. Griggs (Eds.), Special Issue: Learning Styles and Urban Education. *National Forum of Teacher Education Journal, 9*(1), p. 79. Monroe, LA: Louisiana University.

Dunn, R., Griggs, S.A., Olson, J., Gorman, B., & Beasley, M. (1995). A meta analytic validation of the Dunn and Dunn Learning Styles Model. *Journal of Educational Research, 88*(6), 353–361.

Edelman, Susan. (1998). Showdown looms as two Rudys vow special-ed revamp. *New York Post*, June 10, p. 6.

Elliot, I. (1991, November/December). The reading place. *Teaching K–8, 21*(3), 30–34.

Gadwa, K., & Griggs, S.A. (1985). The school dropout: implications for counselors. *The School Counselor, 33*, 9–17.

Klavas, A. (1993). In Greensboro, North Carolina: Learning style program boosts achievement and test scores. *The Clearing House, 67*(3), 149–151.

Kyriacou, M., & Dunn, R. (1994). Synthesis of research: Learning styles of students with learning disabilities. *Special Education Journal, 4*(1), 3–9.

Orsak, L. (1990, October). Learning styles versus the Rip Van Winkle syndrome. *Educational Leadership, 48*(2), 19–20.

Perrin, J. (1990, October). The learning styles project for potential dropouts. *Educational Leadership, 8*(2), 23–24.

Quinn, R. (1993). The New York State compact for learning and learning styles. *Learning Styles Network Newsletter, 15*(1), 1–2.

*Research on the Dunn and Dunn Learning-Style Model.* (1999). Jamaica, NY: St. John's University's Center for the Study of Learning and Teaching Styles.

Stone, P. (1992, November). How we turned around a problem school. *The Principal, 71*(2), 34–36.

*Chapter 18*

# Where in the World Is Carolyn Brunner? Learning-Styles Training in International Schools

*Karen Burke and Rita Dunn*

It was August 7, 1998 and stunned Americans were staring at television images of rubble and carnage at what had been the U.S. embassies in Nairobi and Dar es Salaam. As the reality of the deadly terrorist attacks in Kenya and Tanzania sank in, most Americans realized that they knew little about these places and wondered if they ever had heard of them in any social studies class. Reporters and viewers were grateful if they even could pronounce the names of these esoteric locations or pinpoint them on a map. Few could relate to any personal experiences of the people living in these nations.

That same sense of confusion was repeated on Thursday, August 20, 1998 when Americans received news of the United States' retaliatory actions. In the Red Sea and the Arabian Sea, Tomahawk cruise missiles roared from the decks of American warships, bound for targets in Zhawar Kili Al-Badr, about 90 miles south of Kabul, Afghanistan and Khartoum, the capital of Sudan. Throughout the television reports transcribing videotapes and photographs taken in Khartoum, we observed wide dirt roads, sprawling factory complexes, and squat mud homes. We witnessed anguished faces of the children and people, and we struggled to relate to them personally.

Not quite 24 hours after the cruise missiles hit a factory in a decrepit industrial area of this capital, clouds of white smoke still hovered over the site. Two days after the plant on the outskirts of the town was destroyed, pictures of young anti-American demonstrators, allowed to leave their schools early, were beamed into our living rooms. In the dusty streets, teen-aged students dressed in the camouflage guerilla-style uniforms that are the standard school garb for boys and girls, marched by. We knew so little about these people and understood even less.

## THE WORLD SHRINKS AS WE WATER DOWN THE DIFFERENCES AND WASH AWAY THE STRANGENESS

It's a long way from Buffalo, New York to the sprawling capital of Khartoum on the banks of the Blue Nile—and nobody knows that better than Carolyn Brunner. She has traveled to many countries on the continent of Africa, as well as 50 other nations, to address parents, students, teachers, and administrators about learning styles. In each nation, she has learned about the people and noticed a common thread—support for teaching to their children's individual learning styles. Therefore, when Carolyn heard the names Khartoum, Kabul, Nairobi, and Dar es Salaam, she saw the faces of real people who wanted to provide the best possible education for the children of their nation.

## A LEARNING-STYLES MEMORY FROM DAR ES SALAAM

While many Americans were trying to locate these distant places on a map, Brunner was recalling the names and faces of the many people she had met in these geographic sites. She remembered the look on a boy's face in Nairobi when she handed him a Chicago Bulls basketball cap. As strange as it seemed to his teacher, Brunner knew that reducing the amount of light on his eyes with a cap that sported a visor would increase the young man's ability to concentrate. In addition, he probably would remember more new and difficult academic information than he had previously. Furthermore, it was likely that his teacher's perception of him as "hyperactive" would change too. Carolyn Brunner thought of her son Michael's good friend who needed low light to learn (Studd, 1995). The two young men were separated by thousands of miles, but they shared something very similar—a need for low light when concentrating.

## A LEARNING-STYLES SCHOOL IN KHARTOUM

As news reports focused in on the demonstrators in Khartoum, Brunner recalled a school administrator, Richard Eng. Although she worried about Dick's safety, a smile crossed her face. She recalled the enthusiasm of Dick's staff as they proudly shared stories of bringing learning styles to their school. Dick had brought her a note that one of his students had written and asked him to forward to Mrs. Brunner: "Thank you for telling our teachers about learning styles. We now have the best school in Khartoum. It's not boring like other schools."

## A LEARNING-STYLES SOCCER TEAM IN THE IVORY COAST OF WEST AFRICA

As Brunner packed for her trip to Turkey the next day, it was the dusty terrain in Dar es Salaam that led her to reminisce about the day she spent on the International Community School of Abidjan's soccer field in that city, thousands of miles away—but she recalled thinking of her husband Ron. He had used learning styles to lead his wrestling team to state championships (Brunner & Hill, 1992). The coaches and teachers on the soccer field eagerly awaited any information that would help them improve the natural abilities of their young athletes. They were intrigued as Brunner drew pictures, told stories, and introduced them to various tactual and kinesthetic materials that they could use with these children. [The photograph of their championship soccer team that they mailed to her holds a prominent place on her wall!] Yes, they were real people, with real learning styles, living in real places.

## ONCE UPON A TIME

Brunner has not always had this understanding of cultural diversity and learning styles, but certainly the international and multicultural attraction was present many years ago. She began her teaching career as a student teacher in Panama City, Panama. Immediately following this experience she secured her first teaching position with children of migrant farm workers in Florida. Never did she doubt the virtues of individualizing instruction. Unfortunately, it never really was clear how teaching could be both individualized and practical.

Like many of her colleagues, Brunner began the search through the "hot" topics and latest trends to find answers. For over 15 years, she practiced many of the hit-or-miss teaching methods touted in educational journals, textbooks, and workshops. Although she experienced many successes with students, she also experienced failures. She couldn't understand why some things worked so well with certain students but not with others. Then came learning styles!

## INTRODUCTION TO LEARNING STYLES

By 1987, Brunner had secured a position as the Special Education Teacher Trainer for two New York school districts. Her job was to help teachers increase success for Special Education students. The director of Special Education, Walter Majewski, suggested that she attend a weeklong institute on learning styles with Drs. Rita and Ken Dunn. Although she had read articles about learning styles and had attended training sessions in another system, she had been disappointed in its literature that described "individualizing instruction through learning styles" when, after training, she found that it actually segmented each class into four groups in which every student experienced the same instruction in the same sequence for the same amount of time. In that system, there was no identification of, or teaching to, individuals' learning styles.

Although she enrolled in the St. John's University Learning-Styles Institute reluctantly, it didn't take long for her skepticism to reverse to optimism, enthusiasm, and commitment. She attended the sessions each day and spent every evening reading everything that had been distributed during the day. She completed every required instructional resource—including one each of a Contract Activity Package, Programmed Learning Sequence, and Multisensory Instructional Package. Although Brunner did not attend a single social function while in New York, she was having fun!

Mrs. Brunner learned that learning styles was not just for Special Education. Students at all levels of academic proficiency had evidenced statistically higher achievement—and attitude—test scores when taught through their learning-style strengths. Questions she had struggled with for many years were answered. For the first time, she not only understood *why* students learned in different ways and required different methods; she understood how to match classroom instruction and environments to improve student performance.

## SUCCESSFUL LEARNING-STYLE APPLICATIONS WITH SPECIAL EDUCATION STUDENTS

Carolyn Brunner returned to her district and began training the Special Education teachers to use learning-style strategies. Just as had been described in the research, the mildly handicapped high school students evidenced increasingly higher achievement over the next two-to-three-year period when taught through their learning-style preferences! In June 1987, prior to learning-styles instruction, only 25 percent of the students in Frontier's Central High School in Hamburg, New York passed the State Competency Tests to receive diplomas. During 1987–1988, the first year that Brunner introduced learning styles, that number increased to 66 percent. During 1988–1989, the second year, 91 percent were successful and in 1989–1990, the results remained constant at 90 percent (Brunner & Majewski, 1990). With great pride and enthusiasm, Brunner reported that a greater ratio of "handicapped students" passed State Competency Tests that year than regular education students!

## WHERE DID SHE GO FROM THERE?

These successes led Brunner to the position of director of the International Learning Styles Center co-sponsored by ERIE 1 Board of Cooperative

Educational Services (BOCES) in Cheektowaga, New York and the Association for the Advancement of International Education (AAIE). In that capacity, she worked with both parents and teachers in Brazil, Brunei, Columbia, Costa Rica, Dominican Republic, Ecuador, Guatemala, Finland, France, Honduras, Japan, Malaysia, Mexico, Mozambique, Norway, Peru, Singapore, Sudan, Taiwan, Turkey, and Venezuela. Most verbalized support for teaching to individual learning-styles and a willingness to adapt their schools to the extent feasible in their unique situations. It quickly became evident to her that, regardless of the geographic location, people were relieved when she confirmed that: (1) each child has a unique style; and (2) when permitted to learn through individual style strengths, each achieves better than when required to conform to stereotypical guidelines for learning or studying.

As part of the learning-styles training she provides through AAIE, Brunner introduces people in diverse nations to the Dunn and Dunn Learning-Style Model. Several overseas schools have chosen to administer the *Learning Style Inventory* (LSI) and provide their students with accurate, personalized prescriptions for studying and doing homework through their own learning-style strengths. Teachers became familiar with several small group techniques—Team Learning, Circle of Knowledge, Case Studies, and Brainstorming to use with peer-oriented students. Teachers who had initially expressed reservation about hands-on instructional resources such as Flip Chutes, Task Cards, Pic-A-Holes, and Electroboards, described the excitement they felt as tactual children gradually learned to teach themselves and each other by using these resources independently. Teachers who previously never would have permitted mobile, "hyperactive" students to get out of their seats, experimented with kinesthetic Floor Games for them and later described the students' joy when they earned 85 percent or better on subsequent tests!

## AMERICAN OVERSEAS SCHOOL SUCCESSES

Fewer than five years after attending the first Learning-Styles Institute in New York City, Brunner realized some overseas success stories. In 1992, the Colegio International de Caracas was recognized as the first overseas Learning-Styles School of Excellence. In 1993, the American School of Tegucigalpa and the Mazapan School of Honduras were recognized as Learning-Styles Pilot Schools and, one year later, both became Learning-Styles Schools of Excellence. One year later, in 1995, three more schools became pilot schools—the American International School of Mozambique, the Costa Rica Academy, and the Lincoln School of Costa Rica. That same year, the Colegio Nueva Granada of Bogota, Colombia was honored as a School of Excellence! Between 1996 and 1998, the following additional Pilot Schools emerged:

- American School of Puerto Vallarta (Puerto Vallarta, Mexico, 1996);
- American School of El Salvador (San Salvador, El Salvador, 1996);
- Bilkent University Preparatory School (Ankara, Turkey, 1997);
- Inter-American Academy of Guayaquil (Guayaquil, Ecuador, 1997);
- International Community School of Abidjan (Abidjan, Cote d'Ivorie, 1997);
- Colegio Karl C. Parrish (Barranguilla, Colombia, 1998);
- Khartoum American School (Khartoum, Sudan, 1998).

In addition, the following Schools of Excellence were recognized by the Association for the Advancement of International Education (AAIE):

- Lincoln School (San Jose, Costa Rica, 1996);
- American School of El Salvador (San Salvador, El Salvador, 1997);
- Costa Rica Academy (San Jose, Costa Rica, 1998);
- International Community School of Abidjan (Abidjan, Cote d'Ivoire, 1998).

The ever-increasing requests for university graduate courses in learning styles from overseas schools prompted Carolyn to accept a new position in 1997. She currently serves as director of the International Learning Styles Center of the State University College of New York at Buffalo and AAIE.

Many International Learning-Styles Schools continue to seek her assistance. It is evident that, to Carolyn Brunner, the best accolades come from the students who recognize the benefit of the learning-styles program they attend. It is because of them that we may ask, "Where in the world is Carolyn Brunner?" The answer often is, "out of the country in a land whose name is unfamiliar and whose people we do not know." However, Carolyn Brunner hears the name of that foreign nation and, more often than not, remembers a person and an interesting, personal story about real people, living in real places, with real learning styles.

## REFERENCES

Brunner, C.E., & Majewski, W.S. (1990, October). Mildly handicapped students can succeed with learning styles. *Educational leadership, 48*(2), 21–23.

Brunner, R., & Hill, D. (April 1992). Using learning styles research in coaching. *Journal of Physical Education, Recreation and Dance, 63*(4), 26–61.

Studd, M. (1995). Learning-style differences. *The Clearing House, 69*(1), 38–39.

# Chapter 19

# Jack Gremli and Music Education: Marching to the Beat of a Different Drummer

*Karen Burke and Rita Dunn*

Louis Armstrong was born in a shack in New Orleans with no running water and no toilet. He didn't own a pair of shoes, and food was hard to come by. Never in his life did he have a real music lesson and, until age 17, he lacked enough money to buy his own musical instrument. However, Louis was a genius and he not only changed the course of music in America, but also became the greatest jazz musician who ever lived.

## LOUIS ARMSTRONG: A MASTER MUSICIAN

He sang for pennies with a street group when he was only eight and hung around the honky-tonks at night. He developed his craft in spite of little or poor musical training. He *listened* in those dance halls and on the streets of that seaport city, and he learned. Armstrong would not learn to read music until he was more than 20 years old, and for the whole of his long career he played so incorrectly that he permanently damaged his lip. Nevertheless, he grew up to play for presidents, kings, and queens and was revered as one of the most famous entertainers of his time.

Louis Armstrong, or "Satchmo" as he affectionately was called, was naturally gifted. Few humans are born with so much very special talent that seems to emerge from the depth of their souls. Of course, there are people with a talent or an aptitude for music. These might not be thought of as being musically gifted, but often they are motivated to become the best musicians they possibly can. Such musicians recognize their limitations and know that they will need to devote an endless number of hours and a great deal of energy to developing the talents they do have. Often, because of their acute motivation and perseverance, they become better musicians than would have been possible had they not devoted their heart and effort toward that task. And then there are the many young people who enjoy music because of the personal pleasure they derive from either active participation or peaceful absorption. When they are lucky, they meet someone who instills in them a desire to learn. If they are super lucky, they recognize that few students can even begin to compare with a Louis Armstrong, but that each has a special ability to learn about or appreciate music when they are taught according to their own learning style.

## JACK GREMLI: A MASTER MUSIC TEACHER

Jack Gremli, director of music for the Nanuet Union Free School District, is a sensitive human being who realizes that music students come in varied classifications. There are the few who are obviously gifted, and the some who seem talented and motivated but rarely demonstrate unusual perform-ance. There are others who are above average and may develop musical expertise if they are taught with methods congruent with their learning style. However, there also are many who are gifted in other areas, but only barely pass required music classes. And there are some for whom music may be a nemesis.

Gremli, a lover of music, understood that the school district was required to provide formal training for each youngster, but that the training need not be identical for all. He began to ask professional questions: (1) How can we address diverse students' learning styles in general music?, (2) What do we need to change?, (3) Can we deliver music better than we currently do?

Several district music teachers had observed that different students ap-peared to gain more-or-less from various strategies they had used. They recognized that their students were responding differently to techniques that were "supposed to work for everyone"—but apparently did not. However, the teachers were not able to specifically identify why—or what they could do about it.

Out of curiosity, Mr. Gremli administered the *Learning Style Inventory* (LSI) (Dunn, Dunn, & Price, 1990) to all the middle school youngsters in the music program and shared the results with their teachers. Those pro-fessionals immediately became interested in identifying how various students learned best and were motivated to explore responsive techniques for teach-ing them. However, everyone knew that they needed a stronger knowledge base before they could effectively experiment with alternative strategies for exposing students to the required music curriculum.

## THE FIRST STEPS TOWARD IMPROVEMENT

In spring 1995, Gremli enrolled in the Instructional Leadership Doctoral Program at St. John's University. That program focused heavily on the identification of students' learning-style strengths and the provision of complementary instruction for individuals. Gremli became intrigued with the extensive research behind that model and perceived that learning styles would be a logical beginning point for further expanding the music teachers' skills.

Learning styles had been a topic of discussion among a group comprised of the district's administrative team, middle school grade-level teams, and coordinators in 1994. Jack Gremli had chaired those meetings and thought that several of its members would like to know more about the topic. He applied for and received a staff development grant and then invited a few of his colleagues in the doctoral program to provide practical demonstrations of how to teach adolescents through their learning styles. That thrust then became a significant aspect of both their formative and summative evaluations.

The staff was pleasantly surprised to see how their first impressions of students changed after they understood the youngsters' learning styles. Those students who initially seemed to be gifted often were highly auditory—capable of remembering at least 75 percent of what they heard during a lecture. The majority of the boys, however, were neither auditory nor visual and were poorly equipped to learn by listening. That became a concern of those teachers who knew they were presenting most of their music instruction by talking and lecturing—as most teachers do.

The Nanuet music teachers also discovered that many of their middle school charges who, at first, seemed unpromising as musicians often had highly tactual or kinesthetic learning styles. Those adolescents needed to *do* something; they needed to be actively engaged if they were to succeed as learners! Worse, they were brimming with energy (highly kinesthetic and in need of frequent mobility). Indeed, many of them had been labeled "hyperactive" by their teachers, who felt uncomfortable with the students' vitality and exuberance.

Gremli began to respond to some of the teachers' concerns by providing learning-styles training as an alternative to lecture. Before long, he noticed a number of teachers using tactual and kinesthetic resources with their classes and, shortly thereafter, those were combined into Multisensory Instructional Packages (MIPs) (Dunn & Dunn, 1993). Teachers began requesting published articles related to learning styles and Jack understood that they wanted to learn more; he had felt the same way! Before long, it was evident that the music teachers had "bought into" the program. The music curriculum suddenly included Floor Games for kinesthetic learners, tactual materials for the hands-on learners, small group techniques for the peer-oriented, and Contract Activity Packages for the bright, motivated learners. Success stories emanated from every class and both teachers and students became exuberant!

## LEARNING-STYLE APPLICATIONS TO FACULTY INTERACTIONS AND RELATIONSHIPS

Gremli was delighted with the effect learning-styles implementation was having (Gremli, 1996), but realized that it also was affecting his administrative role as the Director of Music. He related the following anecdote to describe when he realized that something different was happening to him and his staff.

"Jennifer" was the newest and youngest member of the district's accomplished music staff. She had been employed as a "utility" teacher. Her education and experience were in both the instrumental and vocal music field. Although her fifth- and sixth-grade band students' achievement was commendable and the number of students who attended and succeeded at the New York State School Music Association (NYSSMA) festival had increased, "something" bothered Gremli about Jennifer as a member of the music department team. For two years, while she had been working part time, he had attempted to guide her toward "fitting in" where he believed she would be most effective.

Regardless of how hard he tried, nothing seemed to work. Jennifer remained part of the music faculty primarily at the request of the seventh- and eighth-grade band director whose opinion Gremli respected and whose ensemble was fed into directly by Jennifer's students.

At the beginning of her third year of employment, but her first year as a full-time teacher, Jennifer took the *Productivity Environmental Preference Survey* (PEPS) (Dunn, Dunn, & Price, 1990)—the adult learning-styles identification assessment. It was available at the beginning of the semester when all the incoming fifth-graders were administered the LSI. When the results of Jennifer's PEPS were available, Gremli examined Jennifer's *Individual Printout* and realized how different the two were!

- One of Jennifer's pivotal emotional styles was the exact opposite of Jack's. Jennifer was a *non-conformist* and was inclined to do the opposite of what any authoritative person told her to do, whereas Jack was *authority-oriented* and tended to be directive and explicit. No wonder she had balked at every word of "advice" he had given to her!

- Jennifer was peer-oriented, liked to do things her way, but could work well with colleagues in a small group. She appreciated neither the authority figure that Jack represented nor the structure he imposed.

- Jack was primarily an auditory learner; therefore he repeatedly had *told* Jennifer how to "fit in and succeed." Conversely, Jennifer was visual and tactual; she needed to receive his guidelines first in writing. After having read them, she would have highlighted or asterisked the points with which she wanted to comply!

When he understood this information about Jennifer's learning style, Gremli wrote her a note and invited her to meet with him and a few other members of the music staff. He suggested that it might be advantageous for the group to chart everyone's learning-style differences and similarities so that they could work together optimally.

Jennifer and Jack both adjusted the way in which they communicated with each other. For example, Jack now writes her notes, gives her choices, has her work with other instrumental teachers, and changed her schedule so that she primarily can interact with colleagues in small groups. Although Jennifer tends to be impulsive, she now gives Jack the information he requires on time. That permits him to reflect on each concern and decide how it should be reconciled. Jennifer now understands that Jack is reflective and despises working in groups.

When Jennifer tells Jack something, she knows that he will remember it sentence by sentence—and will hold her to her word. In addition, he persists in completing every task undertaken by the department. She acknowledges his perseverance and that he works very hard. Therefore, she tries to complete quickly those assignments for which she has assumed responsibility.

Gremli now has an excellent working relationship with Jennifer. He fully expects that when the building principal asks his opinion concerning tenure, he will suggest that the decision be favorable.

## RESEARCH WITH MUSIC AND LEARNING STYLES

Although delighted with the apparent effects of learning-styles-based instruction on Nanuet's middle school music students' grades and attitudes (Dunn & Gremli, 1999), Jack wanted quantifiable data to be certain that the positive outcomes he perceived were substantial. During a three-year period, his students had performed admirably through a system of alternative instructional strategies designed to teach the identical knowledge in different ways to students with diverse learning-style strengths. Thus, he designed research to determine the relative effects of traditional versus Contract Activity Packaged (CAP) versus Programmed Learning Sequenced (PLS) on both the achievement and attitude test scores of general music students (Gremli, 1999).

His data evidenced that significant differences occurred between each of the three methodologies. Students' achievement test scores were statistically higher in both of the learning-style-responsive strategies than in the traditional format ($p < .001$). Attitudinal test scores were significantly higher ($p < .05$) when congruent with students' highest achievement scores and learning-style preferences (see Figure 19.1 and Table 19.1).

## OTHER GAINS SINCE THE LEARNING-STYLES PROGRAM BEGAN

This story is just one example of the faculty and/or student achievements and gains that have been credited to the implementation of the Dunn and

**Figure 19.1**
**Percentage of Highest Achievement Scores According to Instructional Methodology**

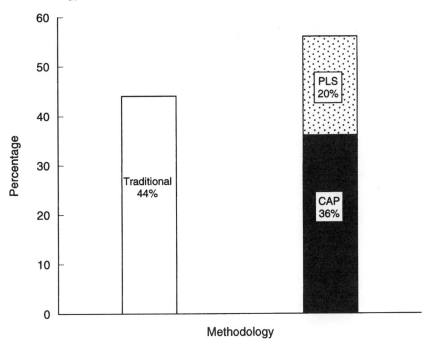

Dunn Learning-Style Model by the Nanuet School District Music Department. The district also was the recipient of the 1996 New York State Music Association's Presidential Citation for Excellence in Music Education. This award is presented to only one school district per year and is not awarded every year.

The number of students selected to participate in all-county and all-state music ensembles has risen to and remains similar to other county school districts that have at least four times the student population of Nanuet. Four of the ninety students selected from a nationwide pool to enter a student composition competition in music were from Nanuet. That feat was a direct outgrowth of the students' Contract Activity Package Activity Alternative creative projects (Dunn & Dunn, 1993).

Members of the music faculty have been invited to serve on committees to establish national music content standards and appropriate representations for benchmarks of student achievement. There has been an addition of at least one part-time position to the music staff because of increased student enrollment in the district every year since the learning-styles implementation process began.

Table 19.1

**Linear Regression Statistics for Attitude Toward Instructional Methodologies and Learning-Style Preferences**

| Methodology | Element | $t$-ratio | $p$ value |
|---|---|---|---|
| Traditional | visual | 2.14 | .036* |
| CAP | light | − 1.28 | .039* |
| | parent motivation | 2.56 | .019* |
| | teacher motivation | 2.42 | .012* |
| PLS | motivation | 2.01 | .007** |
| | teacher motivation | 1.61 | .020* |
| | sound | − 1.07 | .090 |
| | visual | 1.13 | .080 |

\* = significant at the 95% level of confidence.
\** = significant at the 99% level of confidence.

Rehearsals for extracurricular activities, including theatrical productions, marching band, jazz band, and small orchestral ensembles have been established in accord with students' time-of-day preferences. Enrollment in the elective high school vocal music program, taught exclusively through learning-style preferences, is so high it necessitated that the chorus be divided into two groups. Even that division did not provide enough room on the choral risers for all the students in each of the choirs.

Dr. Jack (Gremli, 1999) knows that few students in the Nanuet School District's music program will become a Louis Armstrong. But a learning-styles perspective has convinced him that education can be addressed successfully by identifying both students' and colleagues' strengths and then teaching and guiding through those strengths. Intrinsic motivation, achievement and attitude test scores, and enrollment all increase when learning and teaching styles are accommodated. The Nanuet Music Department evidenced that!

## REFERENCES

Dunn, R., & Dunn, K. (1993). *Teaching secondary students through their individual learning styles: Practical approaches for grades 7–12.* Boston: Allyn & Bacon.

Dunn, R., Dunn, K., & Price, G.E. (1975–1996). *Learning Style Inventory.* Lawrence, KS: Price Systems.

Dunn, R., Dunn, K., & Price, G.E. (1979, 1980, 1990). *Productivity Environmental Preference Survey.* Lawrence, KS: Price Systems.

Dunn, R., & Gremli, J. (1999). Teaching urban students with contract activity packages: Rap, rock, and ragtime—a rational approach. *Journal of Teacher Education, 9*(1), 27–42.

Gremli, J. (1996). Tuned in to learning styles. *Music Educators Journal, 83*(3), 24–27.

Gremli, J. (1999). Effects of traditional versus contract activity packaged and programmed learning sequenced instruction on the short- and long-term achievement and attitudes of seventh- and eighth-grade general music students. (Doctoral dissertation, St. John's University, 1999).

*Chapter 20*

# Denise Parker: Oakland's Reading Expert

*Thomas C. DeBello*

What does it take to get junior high school students to ask for more reading classes? Just ask Denise Parker, reading expert of the Oakland Public Schools, Columbia, Missouri. Since 1988, she and her staff have been increasing achievement and motivating students to read more, and better, through their learning styles. As this reading specialist tells it, she was looking for a way to help students experience success and become "hooked on reading!"

The first group with which she experimented was comprised of eighth-graders who tested below grade level in reading. Many had experienced repeated reading failures in school. After only one inservice workshop presented by her (then) principal, Dr. Mary Laffey (see Chapter 8), Denise began extensive reading about learning styles. She recognized that she, personally, had specific style needs that had to be met if she were to learn something academically new or difficult. Thus, Denise asked herself a basic question:

> If *I* have to design my own environment in a special way for *me* to concentrate on what I am learning, isn't it possible that my students also need variations of the conventional classroom setting for them to focus well? Perhaps many of them don't even realize that they need something different. Perhaps they are unaware of how to change their environment to respond to their personal learning styles.

Out of that experience grew a continuing interest in learning styles and a program that ultimately has helped countless students during the past 10 years since Oakland's learning-styles-based reading program's implementation. With Dr. Laffey's support and guidance, Denise began by experimenting with learning-styles-based environmental practices in her classroom before even attempting to identify her students' learning styles. At various times, she:

- tried playing baroque music as opposed to requiring that the students read in quiet;
- arranged for two softly lit sections of the room as well as the usual bright illumination;
- permitted comfortable seating on a couch, pillows, and lawn furniture that had been donated by parents; and
- permitted sweaters for students who required more warmth than others.

These simple strategies that she tried gave her students the chance to become familiar with various learning-style elements. Her classroom experimentation also took the form of either (1) lowering or increasing the lighting on a particular day or (2) allowing the room to be a little noisy one day and requiring extreme quiet on another day. Students experienced many situations and were invited to articulate their feelings about each prior to actually taking a learning-styles assessment.

Discussions related to the changing classroom pointed out to the class that it was comprised of many individuals with varied needs. When concentrating previously, they all had been required to function as a group—all learning in the same way. As Denise led the discussions, they evolved into problem-solving scenarios.

- How can we meet the style needs of all the learners in our room?
- How do we choose which styles need to be addressed?
- Whose responsibility is it to meet those needs?
- What can we do when one student's learning style distracts another student's learning style?

These provocative topics set the stage for students' styles to be assessed with the *Learning Style Inventory* (Dunn, Dunn, & Price, 1987). That instrument provided an excellent approach for introducing learning styles into the junior high school setting. With the results of the LSI to guide her, Denise formed reading groups, developed instructional materials for each group, re-designed her classroom, and introduced new and difficult material through a variety of perceptual strengths—so that each student could succeed (Dunn & Dunn, 1992). She also showed her students how to use her classroom Learning-Styles Charts to choose partners or groups with similar styles for assignments, homework, or help in understanding their own style or that of a partner.

The results of Denise's first attempts were astounding. Only 12 percent of her students in the previous year's classes had reached nine months or more of growth. Utilizing learning-styles-appropriate strategies, 64 percent of her students reached four or more months of growth in only the first third of the year! Denise has continued to yield similar results year after year!

Those results did not go unnoticed. Quickly, colleagues became interested in using their students' learning styles for whatever they taught. The previous year, principal Mary Laffey had attended the Annual Leadership Certification Institute sponsored by St. John's University in New York City. That year, Dr. Laffey returned to New York with Denise and three other teachers from Oakland Junior High School who formed the nucleus of a group committed to improving teaching and learning through learning styles. Denise's leadership in reading expanded as she added to the repertoire she had developed with the strategies she had absorbed at the Institute. She conducted additional inservice workshops to help colleagues use learning-styles approaches in mathematics and language arts.

With Dr. Laffey' support, reading became the hub of the initiative. Denise Parker's portable classroom was transformed into "The Reading Place" (Elliot, 1991) She created an environment in which students with diverse styles could read and learn to read better. Denise furnished it with cast-off furniture, coffee tables, lamps, and so on.

Then, through a State Incentive Grant, the room also was provided with a computer and printer, software, walkman cassette players, an assortment of instrumental music tapes, and many interesting books. Students were taught to analyze and understand their learning styles. They were shown how to use their strengths whether they were required to work:

• in teams or alone;
• near the teacher or in a section removed from an adult;
• in silence or with soft music;
• near a window for bright light or in a less well-lit area of the room;
• when permitted mobility and when denied it; and
• with or without snacks (intake).

They took responsibility for their own learning by making decisions about how they would attack assignments or studies based on their learning styles.

Collegiality and teamwork among the teachers also helped to establish a unified program. Having the same approach to reading in seventh, eighth, and ninth grades made it easier for the students to progress. And progress they did! In response to the program, students were so motivated to read that they requested an elective class on reading be added to their schedule. In its first year, 33 students enrolled; by its second year, 77 students signed up for the class.

Creating lifelong learners is a goal that many educators established as their top priority. Clearly, because of the leadership of Denise Parker, Oakland's students now have a way for that goal to become a possibility. Teachers have seen the impact of teaching students to understand their own learning styles in increased achievement and improved attitudes toward learning!

## REFERENCES

Dunn, R., & Dunn, K. (1992). *Teaching elementary students through their individual learning styles: Practical approaches for grades 3–6.* Boston: Allyn & Bacon.

Dunn, R., Dunn, K., & Price, G.E. (1975–1996). *Learning Style Inventory.* Lawrence, KS: Price Systems.

Elliot, I. (1991, November/December). The reading place. *Teaching K–8, 21*(3), 30–34.

*Chapter 21*

# Bill Turns Over a New Leaf
# in Rural Cascade, Idaho

*Jeannie Ryan and Rita Dunn*

Bill Leaf has seen increased student achievement since his school adopted a learning-styles approach. But he is not willing to rest on that accomplishment. Leaf, principal of the Cascade School District in Cascade, Idaho, is proud of his teachers and both their ability and flexibility to respond to many students' instructional needs. However, his goal is to have his school become a learning-styles school for 100 percent of the students 100 percent of the time!

He is not the only one who has noticed tremendous change in Cascade! People throughout Idaho and nearby states have been noticing changes too! Learning styles played a significant part in the school's paradigm shift away from the old, traditional program to one that has now been recognized as a model for others to emulate. Last year, the school received visitors from 16 different districts—representatives who visited for one or more days and left enthralled with the wonderful things they had seen. Often they came to observe how the 95-minute block schedule worked as teachers used various learning-style instructional strategies to engage their students in active participation. Sometimes they came to see how the advanced technology was utilized. Whatever their reasons for visiting, they invariably left impressed by Cascade's commitment to learning styles and especially by Leaf's belief that "technology can be the link between individual learning-style strengths and teachers' best teaching styles. It makes individualization workable for both students and teachers!"

## IT ALL BEGAN IN THE LITTLE TOWN OF LEWISTON, IDAHO MANY YEARS AGO

Bill's interest in learning styles started more than a decade ago in a little university town tucked away in the hills of Idaho. He had attended a one-week seminar on campus and was impressed with the hands-on practical applications behind the concept that, to him, "made such sense." That year he tried several of the suggested learning-style strategies and was pleased with their results. He intended to keep working with styles in more depth, "but just somehow never quite got around to it!" And then one day, half a dozen years later, he realized how much time had elapsed, and decided to follow through.

Like many who have been to the Learning-Styles Institute in New York City, Bill Leaf was "absolutely convinced that we could increase the likelihood of all students being successful if we implemented these strategies and techniques." He was fortunate that his enthusiasm, combined with hard work, won the district a grant that enabled him to begin the long, successful journey toward increased student achievement.

During autumn 1995, Bill acquired funding to bring Dr. Rita Dunn to his small, rural district in the scenic western portion of the Rocky Mountains of central Idaho. He then applied for another grant to cover three years of additional funding for learning-styles implementation.

When he received that second grant, Bill decided to focus the available monies on various technologies that would "provide additional avenues to meet the challenges faced by diverse learners." With those funds, the Cascade District purchased 60 small laptop computers that could be checked out and taken home by students. He anticipated that the laptops would complement the learning styles of tactual learners—and it proved to be a wonderful tool for them! Science probes also accompanied those machines, so that the laptop could be used in other laboratory and field learning experiences. Currently, mathematics classes all have classroom sets of TI-92s that provide additional tactual experiences for students.

Laptops and grants are exciting, tangible signs of the commitment to change for the better in Cascade, Idaho. However, the intangible indicators of success, increased student achievement and direct observation of a variety of techniques and strategies, are equally exciting. During the spring quarter of 1994, before the school did any significant work with learning styles, 40 percent of the high school students received grades of B+ or better. After three years of working with learning styles and the increased use of technology, the number of students with B+ or better rose to 47 percent. The junior high school evidenced similar gains in the same time frame, moving from 40 percent receiving B+ or better in 1994, to 49 percent in 1997.

Cascade's American College Testing (ACT) composite scores also improved. During the 1993–1994 school year, before Leaf formally implemented learning styles, students in the college preparatory classes scored at 22.2; those who did not complete the core college preparation classes scored 17.0. Just three years later in 1996–1997, the students with the core class backgrounds increased their scores to 22.8. The state score for this group of students was 22.6 and the national score was 22.1! However, the non-core class students raised their score to 21.0. Leaf noted, "This indicated to me that we were probably educating our general population students better now than we had been before we started our learning-styles project. All students showed gains, but those not specifically taking college preparation courses showed remarkable gains." Before the learning-styles implementation, the non-college core students had scored below the state and national averages. Now, they too were above the state and national averages!

## TEACHING EFFECTIVENESS

Leaf not only sees academic success, but behavioral improvement as well. He believes that when students are feeling successful in school, discipline problems evaporate. That has been the case in the Cascade School District, thanks to learning styles. Leaf and his staff are aware of an improved school climate that they attribute directly to students and teachers feeling better about the learning that occurs in Cascade.

Leaf hesitates to take all the credit for the success of the program. After all, it is the teachers who have to believe in the instructional guidelines and implement them. Mathematics teacher Sally Wise best exemplifies what can be achieved when learning-styles strategies are implemented in the classroom. She uses the technology to identify the learning-style characteristics of students in each of her classes. She then tries to accommodate as many of their traits as she can. She has made major changes in her own teaching style to better meet the needs of her students, especially for her at-risk classes that often are filled with global-tactual students. Mrs. Wise has become an expert with hands-on instructional resources, particularly Electroboards. Of the 120 students she taught last year, not one student failed one of her classes, and most students earned As or Bs.

Leaf speaks with pride about his teachers. He is thankful that Rita Dunn was able to visit his community because, "the keynote speaker or major presenter must be credible beyond any doubt." It often is difficult to re-train teachers and convince them that their previously tried-and-true methods are not reaching all their students.

Leaf attributes much of Cascade's success to the support of three major groups—the administration, the teaching staff, and the students. He stated that learning styles cannot be the dream of only one of these three forces. Rather, it must represent a means to achieving their common goal—that all students have the best opportunity to learn. Although Mr. Leaf provides most of the staff development for his district, he does share that role with teachers who have become outstanding in one or more specific techniques.

Mr. Leaf's district is particularly proud of its response to students' varied time-of-day preferences. The school adopted an alternating block schedule to reflect the time preferences of its calculus students as revealed through the *Learning Style Inventory* (Dunn, Dunn, & Price, 1996). Ninety-two percent of the calculus students tested as preferring early afternoon as their best learning time. Consequently, calculus was taught right after lunch, debunking the myth that the toughest academic subjects should be taught in the morning. And it paid off in terms of grades and students' appreciation!

The Cascade District is successful in that it perceives of its administration and teaching staff as being "warm, caring, and generally quite supportive." The District cites three strategic pillars as the focal point for the success of its schools. Learning styles represents the instructional pillar and it is combined with the use of technology—the second pillar; the Quality School Model for Behavior is the third pillar. Bill Leaf sees these three pillars as compatible when establishing a foundation for success. By validating the instruction for each person as an individual, Cascade truly provides the supportive environment it established as its goal.

Along with the schools' transformation came a personal transformation for Mr. Leaf. He explained:

> I am not the same person I was before I became somewhat knowledgeable about learning styles. I have changed in my relationships with my own family. Before, we simply expected all our children to study and learn in the way we thought to be appropriate. Now, we respect each other's personal traits.

Although he cannot temper his enthusiasm for learning styles, Bill Leaf knows that he must be patient. "I now expect all my teachers to implement learning-styles strategies most of the time. I have found that while that is certainly the goal, I need to be patient and help teachers move in that direction so that we can become the learning-styles demonstration district we should be."

## REFERENCE

Dunn, R., Dunn, K., & Price, G.E. (1975–1996). *Learning Style Inventory.* Lawrence, KS: Price Systems.

*Chapter 22*

# Over the Rainbow with Dorothy Logan-Alexander in Brookhaven, Mississippi

*Thomas C. DeBello*

How can a central office administrator and a building principal work to-gether successfully to improve test scores? Just ask Dr. Dorothy Logan-Alexander and Mr. Dan Brown. Dorothy is assistant superintendent and Learning-Styles Trainer for the Brookhaven School District in Brookhaven, Mississippi, and Dan is the former principal of Alexander Junior High School in that district. Dan's school suffered from decreasing test scores in reading and he asked Dorothy if she could help by providing inservice for his staff in learning styles.

## HOW THE PROGRAM BEGAN

In response to Mr. Brown's request, Dorothy conducted three overview sessions at the next few faculty meetings. She explained what learning styles are, how they differ by age, achievement level, and gender (Dunn & Griggs, 1995), and suggested two or three easy-to-use techniques for responding to some basic individual differences. The first result was that *one* eighth-grade social studies teacher volunteered to begin a small, pilot program; others said that they "might be interested" after they saw what happened with their colleague's beginning efforts.

That one teacher wanted to "try everything!" To Dorothy, that meant that, rather than gradually implement, the teacher wanted to:

• add some informal furniture to relieve some pressure on those adolescents who appeared unable to sit "properly" hour after hour in their wooden, steel, or plastic seats and desks;

- some extent, control for illumination to provide one or two softly illuminated areas and reduce tension for youngsters for whom fluorescent and bright lighting *caused* hyperactivity;

- provide headphones to establish quiet for students who needed it or did not read well but could learn academic material by hearing it with tape-recorded books (Carbo, Dunn, & Dunn, 1986);

- develop multisensory resources for students who learned best tactually;

- develop Floor Games for students who learned best kinesthetically;

- introduce small-group instructional strategies like Team Learning, Circle of Knowledge, simulations, Brainstorming, and Case Studies for those who were peer-oriented;

- experiment with starting new and difficult lessons globally rather than analytically;

- design a few Programmed Learning Sequences for youngsters who required a great deal of structure and were visual and/or tactual; and

- try Contract Activity Packages for motivated students or non-conformists (Dunn & Dunn, 1978, 1993). To do all this would require lots of materials, motivation, persistence, and time.


## REACHING FOR A RAINBOW

District funds were extremely limited, but Dorothy had her mind set on finding, if not a pot of gold, then "a rainbow to give these kids a chance!" She and Dan creatively approached a local bank for assistance in sharing the cost of implementation! As it happened, the bank's manager and Board of Directors each had a "heart of gold!" With finances settled, they continued the training.


## THE NEXT STEP

Next, Dorothy and Dan tested all the eighth-grade students with the LSI (Dunn, Dunn, & Price, 1980). They made students aware of their individual learning-style preferences; their parents were apprised of their offsprings' styles as well.


## THE STEP AFTER THAT

That first year, the environmental elements of light, sound, and seating designs were addressed, as well as intake, mobility, perceptual modalities, the sociological elements, and global/analytic orientations. All eighth-graders participated in this pilot program, including Special Education students.

## AN IMMEDIATE OUTCOME

One outstanding result was that student attendance increased immediately to an all-time high, and disciplinary problems were greatly diminished—just as occurred in the Buffalo City Schools (DeBello, Chapter 22). When asked to explain that phenomenon, Dr. Logan-Alexander credited awareness of students' preferences concerning light and room designs, and the implementation of instructional strategies using sociological preferences as having had the greatest effects. Additionally, everyone in the school—teachers, members of the clerical and custodial staffs, and Dan Brown, the principal—reported that students appeared happier, more cooperative, more attentive, and for the first time in years, "eager to learn." Quite noticeably, students' self-esteem had risen!

## INVOLVING PARENTS

To develop and maintain community support, the school district provided an evening dinner for the parents of the 127 students in that pilot program. At that time, they were oriented to the Dunn and Dunn (1978) Learning-Style Model. Parents received a packet of information about the program and a copy of their child's *Learning-Style Profile.* Subsequent evening sessions were held with small groups of parents who had volunteered to assist teachers in developing tactual instructional resources—items that had not been incorporated into the school's instructional agenda prior to the implementation of learning styles. Those meetings reflected the Board of Education's and the community's support for what was emerging from the learning-styles program at the junior high school! In addition, several descriptive articles explaining the program appeared in local and state newspapers.

## EXPANDING THE PROGRAM

Based on their initial success, the Brookhaven School District encouraged Dorothy Logan-Alexander to continue an annual K-12 staff development program that focused on teachers who were motivated to implement learning styles in their classrooms. Attracted to the Dunn and Dunn model because of the ease with which they could administer and implement it, the Brookhaven teachers also appreciated the LSI's ability to clearly and concisely identify their students' styles. Teachers were given the latitude to implement those aspects of the model that they felt most competent in initiating.

Many kindergarten teachers incorporated several aspects of learning styles and all elementary school teachers became involved with many, if not all, of the learning-styles approaches. In the secondary schools, the environmental and sociological strands as well as perceptual modalities were focused on. Whereas this district reported being in only the "second stage of implementation" (Dunn & Dunn, 1993), even many secondary teachers were using specific instructional resources to accommodate their students' preferences.

## ANALYZING RESULTS

What really made this program successful? Dorothy Logan-Alexander's belief in learning styles as an effective tool and her commitment to it played a powerful role! Principal Dan Brown's recognition of the importance of providing ongoing support to his faculty was a second crucial factor. By allowing Logan-Alexander to work two days each week with the junior high school pilot teachers for the duration of the program, he clearly demonstrated his support of the program. In addition, he encouraged non-participating teachers to visit the pilot classes during their planning periods to observe the program's progress and the instructional strategies that the participating teachers were using.

Brookhaven's success also can be attributed to Dorothy's effective and ongoing staff development. In time, she brought the junior high school students' grades "somewhere over the rainbow"—but in Mississippi rather than in Kansas. Dan Brown's encouragement and staff leadership established the climate. And the inclusion of administrators, teachers, the Board of Education, parents, and the children effervesced the entire process.

## THE RELATIVE IMPACT OF MONEY VERSUS COMMITMENT AND ENERGY

Dr. Logan-Alexander stressed her belief that cost should never prohibit the implementation of a good program. This experience taught her that traditional instruction is far more expensive than learning-styles-based instruction, because it requires more time, materials, and effort to teach all children the same way at the same time.

## THE POWER OF PARENTAL BACKING

One crucial outgrowth of the learning-styles program was to increase substantially parental involvement in their children's learning. Brookhaven parents gave their time and energy to develop resources. They built, painted, traced, drew, provided nourishing snacks, and, in the process, learned a great deal about (a) their own children and (b) how to teach to diverse children's styles. They also learned that they were welcome in their children's classrooms and, indeed, teachers were grateful for their contributions. Dr. Logan-Alexander observed a notable bonding effect as a result of the learning-styles program, and she was impressed with its effects on overall student—teacher relationships.

Brookhaven's learning-styles' success was celebrated by the entire community through articles in local and statewide newspapers. Dan Brown was quoted in a major state newspaper as saying that "learning styles is one of the best programs ever brought into our school!"

## CAN WE MEASURE THE IMPACT ON STUDENTS?

During the second year of the program, a group of 40 junior high school students asked to meet with Dr. Logan-Alexander. When she arrived, they handed her a huge Christmas card that they requested she mail to Dr. Rita Dunn—the "lady in New York who taught you about learning styles!" Each had signed the card and written inscriptions on it. Among some of the more poignant statements on it after "Dear Dr. Dunn," were the following:

- You changed my life when you taught Dr. Alexander about learning styles.
- My heart says, "Thank you"!
- This is the first time I ever passed everything.
- My family is proud of the new me.
- How much does learning style mean to me? My life!
- We will always remember you!
- Someday, I will come to meet you.

## EPILOGUE

Dr. Dunn was so touched by the youngsters' expressions that she mailed a response to the group. She told them how much their card had meant to her and invited them all to attend St. John's University when they completed Brookhaven High School! She eagerly awaits them.

## REFERENCES

Carbo, M., Dunn, R., & Dunn, K. (1986). *Teaching students to read through their individual learning styles.* Englewood Cliffs, NJ: Prentice-Hall.

Dunn, R., & Dunn, K. (1978). *Teaching students through their individual learning styles: A practical approach.* Reston, VA: Reston Publishing Company.

Dunn, R., & Dunn, K. (1993). *Teaching secondary students through their individual learning styles: Practical approaches for grades 7–12.* Boston: Allyn & Bacon.

Dunn, R., Dunn, K., & Price, G.E. (1980). *Learning Style Inventory.* Lawrence, KS: Price Systems.

Dunn, R., & Griggs, S.A. (1995). *Multiculturalism and learning styles: Teaching and counseling adolescents.* Westport, CT: Greenwood.

# Chapter 23

# The Educational *Spirit* of St. Louis: Sr. Natalie Lafser Brings Learning Styles to the Archdiocese

*Nancy Montgomery and Rita Dunn*

Just as St. Louis is the "Gateway to the West," the Dunn and Dunn Learning-Style Model is the Gateway to Education.
—Sr. Natalie Lafser, 1998

Sr. Natalie Lafser has enjoyed a 32-year career encompassing 9 years of teaching, 17 years of counseling, and 6 years as Director of the Office for Learning Style in the Archdiocesan School System of St. Louis, Missouri—the largest school system in the state. Before her retirement in 1995, she produced four videotapes approved by the Learning Styles Network and used widely for teacher training throughout the country, particularly for those new to the profession and those in remote, rural areas. Those videotapes model exemplary practices in the implementation of learning-styles programs. They include clear directions for specific small group instructional strategies for peer-oriented students; capitalizing on individuals' perceptual strengths and adapting teaching for tactual and kinesthetic learners; and interpreting individual students' learning-style profiles. Available for purchase, the videotape set further spreads the word of how to use learning styles effectively beyond the many places where Sr. Natalie was able to travel to present workshops, such as Chicago, Kansas City, and Baltimore! How was such a demand created for her guidance in learning-styles implementation?

## FATE INTERVENED: A ONE-HOUR RADIO BROADCAST

As an active learning-styles staff developer for the Archdiocesan high schools during the 1980s, Sr. Natalie was invited to be the guest on a one-hour afternoon talk show on KMOX in St. Louis, hosted by Anne Keefe. This popular program featured interviews with well-known people from the community, after which callers could telephone in with questions.

After the interview, Sr. Natalie was astounded to learn that her introduction of learning styles to the KMOX radio audience had elicited almost 1,000 long distance phone calls and letters. Sr. Natalie recalls with amazement how "the phone lines never stopped lighting up!"—attesting to the level of the need and interest in the Dunn and Dunn Learning-Style Model.

Sr. Natalie remembers how people teased her after the show, saying that she could have had a career in sales! She admits that when she is convinced of the value of a pedagogical model, she confidently recommends it to others. How did she "sell" 1,000 radio listeners on learning styles? What energized people into paying for long distance charges to St. Louis and to St. John's University in New York for more information? How did Sr. Natalie develop the strong belief that the Dunns' model could make such a difference in helping young people become effective, lifelong learners? Let's take a closer look at the unique career of Sr. Natalie Lafser—a dynamic force in the educational spirit of St. Louis.

## THE NEED FOR LEARNING STYLES FROM A COUNSELING PERSPECTIVE

During her early teaching experiences in elementary and junior high schools in Michigan and Wisconsin, Sr. Natalie became concerned about the needs of children as human beings. During that period, the term "the whole child" was popular, and she translated it to mean that each person's emotional, physical, and psychological traits contributed to the ability or inability to learn well. She decided to return to school—Indiana University at Bloomington—to earn a master's degree in Counseling, which she used to garner counseling expertise in grades K–12.

Many youngsters of all ages and grades experienced some academic problems. However, to Sr. Natalie's perception, the pressure to obtain higher grades and pass important tests caused many senior high school students serious academic and personal tensions that mandated the availability of counseling at that level. Too often, in desperation for a "quick fix," teachers tried scattered approaches. They seized the latest fad of the moment and, if it didn't produce fast results, they would try another fad until no additional time was available.

In addition, there was a prevailing belief that students who were failing were not "trying"; they simply "weren't working hard enough." When teachers had no other alternative approaches available, they suggested that the student might have a "learning disability." The bottom line invariably was that students were blamed for their failures.

## WHY THE COMMITMENT TO LEARNING STYLES BEFORE LABELING

Sr. Natalie described this real incident. The parents of an eighth-grade girl who was failing English came in to request that their daughter be given the *Learning Style Inventory* (LSI) (Dunn, Dunn, & Price, 1985) because they were aware that the school was committed to the learning-styles approach. They did not admit to Sr. Natalie, their daughter's counselor, that she already had gone through a complete battery of psychological testing.

When the LSI had been interpreted, Sr. Natalie explained the student's learning style: she was both low/visual and high/auditory. Therefore, the English teacher's procedure of assigning readings *first* (visual) and then testing the class before any discussion or reading aloud in class (auditory) was not accommodating their daughter's perceptual strengths. Through interpretation of the LSI, Sr. Natalie recommended that the student *listen to the passages read aloud first* (auditory). All she needed to do was:

* read the text aloud onto a tape recorder, and then
* listen intently as the tape recorder played back her own voice reading aloud. An alternative was to:
* read aloud with peers first;
* discuss the meaning of the required reading;
* answer questions related to it (normally found at the end of the chapter); and then
* re-read the material at home that evening.

Sr. Natalie then continued and told them about other aspects of their daughter's learning style. After interpretation of their daughter's LSI profile, the girl's mother opened her purse, brought forth a thick stack of papers, and announced:

> Sister Natalie, we were so concerned about our daughter's grades that we had a battery of psychological testing done. Look at these recommendations given to us by the team of experts who evaluated the tests. They described her problem just as you did, except that you have told us what to do to help her!

Sr. Natalie's analysis had been the result of using only the LSI! She was able to make the same diagnosis, but she also was able to suggest two possible homework prescriptions that would eliminate the student's problems. In addition, her solution was provided without the exorbitant cost in time, money, and emotional strain on the parents and the adolescent!

## SELECTING A LEARNING-STYLES MODEL: UNIQUE EMPHASIS ON STUDENTS

During the late 1980s, while she was head of the guidance department at Aquinas Mercy High School, Sr. Natalie found herself on the Archdiocesan Committee for Planning the Annual Secondary-Teachers' Institute. When someone loaned her an audiotape of Dr. Rita Dunn speaking about learning styles, she was impressed with the approach. She particularly liked the emphasis on the concerns of pupils and their parents; most methods focused on teachers' perspectives. Sr. Natalie had observed that, as students moved up the grade-level ladder, teaching became *less student-centered* and *more content-centered*—on math, science, history, grammar—but not the learner. Hence, more secondary than elementary students "got lost."

In sharing Dr. Dunn's audio presentation with the Committee, it was decided that, for the upcoming institute, instead of a series of staff development workshops on diverse topics, why not select one important subject for in-depth analysis and application? After extensive discussion, members chose learning styles as the topic and the Dunn and Dunn Model because "they didn't want to spend a lot of time, effort, and money on a model that was not well-researched." They also appreciated its already-in-place structure for identifying and prescribing for individuals' styles.

Sr. Natalie was thrilled to secure Dr. Dunn as the presenter for the institute. She and the Committee decided that, for the first time, they would bring together all the faculties, staffs, and administrators of all the Catholic elementary, middle, and high schools in the city of St. Louis and the surrounding countryside. In addition, to expose as many professionals as possible to this researcher and her model, the Committee also invited educators from 32 secondary schools, 88 middle schools, and more than 200 elementary schools. They reasoned that a common knowledge of learning styles would create an atmosphere of open experimentation and excitement about new paths to student academic success. Even if some of the participants were loathe to "buy into the program" at first exposure, they would be less prone to deny support to those who did. Anticipating possible reactions to a new approach to teaching by essentially conservative teachers, Committee members reasoned that there would be more tolerance for some of the learning-styles suggestions if "the teacher next door" understood the basis for students' prescriptions. They were aware that, at the secondary level, fledgling learning-styles implementation can be misunderstood. In addition, widespread exposure to the construct addressed the problem of a lone teacher or two experimenting with learning-styles strategies on their own and being somewhat threatened by the aspersions of their peers.

## DIRECTOR OF THE OFFICE FOR LEARNING STYLES OF THE LARGEST SCHOOL SYSTEM IN MISSOURI

Teachers surveyed after the institute were overwhelmingly positive in their evaluations. However, attending a workshop with thousands participating does not give educators enough to implement a program without the appropriate, ensuing support and follow-up. Sr. Natalie approached the superintendent with a suggestion. The archdiocese had taken a forward-looking step and invited Dr. Dunn to introduce her learning-styles model to the entire system. Both teachers and administrators had been most receptive to the concept. Therefore, why not invest in the complete training of a small cohort of enthusiasts by sending them to the Annual Leadership Certification Institute in New York? In that way, experienced staff developers would be available to guide archdiocesan teachers trying to implement learning-style strategies.

The superintendent appreciated and supported that idea. With the assistance of several certified archdiocesan experts over the next few years, Sr. Natalie established the Office of Learning Styles for the Archdiocese of St. Louis. Serving as its director between 1989 and 1995 enabled her to use her skills in both teaching and counseling. She visited and assisted every K–12 teacher who requested her presence in 125 of the 200 elementary schools in the system.

Sr. Natalie described this far-reaching training to teachers, students, and parents as the greatest challenges and rewards of her career. Success bred success exponentially as teachers were influenced by their peers' positive experiences with learning styles in their own building. Teachers who had not been on staff at the first archdiocesan institute were inspired to seek training and pressured their administrators to invite Sr. Natalie and her staff to visit their campuses.

## WORDS OF WISDOM FROM A SPIRITED LEARNING-STYLES STAFF DEVELOPER

This successful learning-styles staff developer offered the following guidelines for educators interested in improving students' achievement.

### 1. Take "Baby Steps"—But Do Keep Stepping!

Sr. Natalie's suggestion to teachers is to begin wherever they are comfortable. Adapting how instruction is delivered to students is a start. Success with one or two elements produces the confidence to experiment with other elements. Sister has heard things like, "Accommodating pupils' preferences is working very well, but I will *never* allow eating in my class. Do you hear me?" However, sure enough, down the line, initial resistance dissipates in the face of multiple successes.

Another advantage of addressing the elements gradually and systematically is that it is easier to document reliably the effect of that element on different students' grades.

Sr. Natalie believes that learning styles is not an all-or-nothing, now-or-never proposition. Teachers have control over their classrooms and have countless ways, if they choose, to resist any innovation mandated for them. However, despite constraints on their time, energy, and budgets, teachers want methods to enhance student achievement. When staff developers demonstrate that what they offer is helpful rather than burdensome, teachers are appreciative and cooperative. They *want* to understand how to help their students learn.

### 2. Prepare Well for Using and Interpreting the *Learning Style Inventory* and the Individual Profile It Provides

Sr. Natalie reminds us that thoughtful, in-depth preparation of students for taking the LSI is of paramount importance. Any child beyond third grade who sees questions calling for answers written on a piece of paper automatically thinks it is a test necessitating "right" responses. She suggests that counselors or teachers do things like turning off the lights and asking the class, "How many of you might learn better with the lights off like this rather than with them on?" After flipping the lights back on, "How many prefer learning this way?"

Another illustration would be to talk about persistence—which students invariably equate with always being a positive quality. Discuss possible advantages of not being persistent (Sr. Natalie herself is not). When we say that all truthful answers to the LSI questions are acceptable, we mean it!

Depending on the grade level and knowledge of the students' persistence quotient, teachers should divide the LSI questions into segments to prevent fatigue. Read the questions aloud to non-visual youngsters. When the LSI is completed, scores will be more reliable because of this detailed preparation.

Interpreting students' results for parents and children is critical. This requires introducing learning styles to families. It also is effective to administer the adult version, the *Productivity Environmental Preference Survey* (PEPS), to parents.

### 3. Involve Parents and Community Members

It is important to involve and educate parents and the community. Most people have been "brainwashed by school systems and are convinced that there is only one correct way to do homework and to learn." Nevertheless, Sr. Natalie recounts what can happen when parents' thinking is broadened.

> At one faculty meeting, a teacher told me that when her own daughter was in fifth grade, the two had fought every night over homework. The mother admonished the child to "put on the brighter light, sit at the desk, and turn off that stereo!" This same mother, who eventually became a teacher, had attended a PTA meeting at her daughter's school. I was the guest speaker on learning styles.
>
> During the lecture, I apparently used the very same words that mother—and many others in the auditorium—had used with their children repeatedly. Many parents speak to them nightly without understanding that they only are appropriate for analytic children. This particular mother was desperate to end the family fights and help her daughter achieve well in school. The very next night, she told her child, "Go ahead and lie on the bed, read in dim light, listen to your music, and snack while you study. If your grades are better, I'll leave you alone!"
>
> When she became a faculty member, she asked to be on our staff development team. As a teacher, she finally expressed her gratitude. She told me, "I've wanted to thank you for three years for a better relationship with my daughter and for helping her find success in school. Your suggestions for allowing her to do homework in her style really worked!"

## 4. Stop Guessing about What Might Work; Use Learning-Styles-Responsive Approaches, Particularly for "T/K" Students

"What is so wonderful about learning styles is that we don't have to play guessing games any more!" Sr. Natalie stresses the urgency of using tactual or kinesthetic (T/K) materials with secondary pupils whose needs are slighted as they progress through the grade levels. For example:

- A demoralized sophomore who failed the fourth history course in a row appealed to Sr. Natalie for help. Sister showed her how to make simple question-and-answer Task Cards (Dunn & Dunn, 1993)—which she did at the bus stop and everywhere around the campus. One day shortly thereafter, she "bounced" into the guidance office to report that she had "aced the test" with the use of that one manipulative.

- A principal told Sr. Natalie about a freshman who had come into the office in tears. "I'm a failure in school," she cried. Her profile clearly indicated that she had tactual and kinesthetic strengths. That principal taught the youngster to study Spanish with Flip Chutes and Electroboards (Dunn & Dunn, 1993). Incredible as it may sound, the girl was soon on the honor roll. She repeatedly returned to the principal during lunch hours to introduce other students who were having trouble in school. She thought they might profit from the same kind of resources that had helped her. However, those secondary students wanted to hear directly from the principal that it was acceptable for them to learn with the "magical hands-on materials that worked!"

• A public librarian called the school to say that one particular student often studied at the library. The librarian asked, "What has happened to that child? She used to be so morose and down in the dumps, and now she is flying high!"

What can teachers and counselors do to ensure more successes at the secondary level? Sr. Natalie's staff-development sessions on making tactual and kinesthetic materials were such a hit that she scheduled "T/K Days" at each of the schools. Parents volunteered in droves, attended, and created manipulatives with the teachers! Parents became involved in their children's education, made time, energy, and material contributions to the schools, got to know the teachers, and learned how to make resources to help with their own—and other people's children's—homework assignments.

## CAN LEARNING STYLES BE TAKEN TOO FAR?

When asked whether learning-styles-based instruction could be taken too far, Sr. Natalie reflected. She said that, at times, she could almost see the figures churning in the minds of the staff during training sessions: "21 elements times 35 students in my class . . . impossible!" She joked, "It scares them to death!" Instead of multiplying the numbers, she advises teachers to consider the plight of the students who fail—or perform poorly—with traditional teaching.

> Pull out the youngster's learning-styles profile. Locate the one element that "jumps off the paper at you," and tell the student how to work with it! No teacher has to teach everything with learning styles. We don't even have to use every one of the elements. However, sometimes, there are certain elements with which individuals need to come to terms. I know that as well as anyone else!

As an example, Sr. Natalie explained that, although she had been impressed with everything she tried with the Dunn and Dunn Model, "a little voice inside" her head said to her, "This cool and warm stuff (temperature effects); I don't need either. How could that really matter to anybody?" That doubt made her understand that there probably was an element or two that every teacher and administrator had "trouble swallowing." However:

> One student who always had done well in history was failing that one semester and blaming the teacher. Everything on the youngster's profile pointed to the need for a cool environment when concentrating. Feeling "a little foolish and un-guidance-counselor-like," Sr. Natalie sheepishly inquired about the location of the classroom, the student's seat, and the

time of day of her current history class. It turned out that the class was on the sunny side of the building, the adolescent's seat was directly adjacent to a row of windows, and the time of day was right after lunch. She was reduced to offering this "expert" opinion: "My advice, as your guidance counselor, is to ask your teacher if you can move to the other side of the room near the door for cooler ventilation."

The student immediately began passing history with flying colors. Sr. Natalie's response was, "Who cares? If it works, do it!" According to Sister, "No, you can't take learning styles too far."

Sixty-five percent of most instructors are analytic. She asks teachers during staff development, "How well would you do and how long would you remain motivated if you had to come to school every day and learn difficult information while (1) sitting on beanbag chairs or lying on the carpet, (2) studying in subdued lighting, and (3) listening to music? That's exactly how alien your analytic teaching is for global students when you make them concentrate in plastic, wooden, or steel seats and desks, bright light, and quiet!"

Sr. Natalie clearly remembers the words and tone of the student who needed a cool environment to concentrate: "I thought there was something wrong with me. Now I feel good about myself again and I like the way I learn."

Sr. Natalie Lafser would like to leave educators with this rebuttal to the first response many have when they hear about yet another new pedagogical innovation. Children have always had their own individual learning styles, and they always will. The Dunn and Dunn model is not a current fad; it is based on 30 years of empirical research. Learning styles will only be "the latest trend" if you let it be! Don't allow that to happen!

## REFERENCES

Dunn, R., & Dunn, K. (1993). *Teaching secondary students through their individual learning styles: Practical approaches for grades 7–12.* Boston; Allyn & Bacon.

Dunn, R., Dunn, K., & Price, G.E. (1975–1996). *Learning Style Inventory.* Lawrence, KS: Price Systems.

Dunn, R., Dunn, K., & Price, G.E. (1979, 1980). *Productivity Environmental Preference Survey.* Lawrence, KS: Price Systems.

Lafser, Natalie. (1998, September). Personal interview with Dr. Nancy Montgomery.

*Chapter 24*

# Heralding a Hudson Valley Highlight: Regina White, the First Internationally Awarded Pioneer in Learning-Styles Research

*Nancy Montgomery and Rita Dunn*

In February 1971, Regina White attended a workshop conducted by Dr. Rita Dunn, whose pioneering work on individualization would become the prototype for the Dunn and Dunn Learning-Style Model. Dr. White reflects: "I have had the pleasure of a close, collegial relationship with Rita, my mentor and my friend, for 27 years. She changed my life; it has never been the same since I met her!"

## ALMOST THREE DECADES AGO . . .

Tracing Dr. White's illustrious career as a teacher, administrator, and curriculum supervisor in a number of K–12 school systems in New York and New Jersey is fascinating. She has experienced (1) personal obstacles of single parenthood and illness, (2) challenges to her innovative ideas for staff development, (3) groundbreaking scholarship in learning-styles research that won for her an international research award, and (4) professional recognition by national media (Elliot, 1997). Regina White forged a distinctive career featuring milestones in learning-styles research and publications, in pedagogical and administrative leadership, and in extremely successful, practical applications of theory in her own classrooms and in her subsequent staff development for teachers. In a sense, her own career paralleled the emergence and development of the learning-styles construct.

## THE LADY WITH TWIN TWO-YEAR-OLDS WHOSE LIFE HAS NEVER BEEN THE SAME

In 1971, Regina White taught seventh-grade social studies in Seaford, New York, a small district on Long Island. When the curriculum director requested her participation as one of ten teachers in the system approved for attending an inservice workshop on individualization of instruction, Mrs. White's impulsive response was: "I can't possibly go! I have twin two-year-old sons, and I cannot get home at 6:00 P.M.! I am not ready for something like that!"

Despite her protests, one week later she found herself crossing the courtyard from the junior high school, where she taught, to the adjacent high school where she had student-taught and graduated from—to listen to Dr. Rita Dunn. The rest is history!

## THE YOUNG SOCIAL STUDIES TEAM LEADER

After two hours of exposure to Dr. Dunn's presentation, Regina White felt compelled to sign up for Dr. Dunn's course. She then became the social studies team leader in her school, which had heretofore been ultra-conservative. Indeed, some students likened it to a parochial school with classes passing each other in lines on the right side of the hallway. The current administrator, who had been Mrs. White's principal when she was a high school student, did not fully understand the team's experiments with individualization, but she credits him with allowing them to "try it anyway!"

Before long, she and the two colleagues she was informally training were implementing Contract Activity Packages (Dunn & Dunn, 1992, 1993; Dunn, Dunn, & Perrin, 1994). They also changed designs of classrooms from rigid rows of desks to areas for puppet shows, game playing, and film watching.

At that time, the team had a seventh-grade student who was almost 16, but reading at only a first-grade level. The administration merely was waiting for him to turn 16 and leave school for the job market. However, when the team teachers began re-designing their classrooms and initiating learning-style activities, they noticed a change in Seth. Suddenly, he had become aware of everything that was happening around him. He paid attention to every lecture and discussion, became involved in unit activities and, for the first time, got a test score of 100 on the material! The reversal of underachievement in that one boy merely because he could sit informally and work with tactual instructional resources astonished every teacher on that team.

At the end of the school year, as they marked final exams for the 15 seventh-grade classes, teachers began to run in and out of each other's rooms to share their amazement. The students' test results for units taught through Contract Activity Packages—one learning-style strategy—stood out far and above the test scores for units taught traditionally. "What totally blew our minds," remembers Dr. White, "was that even the essays were far superior to those written about traditionally taught themes."

## NEW DIRECTIONS

Although Regina had considered entering law school, Dr. Dunn encouraged her to enter a (then) new doctoral program at St. John's University in Jamaica, New York. Dr. White reports that "Rita prevailed as only Rita can. She sparked my enthusiasm about a novel course of study entitled PACE— Program for Agents of Change in Education." In the meantime, word of the high test scores of Seaford's social studies students became the topic of conversation in that region and representatives of the surrounding school systems began visiting the district's classes under Dr. White's supervision.

## PUSHING THROUGH THE PAIN

Sadly, in the midst of these exciting developments in her work on individualizing instruction through students' learning styles and studying for an advanced degree, Regina White seriously injured her back and was ordered to rest in bed for four months. When she recovered, her physician permitted her to drive only the one mile to school and back during the following term. However, Dr. Dunn summoned her back: "Regina, we're conducting inservice workshops in Island Park and need your expertise in the individualization of social studies." Despite Regina's protestations, Dr. Dunn and the work prevailed again. A colleague was sent to transport Regina White, who reclined in the back of a station wagon to rest on the way to the site! However, the story ends happily, with a return to good health and an ensuing job offer to chair the social studies department in the Island Park (K–8) school district. That invitation was a direct outgrowth of the outstanding impression Regina White had made on the social studies faculty and others who attended the workshop. With no previous interest in administration, but with Dr. Dunn's recommendation and support, Regina accepted the position. Apparently, she had little choice, for the principal told her, "the hiring committee will accept no one but you!"

## EARLY SUCCESSES WITH THE EMERGING DUNN AND DUNN MODEL

At Island Park, beginning in 1974, Regina modeled how teachers could work toward individualizing instruction. She often combined two or three classrooms of students for such demonstrations. Simultaneously, Drs. Rita and Kenneth Dunn were developing the *Learning Style Inventory* (LSI). Helping to test that instrument through her doctoral studies at St. John's University, Regina White decided to test the emotional elements—responsibility, structure, motivation, and persistence—by creating four different social studies classes based on pupils' learning-styles profiles.

Regina was ebullient about researching the LSI in its early stages. She placed students into one of four different treatments. Environments ranged from traditional to independent studies classes in which students worked with one of the five different strategies for teaching the identical academic information through different instructional approaches—each responsive to diverse individuals' learning-style strengths. Thus, in one classroom, Contract Activity Packages (CAPs) were used independently by students with their teacher serving as the facilitator, whereas in another classroom, structured, teacher-directed conventional lessons were provided on the same topic. Student improvement that year supported the reliability of the elements comprising the emotional strand of the LSI and provided support for the use of CAPs over traditional teaching.

Regina White's research also revealed that CAPs were extremely effective with adolescents with specific learning-style traits. She found that nonconformists responded well to three teacher behaviors:

1. Permitting choices;
2. Explaining why, what was required, was important to the teacher; and
3. Speaking collegially rather than authoritatively.

She also found that motivated students who were either auditory or visual achieved extremely well with CAPs. That year, Regina was the recipient of Delta Kappa Gamma's International Award for the quality of the research she had conducted.

## WORD SPREADING AMONG HIGH SCHOOL FACULTY ABOUT JUNIOR HIGH SCHOOL SOCIAL STUDIES SUCCESSES

When Regina White visited the receiving district's high school to coordinate the social studies program, "teachers there already knew that I was a strong advocate of individualization. Now, after the research findings, I was exuberant over what they thought was something new—learning styles! Many did not know the difference between the two!" (Individualizing instruction is what we want to do; learning styles is how we do it.)

During that visit, the ninth-grade high school teachers told her that "they knew immediately who the Island Park graduates were because, 'those kids know how they learn'!" Apparently, the students' learning-styles experiences at the junior high school had taught them how to attack new knowledge with the "right resources for them!"

## APPLYING LEARNING-STYLE CAPs TO SUMMER PROGRAMS

Another innovative application of learning styles was that the district received a variance from New York State that allowed youngsters attending summer school to use CAPs to master only those objectives they had not learned during the year. In addition, the students using the CAPs were required to attend only as necessary for them to master their requirements. That summer program was so successful academically that others came to observe. Another outcome was that Regina White was pressed into presenting learning-styles information even more widely to other districts' staffs. "Nut or not" (her words), she was in demand!

## APPLYING LEARNING STYLES TO SPECIAL EDUCATION

In 1978, Regina continued her secondary-staff development in East Islip, a larger Long Island community of 3,000 students (K–12). Once again, she initiated formal assessment of learning styles in social studies. By then, the LSI had been computerized. Teaching how to address different perceptual modalities, her most important achievement in this district was to use students' learning-style profiles before testing for Special Education placement.

## LEARNING STYLES WHEN THE COACH CANNOT "TAKE IT" ANYMORE!

At a faculty meeting where Dr. White (she earned the doctorate in Instructional Leadership in 1981) was preparing staff to assess for learning styles, Jay, "the assistant football coach and a super teacher," implored her to help. "One boy is constantly darting back and forth to the trash and disrupting the entire class. I can't take any more!" Dr. White tested Jay's class first. Sure enough, that youngster's mobility score on the LSI was 80, much higher than anyone else's score in the school. Because he also needed bright light, he was seated near the window in the back of the room. He was permitted to pace the five feet to the nearest window and then back to his desk as he needed—but without distracting anyone else in the room. At the next meeting, Jay reported ecstatically that the student's grades—and those of the entire class—had risen because they were better able to concentrate on their work. Dr. White concluded the story by saying, "That is why I am so committed to learning styles!" She is less interested in receiving honoraria than she is in spreading the word to help others "turn our young people on to learning."

## RESOURCE ROOM STUDENTS GO MAINSTREAM AND REGENTS SCORES SOAR WITH LEARNING STYLES

The East Islip Learning-Styles Academy was designed through a Carnegie Foundation grant for high school reform. Four teachers of language arts, social studies, science, and mathematics volunteered to use learning-style-responsive instruction with 100 tenth-graders. In addition, three pupils obtained permission from the Committee on Special Education to sign out of Resource Room and into the learning-styles program. After being in the program for one year, the three adolescents were *declassified out of Special Education*, which rarely happens. These three, and the other 97 students in the Learning-Styles Academy, achieved much higher Regents scores than the 100 other tenth-graders taking the same exams!

## A FIRST-TIME PRINCIPAL

As principal of the junior high school in East Islip, Dr. White implemented a learning-styles school-wide assessment of all youngsters. She then provided training for all faculty in how to teach with CAPs and Multisensory Instructional Packages (MIPs) (Dunn & Dunn, 1993).

## A FIRST-TIME ASSISTANT SUPERINTENDENT

In 1986, she became Assistant Superintendent in Wyandanch, New York, an almost 100 percent minority district with the lowest scores in New York State. Despite all the problems generally acknowledged for minority, poverty populations, after working with the principal and third-grade teachers to integrate learning styles, standardized test scores rose 15 percent!

## IF YOU CHANGE THE WAY YOU TEACH, THEY WILL ACHIEVE

In 1988, Dr. White became the principal of a West Orange, New Jersey middle school. At the first meeting with the middle school guidance counselors to determine which students were eligible for Title 1 services for seventh-graders, someone questioned why so many students had been classified for Title 1 since second grade and still required that assistance five years later. Another participant responded that "obviously, these students cannot learn" because they had failed with several different teachers during those years. Everyone was quiet; no one previously had voiced this degree of pessimism toward pupil ability. Dr. White responded, "If we don't teach them the way they learn, they will *never* leave Title 1!"

Dr. White trained one mathematics and one reading teacher to teach in the Title 1 program after testing for learning-styles. The Title 1 students all revealed global processing styles. They also were extremely kinesthetic (in need of learning through active whole-body activities) and had strong tactual (hands-on) modality preferences. In addition, they needed to work in diverse sociological patterns—in a pair, with peers, with teachers, with many manipulatives, with games, and though role-playing and simulations.

An environment was created that included a plethora of multisensory resources to accommodate varied styles. Snacks and music were made available and informal seating was permitted. Dr. White thinks back:

> We simply could not believe the increase we saw in achievement! All made significant percentile gains in math with one child testing out of the Title 1 program in December, three others in April, and all of those going on to do well in regular math. Three more tested out by June and, the following fall, five more. Progress was monitored and all maintained their improved test scores.

## CHANGING NEW JERSEY STATE STANDARDS TO TEACHING THROUGH LEARNING STYLES

From 1992 to 1995, Dr. White led staff development in grades 7–12 in Wood Ridge, New Jersey, with much of the faculty teaching through students' learning styles. All youngsters received their learning-style profiles, and their parents were informed as well. New Jersey maintains specific yearly school goals based on needed change or demonstrated achievement. Wood Ridge's goal was to increase achievement and attitude test scores in global studies by teaching through learning styles. Wood Ridge documented to the state tremendous improvement in achievement and attitude test scores for nearly every student.

New Jersey has state standards outlined for each discipline. Wood Ridge's results confirmed New Jersey's recommendation to teach social studies through not only cooperative learning, but also the Dunn and Dunn Learning-Styles Model!

## REVVED UP IN RHINEBECK

In 1995, Dr. White began her current assignment as middle school principal and district curriculum director for the 1,250 K–12 students in Rhinebeck, in the Hudson Valley area of New York. New York State requires site-based management in its schools. With Dr. White onboard, Rhinebeck's district planning team appreciated having a learning-styles expert in their midst, one who could help pupils accomplish benchmark expositions in grades 5, 7, 10, and 12.

Dr. White began staff development in the winter with an entire session for the staff of the whole district on the superintendent's conference day. Additional courses were offered on how to implement during the summer. In the fall, a follow-up was provided on learning-styles assessment. In time, all students in grades 6–12 had Individual Profiles mailed to them. Presentations were made to inform and involve their parents, and teachers learned to use Flip Chutes, Task Cards, and CAPs in re-designed classrooms.

One global student who had experienced a great deal of trouble in school did a "complete turnaround" after he was taught to help himself to learn through his own preferences. That student was introduced to learning styles in the seventh grade and remained successful through to the eleventh grade. His change was so remarkable that his mother consented to be interviewed about it for magazine coverage.

In spring 1998, middle school children preparing for state assessment tests in reading, mathematics, and social studies were assigned to classes based on their need for quiet or sound, and given a choice of learning in either quiet or with baroque music. Again, test scores rose significantly.

The district's current objectives include administering the *Productivity Environmental Preference Survey* (PEPS) to all twelfth-graders as a "graduation going-away present" to allow them to benefit from their profiles while engaged in college studies or in the workforce. Dr. White believes that systematic, district-wide implementation of learning styles will enable Rhinebeck to have all its students pass the new requirements for the New York State Regents Examinations.

## RESEARCH USING THE DUNN AND DUNN MODEL (1980)

Dr. White was among the first persons to conduct research testing the individual elements of learning styles and to use the LSI as an identification instrument. Because this was uncharted territory at the time, there was skepticism and pressure to change to a more conventional topic and to use an approved instrument. However, persistence (one of the emotional elements) was Regina White's middle name; she was determined to learn how to work with less responsible students.

When she assessed gifted children with the *California Psychological Inventory* (CPI), they scored low on responsibility and insisted on doing math "their own way." Responsibility on the LSI actually approximated conformity on the CPI. Dr. White defended her dissertation in 1980, publishing the first research on the Dunn and Dunn model. She was honored with the Blanton Centennial Scholarship from Delta Kappa Gamma!

## CURRENT HONORS

Eighteen years after that watershed research, Dr. White was invited, along with experts in medicine and psychology, to represent the field of education at a Long Island conference designed to prepare young women and men for the twenty-first century. She addressed them on learning styles because she has seen the rewards reaped by countless students and believes it merits that kind of recognition through a national venue about the future.

## RESEARCH, PRACTICE, AND ASSESSMENT REINFORCING EACH OTHER

An adjunct professor of education at St. John's University, Dr. White has directed staff development in curriculum change in the Carolinas, Tennessee, Illinois, Wisconsin, Oregon, and throughout New York and New Jersey. She has presented at numerous state and national conferences and served as consultant to many school districts. With publications in journals on reading, writing, and learning disabilities, and school research and development, she also has written for the New York State Education Department and authored a text used in every fourth-grade social studies class on Long Island (White & Sesso, 1984).

When Regina White trekked across that courtyard from the junior high school to her old high school on that crisp autumn morning back in 1971 to hear Dr. Dunn speak on individualized instruction, she already was beleaguered with personal and professional responsibilities. However, we have seen that while Dr. White is fully "responsible" in the denotative sense of the word, she is—happily for the field of education—*not* "responsible" (conforming) in the connotative sense of learning-styles lingo.

Never the conformist, Dr. White was indeed "changed for life" through her association with Dr. Dunn and learning styles. Her career continues to be a distinctive one as teacher, curriculum coordinator, principal, assistant superintendent, staff developer, scholar, speaker, and author, Dr. Regina White is truly a Renaissance educator for the twenty-first century.

## REFERENCES

Dunn, R., & Dunn, K. (1992). *Teaching elementary students through their individual learning styles: Practical approaches for grades 3–6.* Boston: Allyn & Bacon.

Dunn, R., & Dunn, K. (1993). *Teaching secondary students through their individual learning styles: Practical approaches for grades 7–12.* Boston: Allyn & Bacon.

Dunn, R., Dunn, K., & Perrin, J. (1994). *Teaching young children through their individual learning styles.* Boston: Allyn & Bacon.

Dunn, R., White, R.M., & Zenhausern, R. (1982). An investigation of responsible versus less responsible students. *Illinois School Research and Development, 19*(1), 19–24.

Elliot, I. (1997, November/December). Off to a running start. *Teaching K–8, 28*(3), 40–43.

White, R. (1981). An investigation of the relationship between selected instructional methods and selected elements of emotional learning style upon student achievement in seventh grade social studies. (Doctoral dissertation, St. John's University, 1980). *Dissertation Abstracts International, 42,* 995A. Recipient: Delta Kappa Gamma International Award.

White, R., & Sesso, G. (1984, revised 1990, 1997). *The Long Island story.* Austin, TX: Steck-Vaughan Berrent Publications.

*Chapter 25*

# Roland Andrews: From the 30th to the 83rd Percentile in Three Years with Poverty, Minority Children!

*Jeannie Ryan and Rita Dunn*

After 24 years in education, nine as an elementary principal, Roland Andrews overhauled his philosophy of education (Andrews, 1996). "I used to place the major responsibility for achievement squarely on the backs of the students," he explained. But after his learning-styles training, he changed his mind and his attitude—and the reading and math achievement of the students in his school!

In spring 1986, Brightwood Elementary School's students scored in the 30th percentile in reading and math on the *California Achievement Test* (CAT). That summer, Roland Andrews, the principal, attended the one-week annual Leadership Certification Institute conducted by St. John's University in New York City. There he was bombarded with information. He struggled to remember all that he could about:

- the prize-winning research that documented the significantly increased achievement, improved attitudes, and better behavior that resulted when students were taught through their learning-style strengths rather than through their teacher's style;
- how to identify students' learning styles at different age and ability levels;
- how to re-design a classroom to respond to students' multiple learning-style traits;
- how to determine which reading approach is best for which child;
- how to use different reading approaches with different children in the same grade at the same time;
- how to work with non-conformists;
- how to work with peer-oriented students;
- how to work with teacher-motivated, but low-auditory learners;

- how to match teachers' teaching styles and students' learning styles;
- how to teach children with different processing styles in the same classroom and at the same time;
- how to teach students with no perceptual strengths and only short attention spans;
- how to teach reading at various children's best time of day; and
- how to use students' strongest perceptual strengths to introduce new and difficult material, their secondary or tertiary strengths to reinforce that information, and how to have them create an original application to secure retention.

But in one week, he could not absorb it all. That fall, Brightwood's teachers began experimenting with what Andrews could share with them. The teachers were given the option of choosing one or more of the learning-styles strategies to experiment with that year. Every staff member volunteered to work with at least one technique, and all but one followed through with the experimentation.

However, Andrews did not leave teachers alone to contemplate their successes and failures.

> Our faculty and I met once each week after school for one hour. During those periods, we discussed and experienced a series of different instructional strategies. We shared what seemed to be working—and with which children.

During that first year, Andrews and his teachers were able to:

- administer, score, and evaluate the *Learning Style Inventory* (Dunn, Dunn, & Price, 1986);
- use small group techniques such as Team Learning and Circle of Knowledge with peer-oriented students (and observed which students could not function well with other children);
- implement tactual and kinesthetic resources for tactual and kinesthetic youngsters; and
- introduce the Contract Activity Package (CAP) and the Programmed Learning Sequence (PLS) (Dunn & Dunn, 1992; Dunn, Dunn, & Perrin, 1994) for students with diverse styles.

Teachers were so enthusiastic about what was happening in their classes that Andrews was impressed with their tremendous energy output.

> I was concerned that they might become weary and burn out, but the reverse occurred. The more improvement they observed, the harder they worked and the more productive they became. Student behavior was so drastically improved, and the students were so cooperative and delighted

with the changes, that our successes were energizing to everyone—
teachers, students, parents, and me!

The more success the students experienced, the more learning-style strategies the teachers tried. Student and teacher morale was on an upswing.
Parents were coming in to find out what we were doing and offering to
help in any way they could!

At the end of only one year of learning-styles implementation, the students' reading and math scores on that same standardized test rose to the
40th percentile in both reading and mathematics. Although that score was
still nothing to brag about, you have no idea of how difficult it is to elevate
an entire school's score by a 10 percent increase across the board! Furthermore, many of the schools nearby were still at the 30th percentile! They
were seeing results!

Teachers were convinced that learning styles were working. More important, teachers were pleased with not only the scores, but the improved behavior and attitudes toward learning in their classes. Parents in this poor
suburban district were so delighted with the improvement in their children
that they collected sufficient funds to send five teachers to the Annual Leadership Certification Institute in New York City during the summer of 1987!

In September 1987, Brightwood Elementary began its second year with
learning styles. The trained teachers who had attended the Certification Institute assumed a leadership role and helped colleagues learn more about
teaching to students' strengths. More teachers began to re-design their classroom environments. They provided for dimmer and brighter areas, informal
and formal seating, and they even experimented with music for those who
needed sound while learning. And school-wide, everyone taught reading in
the afternoon rather than in the morning, because 65 percent of Brightwood's student body evidenced strong preferences for afternoon learning.

In 1988, the CAT scores increased to between the 74th and the 77th
percentile, and Brightwood's African-American students scored 21 percent
above both the district and the North Carolina state average. They also
achieved equally as well as the Caucasian youngsters. Again, parents voluntarily collected monies to send more teachers to study at the summer
Leadership Certification Institute in New York City. In 1989, Brightwood's
CAT scores rose to the 85th percentile in reading and math, which was
among the highest in North Carolina (Klavas, 1993). The African-American
students exceeded this with an average of 88 percent. According to Andrews, "All we did between 1986 and 1989 was change our teaching to
respond to the students' learning styles!" It is crucial to note that students
in Brightwood had consistently shown 15 to 20 percent improvement above
their own previous test scores after their teachers began using learning styles.

Brightwood's teachers and Mr. Andrews learned to disregard demographics like low socioeconomic status, divorce, one-parent families, and under-

achievement. They saw them as unfortunate circumstances, but they knew what happened when students were taught correctly—through their learning styles—and the impact of that energized the staff.

Dr. Roland Andrews changed his views on education (Andrews, 1991).

> Teachers bear the responsibility for identifying each child's learning-style strengths and for then matching those with responsive environments and approaches. Administrators bear the responsibility for providing teachers with monetary, instructional, and emotional support for teaching students through their strengths—rather than through the teacher's style.

Roland Andrews was so pleased with the results at Brightwood that he devised a set of guidelines for administrators considering learning-styles implementation.

- First, he encourages administrators to become informed. He strongly believes that the principal should be totally involved and committed.
- Second, the principal must share his/her knowledge with the staff and parent groups. Use videotapes, magazine articles, outside speakers, faculty meetings, and trips to learning-style schools to educate your community.
- Third, develop staff awareness. Use the learning-style differences within your own staff to allow teachers to relate to the needs of their students.
- Fourth, Andrews encourages administrators to introduce learning styles to the students. This is perhaps the most important step. Students constantly need to be reminded that it is alright for them to learn differently from each another and their friends.
- Fifth, assess the students. Administer the *Learning Styles Inventory* (LSI) (Dunn, Dunn, & Price, 1985) and stress that there is no *right* or *wrong* answer.
- Sixth, share the results of the LSI. Help students understand how they learn best and help teachers prepare a profile for their classes. Help parents know which elements are important for their children.
- Seventh, develop a school plan for success. Use the results of the assessment to diagnose and prescribe teaching techniques to meet identified individual and class styles. Involve parents and teachers in the development of a learning-styles staff development program. Build on the enthusiasm of staff members who express a positive attitude toward learning styles.
- Eighth, Andrew stresses, "Go slowly—although I could not restrain my staff!" If they try to do too much, they may tire of the effort and stop altogether. Of course, when strategies they try are successful, there is no holding them back (Andrews, 1990).
- Ninth, provide ongoing staff development. Establish a regular schedule and use meetings to discuss results, introduce new ideas, reinforce previous sessions, and plan for future sessions.
- Tenth, evaluate progress. Do not expect everything to bloom at once. But do look for changes in behavior, attitudes toward learning, and teacher satisfaction. And

look for improved achievement on standardized tests, class work and tests, and report cards.

In a book devoted to outstanding educators, Dr. Roland Andrews is one of the most inspirational. He is a quiet, self-effacing gentleman in true Southern tradition. Not a person to seek personal acclaim or recognition, he and his staff worked tirelessly to improve the academic abilities of their minority, poverty, often single-parent school population in a region of the United States where many other educators had failed.

As explosive gains were evidenced on standardized achievement tests, the school was (1) examined incredulously, and (2) promulgated into recognition for the quality of its excellent instruction. To its credit, the State Education Department of North Carolina recommended that administrators visit the school to observe, and perhaps emulate, its program. That led to state and national popularity and extensive media coverage, which, in turn, led to the similarly enviable academic gains among previously poorly achieving children in other schools (Stone, 1992) (also see Chapter 21).

## REFERENCES

Andrews, R.H. (1990, July–September). The development of a learning styles program in a low socioeconomic, underachieving North Carolina elementary school. *Journal of Reading, Writing, and Learning Disabilities International, 6*(3), 307–314.

Andrews, R.H. (1991). Insights into education: An elementary principal's perspective. In *Hands on approaches to learning styles: Practical approaches to successful schooling* (pp. 50–52). New Wilmington, PA: Association for the Advancement of International Education.

Dunn, R., and Dunn, K. (1992). *Teaching elementary students through their individual learning styles: Practical approaches for grades 3–6.* Boston: Allyn & Bacon.

Dunn, R., Dunn, K., & Perrin, J. (1994). *Teaching young children through their individual learning styles.* Boston: Allyn & Bacon.

Dunn, R., Dunn, K., & Price, G.E. (1975–1996). *Learning Style Inventory.* Lawrence, KS: Price Systems.

Klavas, A. (1993). In Greensboro, North Carolina: Learning style program boosts achievement and test scores. *The Clearing House, 67*(3), 149–151.

Stone, P. (1992, November). How we turned around a problem school. *The Principal, 71*(2), 34–36.

# Chapter 26

# MagneTech's Gwen Cox:
# The Believe-in-the-Teaching-Staff Lady

*Thomas C. DeBello*

How many educators have fantasized about building a school from scratch, selecting their own faculty, and equipping the building with the latest technological advances? What if you had accomplished all that in three years, and then saw it all go up in smoke—the result of a tragic fire? Well, if you were Gwen Cox, you would roll up your sleeves and start all over again, believing that it would turn out even better next time!

## BACKGROUND INFORMATION

Lawton, Oklahoma is a city of nearly 100,000 people, with approximately 18,000 students enrolled in its school system. Ms. Gwen Cox was Lawton's dynamic Assistant Superintendent for Instruction when the district was faced with the problem of a high percentage of third-graders who were, in Gwen's words, "not yet successful!" Many of those youngsters were seriously "at-risk" for a number of reasons. The typical profile of those students often included:

• low self-esteem
• low reading and math scores;
• non-reading;
• poor social skills;
• discipline problems
• high transience rates; and
• a lack of parental involvement in school—with a population that was highly parent-motivated.

*Board of Education support.* Ms. Cox convinced the Board of Education to provide funding for the establishment of a magnet school to accommodate the approximately 100 identified at-risk third-graders in the district. She was convinced that support for these children through the understanding of the superintendent of schools and the Board of Education was critical to the success of the project. But most of all, she believed in dedicated educators' ability to make academic breakthroughs with children.

*Teacher education.* With a staff and principal specifically selected for this very special program, MagneTech was established as a school-within-a school identified for third-graders. Similarly convinced that what was needed was to find out how these children could learn, Ms. Cox introduced a training program in learning styles for that entire staff.

Principal Ardeth Hearn, Assistant Principal Lisa Robinson, and their instructional staff participated in the training during a two-to-three-year period by attending summer workshops in Dallas, Texas under the auspices of Carole Marshall's Quality Education Systems. While Ms. Cox recognized that the staff was comprised of teachers who had different strengths, she also believed that they all shared a love of teaching, high expectations for their students, and a belief that all children could learn. She liked to say that Ardeth had "empowered" the staff; she "got out of their way and allowed them the dedication, commitment, and professional growth of that entire administrative and instructional staff that contributed to the ultimate success of MagneTech—the learning-styles third-grade school.

## INVOLVING PARENTS

*Reaching out to parents.* Parents also became a key component of the MagneTech learning-styles program. Recognizing that many of the children were very parent-motivated, but that their parents had not previously been involved in their children's schooling, MagneTech's goal was to find a way to draw them in. An extended-day program was instituted so that working parents had time to visit classes in session. Classrooms were opened to parental visitations and notes were sent home to parents in two languages encouraging parental participation. In addition, acceptance of parental involvement on the part of the administration and staff facilitated the active participation of many parents who previously had not been involved in school programs.

*The extended school day.* One exceptional example was the extended day designed for the computer lab in which the children taught their parents how to use computers! In addition, the school purchased life-skills programs for adults, made them available to the parents, and provided assistance so that some parents actually learned to read for the first time!

*State-of-the-art technology and school renovation.* To support learning in a variety of ways, the school was provided with state-of-the-art technology and the opportunity to renovate the facility to accommodate its children's environmental preferences based on their learning-style analyses. To accomplish that, large openings were created between classrooms. Teachers viewed all students as theirs and, indeed, students were given easy access to environments that supported their learning-style preferences.

*Changing the delivery system.* Along with accommodating environmental preferences through classroom re-design, teachers began using small group activities for peer-motivated youngsters. They also adapted lessons for global and analytic learners. Another priority was the conscious effort to respond to students' perceptual strengths as suggested by *LSI* (Dunn, Dunn, & Price, 1990) data—especially the kinesthetic modality which was addressed with whole-body activities and field trips. Tactual resources, such as Flip Chutes and Task Cards, were employed to address the needs of tactual students (Dunn & Dunn, 1992). Students had many opportunities to learn alone, with peers, with an adult, or in any combination of sociological groupings—again, as suggested by the youngsters' LSI information. Given that many of the students had not been successful in traditionally designed programs, such initial steps made good sense and, indeed, produced dramatic results.

## RESEARCH UNDERTAKEN TO DETERMINE MAGNETECH'S EFFECTIVENESS

Through a grant to Cameron University, a research study evaluating MagneTech was undertaken. Both quantitative and qualitative techniques were employed to assess the effectiveness of the program.

*Increased IQ.* The most startling results were in the area of IQ gains! When comparing the participants' mean IQ scores between the fall and spring of the 1990–1991 school year, children gained an average of eight points, as measured by the Otis-Lennon! Thirty-six students had gains of 10 points, and 20 students' IQ scores increased by one standard deviation! According to that report, although 50 percent of the students were expected to miss any question on a norm-referenced test such as the Otis-Lennon, the MagneTech students persevered through the test.

*Improved student performance.* Comparisons between these students' increased achievement test scores between the (then) current semester and for the same time period during the previous year, as measured by the *Metropolitan Achievement Test*, also showed remarkable gains—a 120 percent increase in language, an approximately 85 percent increase in math, a 60 percent increase in reading, and a composite increase of nearly 60 percent!

Reading gains were also measured through a comparison of audio recordings made at the start of the school year and periodically throughout the year. Such gains were revealed in increased sight vocabulary, and the self-confidence to use newly acquired word attack skills. The researchers reported that Ardeth's tone of voice contributed to many of the students' progress from being hesitant to becoming confident and having a sense of power. Additionally, writing samples taken throughout the year showed gains in spelling, handwriting, and the ability to organize thoughts into coherent, logical sequences.

*Social gains.* MagneTech also can boast of gains in students' social skills. Disruptive behavior, whether in class, on the playground, or in the halls, diminished dramatically during the course of the year. The improved discipline accompanied increased academic achievement and self-esteem. Letters from parents have validated the role the school has played in breaking the children's cycle of failure.

## A TRAGIC EVENT

After its second year in operation, MagneTech and the school it was housed in were devastated by a fire that might have made it impossible to continue. Summoning all possible community resources and support, MagneTech reopened in available space within the community. The lack of traditional classroom space might have been a major setback to others, but with Gwen Cox's leadership, MagneTech staff, students, and families pulled together to keep the program alive.

Ms. Cox and MagneTech's staff believe that all children can learn when provided appropriate teaching tailored to fit the child's learning style. That belief has become their core philosophy. In addition, Ms. Cox strongly believes in the power of the instructional staff when it has been empowered to initiate learning-style strategies with substantive training and support.

## REFERENCES

Dunn, R., & Dunn, K. (1992). *Teaching elementary students through their individual learning styles: Practical approaches for grades 3–6.* Boston: Allyn & Bacon.

Dunn, R., Dunn, K., & Price, G.E. (1975–1996). *Learning Style Inventory.* Lawrence, KS: Price Systems.

*Chapter 27*

# With a Song in Her Heart:
# Dee Ainsworth of Manchester, Missouri

*Thomas C. DeBello*

From music teacher to staff developer, and with a song in her heart, Delilah (Dee) Ainsworth successfully introduced learning styles into her school and district. Barretts Elementary School, in the Parkway School District, has an enrollment of little more than 600. There are 26 classroom teachers and 19 support staff, with an average class size of 23. About 15 percent of the students were African American and 2 percent were Asian American. Whereas the majority of students scored above average on math and reading assessments, 9–10 percent received remediation in those subjects and an additional 7 percent were classified Special Education.

Barretts School's community is made up of highly educated and skilled middle-class people from many cultures. Although the demographics of the area vary from one end to the other, the school district maintains a unique, open-minded unity with flexibility and individuality as its cornerstone.

It is, perhaps, those characteristics that provided the fertile ground for Dee to share her enthusiasm for learning styles. Having attended a learning-styles conference in St. Louis, Dee was motivated to implement it with her classes. She began by observing her students and adapting some of the learning-style strategies that she had learned.

After seeing the positive results, her principal supported Ms. Ainsworth's efforts, allowing her to present learning styles to the faculty. Recognizing the successes she had, 14 of her colleagues joined in a pilot program in 1990. That program had a great impact on their school and other schools in the district.

Dee received training as a certified learning-styles consultant after attending the annual Certification Institute in New York City. She then returned to Manchester that summer to conduct a special summer workshop for teachers who volunteered to pilot the program. Those teachers began the 1990 school year by introducing learning styles to their students, assessing their styles, and modifying their instruction to complement student style preferences.

At first students were given the opportunity to discuss their personal preferences and teachers led those discussions, often sharing their own stories. Afterward, they were read *Elephant Style* (Perrin & Santora, 1982) or *Mission from No-Style* (Bralo, 1988) as a preparation for taking the *Learning Style Inventory* (LSI) (Dunn, Dunn, & Price, 1985). When the surveys were returned, teachers created charts identifying each student's style. Those charts were mounted on a wall in the classroom so that each child became aware of other children's learning styles. Right from the start, children were taught to respect the style differences of their classmates.

Teachers then began to modify their classrooms according to students' learning-style preferences. They then introduced Team Learning activities and lessons in students' preferred sociological groupings. Additionally, such materials as Flip Chutes and Task Cards were introduced for tactile learners. The success of the pilot program spread to other classes and, since that beginning, Dee has been invited to conduct workshops every August to the Parkway School District teachers.

Observers to Barretts School can see many examples of learning-styles implementation throughout the school, and in special area classes. Classroom teachers routinely teach to both global and analytic learners simultaneously. Children are allowed to choose assignments in order of their perceptual preferences, and nearly everywhere you will see tactual materials in use. Some teachers have started to use Contract Activity Packages (CAPs) as part of their instruction.

As the school's music teacher, Dee incorporated and modeled learning styles in all her classes. She presented materials in four modalities simultaneously and emphasized that she used more techniques for the global learner than she did in the past. Through story telling, acting, singing, and shaping images with her hands and body, Dee modeled a multisensory approach that broke with traditional pencil-and-paper learning tasks. Since there are few researched approaches to learning styles for music classrooms, Dee has been breaking new ground!

Barretts' physical education teacher, Linda Luttbeg, also employed learning-style strategies in her classes. In a full research study that she completed for her master's degree, Ms. Luttbeg chronicled a learning-styles-based unit that she prepared for teaching archery to sixth-graders. Introducing the unit through students' primary modalities and then reinforcing with their secondary and tertiary preferences produced success for all learners. Students in the study showed significant gains in terms of their pre- and post-test scores, as well as improved attitudes toward learning! One student summed up the responses of the other students: "I learned a lot about archery and had a great time. I also learned more about my own learning style!"

Ms. Ainsworth reported that the first student changes that were noticed were attitudinal. Not only were students better able to do whatever they needed to help them learn better, but students who had been struggling actually reported greater confidence in themselves! In addition, there were fewer discipline problems. Sometimes academic gains occurred when schedules were changed to accommodate time-of-day preferences of mathematics students. Other students evidenced academic gains when the environment became responsive to their light and sound preferences.

Parents were included in the process from the beginning. Ms. Ainsworth gave parent presentations explaining the LSI printouts of their children's learning styles. Parents were encouraged to work together and to form a parent group to create materials for the children to use. Parents also have been involved in projects to support teachers' learning-style efforts and have become strong supporters of the program. Parents also brought awareness of learning styles to their friends and neighbors.

Both parents and her colleagues recognize Dee Ainsworth's commitment and appreciate her efforts on their children's behalf. She often is stopped by a student or a parent who is eager to tell her of yet another learning-styles success story. Those stories range from the:

- Special Education child who improved his math grades while listening to Baroque music;
- male student who was accepted to one of the top law schools in Virginia because of how he applied his learning-style strengths to studying;
- parent who wanted to buy a house in the area because she wanted her child to attend a school that "teaches to children's strengths."

The word of Dee's successes spread throughout the Parkways School District. Because there were so many students and adults who benefited from knowledge of learning styles, teachers from 22 of the 26 schools in the district volunteered to learn more about learning styles. Dee has been busy giving workshops and training teachers to implement learning styles in their classrooms. Recognition of the success of the project has even reached the local private school community, and Dee also has given workshops for the local Lutheran school.

Dee recognizes the hard work and effort it takes to make the impact she and her colleagues have had. She cautions staff developers to start slowly and avoid the appearance of mandating implementation. In addition, she strongly advocates open communication with parents and students, stating that children must know and "live" their own styles.

Based on her experiences, and the successes she has seen, Dee Ainsworth has a definite opinion about what "good" schooling is. In her own words,

"Good schooling is meeting the learning needs of all students. There is no greater gift we can give our children than to teach them to recognize and capitalize on their learning-style strengths and to use those strengths for life."

## REFERENCES

Braio, A. (1988). *Mission from no-style: Wonder and Joy meet the Space Children.* Jamaica, NY: St. John's University's Center for the Study of Learning and Teaching Styles.

Dunn, R., Dunn, K., & Price, G.E. (1985). *Learning Style Inventory.* Lawrence, KS: Price Systems.

Perrin, J., & Santora, S. (1982). *Elephant style.* Jamaica, NY: St. John's University's Center for the Study of Learning and Teaching Styles.

*Chapter 28*

# Joan DellaValle: A New Yorker Brings Learning Styles to Her Long Island School

*Thomas C. DeBello*

"Moxie" is a term that is not used too frequently today. It brings to mind determination, motivation, and know-how, and it seems to fit a quintessential native New Yorker—one whose energy, enthusiasm, and skill are brought to everything she does. Her voice epitomizes New York; her commitment to children and their success in school epitomize her passion.

> First and foremost, I truly believe in the philosophy of learning styles. It makes it possible to examine, without criticism, differences among children, staff, materials, and methodology. That allows us to select the best match for each student.

## BACKGROUND INFORMATION

Dr. Joan DellaValle is no newcomer to the field of learning styles. She received her doctorate in 1985 from St. John's University, where she worked closely with the Center for the Study of Learning and Teaching Styles. She has established herself as a leading researcher in the field of learning styles and has several publications to her credit. Her award-winning doctoral dissertation on some students' need to move while learning (mobility): (1) influenced instructional practices, (2) served as a basis for future research, and (3) received three national prizes—one each from the Association for the Supervision of Curriculum Development, Phi Delta Kappa, and the National Association of Secondary School Principals (DellaValle, 1984).

Through her presentations at the Annual Leadership Certification Institute in New York City, Joan quickly became known as a leading staff developer. She has traveled widely, conducting workshops and conferences, and helping schools and school districts establish learning-styles-based programs.

However, it is at Otsego that she is at home. Otsego Elementary School is located in Dix Hills, Long Island, and is in Suffolk County's economically affluent Half Hallow Hills School District. Joan brought her engaging smile and her own brand of moxie to the school when she became principal in 1986.

How did a well-known researcher and staff developer introduce learning styles to her own elementary school staff? "Slowly" is what she would say. "I brought to Otsego my interest in learning styles and the belief that we must adapt our learning strategies to meet students' differences." It is, perhaps, the knowledge that, as principal, she would have many formal and informal opportunities to expose teachers to learning styles over time that she choose not to take a more aggressive stance.

Instead, Joan invited a small group of teachers to work with her to develop hands-on instructional resources for their classes. Building on the base of Special Education and remedial teaching, others slowly joined. Eventually, an overview was provided for the entire staff, and teachers were encouraged to begin wherever they felt most comfortable. The first sign that the program had gained acceptance was the staff's use of tactual kinesthetic materials to teach children who did not learn easily by listening to lectures or discussions. When they saw that their children were enjoying the Flip Chutes, Task Cards, and Electroboards and learning from them, teachers were hooked!

Meeting in the morning before school, Joan conducted a 15-hour inservice workshop; attending teachers received one inservice credit for participating. By starting slowly, and allowing teachers to "buy into" the program as it met their needs, they began to develop understanding and commitment. Additionally, they recognized that their own style differences were valued and supported by their administrator. Joan accomplished that through her supervisory techniques, and through positive affirmation of the differences between and among the staff.

> I also provided a time for teachers to make materials together. We met in my office on Friday mornings and developed tacual/kinesthetic materials for their students. This increased comradery provided topics for discussion about academic needs and learning styles.

That personalized consideration was part of the approach that built long-term commitment and established a team spirit. Additionally, teachers enjoyed the materials and the Team Learning activities, which they were able to use immediately in their classrooms.

When Otsego's learning-styles program was initiated, the advantages of recognizing differences among students was emphasized. The school's motto, "Everyone Deserves Respect," set the tone and the notion of individual differences in many ways. The use of learning styles also helped to assimilate Special Education students into the mainstream classes.

One of the most critical aspects of staff acceptance and understanding is in their own self-awareness—knowledge of how they learn and their learning styles. The big breakthrough occurred when the teachers were administered an adult learning-styles identification assessment. When the teachers received their own personal profiles, they related the concept of style to themselves and then carried it into the classroom. Through additional staff development, the faculty began to learn about their own styles and the differences among themselves.

> We focused on global and analytic processing and soon teachers were teasing each other about their differences, rather than complaining about the lack of uniformity.

Examining differences among their and their colleagues' styles enabled teachers to consider the placement of students in classes based on the best matches between students' learning styles and their teacher's teaching style.

As a school administrator, Dr. DellaValle found that her understanding of learning styles helped her to encourage teachers to use their strengths, rather than to change their teaching styles. Such awareness ultimately helped to encourage diversity and provided greater flexibility for students.

Teachers also are encouraged to investigate other programs, with the understanding that no single program or method will be best for all students. For example, Cooperative Learning and multiple intelligences have been integrated into the school's learning-styles-based program with, as Joan puts it, "even more flexibility in terms of our understanding of children's styles and their academic needs." Additionally, such strategies as Whole Language and thematic instruction are used when teachers believe they will complement specific children's learning styles.

Joan sees learning styles as contributing to good schooling in that it combines beautifully with and supports any new program, method, and material being introduced into education. Indeed, children's individual learning styles determine *for whom* each strategy is likely to be effective. "And, contrary to the popular bandwagon approach, we have found that *nothing works for even a majority of children!* Furthermore, some things work only some of the time!" She adds:

> Learning styles is a philosophy that provides options in approaches to learning. It removes negativity from a lack of success by providing an alternative reason for failure—a mismatch between the method and the student. This ultimately generates success when the match is made.

Rather than first seeking what is wrong with a student who is experiencing difficulty, alternative approaches based on our knowledge of how that child learns best are what we try.

At Otsego Elementary School, the learning styles of all third-grade students are assessed with the *Learning Style Inventory* (LSI) (Dunn, Dunn, & Price, 1996). The results are shared with parents in the form of the child's LSI printout at parent conferences. The continued dialog and use of materials related to learning styles has helped build the language and climate of the school.

Through parent workshops and meetings, Joan uses a blend of humor and her own experience as a parent of two sons to convey incidents that parents relate to easily. Parents become part of the conversation and share in understanding how learning styles affect their child. They have come to understand that learning styles is neither an added-on program nor a set of instructional strategies; rather, it is infused into the mission and culture of the school.

How does this administrator measure the success of such an approach? Joan has seen attitudinal gains in terms of her students' acceptance of each other as individuals and learners; the same was true for the staff's acceptance of each others' varied styles. Concurrently, Joan attributes a sharp reduction in discipline problems to the fact that students were given more freedom to work in appropriate environments in which they *could* succeed.

Children working either in pairs or in cooperative groups had opportunities to move to comfortable spaces and/or to communicate with each other. They were not being admonished for speaking to their peers because they were allowed to do so.

Contributing to that overall change was the relaxed atmosphere in the rooms of teachers who allowed students to work in informal areas. That, Joan believes, reduced stress for some youngsters, contributing ultimately to their greater success in school both socially and academically.

New York State, like much of the nation, has adopted new standards in all academic areas. Those standards also have performance indicators that clearly identify the types of activities students should be engaged in to demonstrate needed competencies. Otsego students, through their experience with learning-styles-based strategies, have experienced high levels of hands-on activities supported by this approach. Joan anticipates that even with new assessments being implemented during the 1999 school year, students at Otsego will continue to achieve at high levels.

While Joan would be the first to say that her primary commitment is to her students and staff, she has developed an excellent reputation as an author (DellaValle, 1990; DellaValle & Sawyer, 1998; Dunn, DellaValle, Dunn,

Geisert, Sinatra, & Zenhausern, 1986) and a learning-styles staff developer. Joan brings knowledge, skill, and charisma to all that she does, making her a truly successful supervisor!

## REFERENCES

DellaValle, J. (1984). An experimental investigation of the word recognition scores of seventh grade students to provide supervisory and administrative guidelines for the organization of effective instructional environments. (Doctoral dissertation, St. John's University, 1984). *Dissertation Abstracts International, 45,* 359A.

DellaValle, J. (1990, July-September). The development of a learning styles program in an affluent, suburban New York elementary school. *Journal of Reading, Writing, and Learning Styles International, 6*(3), 315–322.

DellaValle, J., & Sawyer, E. (1998). *Teacher Career Starter.* New York: Learning Express.

Dunn, R., Dunn, K., & Price, G.E. (1996). *Learning Style Inventory.* Lawrence, KS: Price Systems.

Dunn, R., DellaValle, J., Dunn, K., Geisert, G., Sinatra, R., & Zenhausern, R. (1986). The effects of matching and mismatching students' mobility preferences on recognition and memory tasks. *Journal of Educational Research, 79*(5), 267–272.

*Chapter 29*

# Susan Wellman: Wisconsin Classroom Teacher Turned Staff Developer

*Thomas C. DeBello*

If a goal of education is to improve students' academic performances, there should be no hesitation in implementing learning styles. That is exactly what it does!

Susan Wellman, teacher at Elm Lawn Elementary School in Middleton, Wisconsin, bases the above claim on repeated personal experiences. When she first introduced learning styles into her classroom, her students, on average, outperformed and had greater depth of understanding than students in classes that "covered" the same material traditionally. That effect has been repeated every year since then.

Like many other teachers, she first became aware of learning styles through a course she took at a local university. Then, through workshops she attended in her school district, in North Carolina and, eventually in New York City, Susan became a certified learning-styles trainer. She has since shared her experiences and knowledge with others in her school and district through inservice sessions and courses sponsored by her district.

Susan's school and district administrators were strongly behind learning-styles implementation. On the district level, Rita and Kenneth Dunn were invited to present two one-week summer workshops for two consecutive summers in 1992 and 1993. The entire staff was invited to have their own learning styles identified through the *Productivity Environmental Preference Survey* (PEPS) (Dunn, Dunn, & Price, 1990). At Elm Lawn, action teams were formed that met on a monthly basis to discuss implementation of the program.

Elm Lawn Elementary School adopted learning styles as a building goal, and time was provided to develop learning-styles materials. Successes were shared, and learning-style updates were published in the school's bulletin.

The plan for implementation began with teachers assessing all of their students, and sharing the results with the children's parents. The school district offered district-wide inservice programs for parents and the Elm Lawn PTA sponsored an inservice program on two different occasions. Parent newsletters contained information about learning styles. This comprehensive community education project genuinely sought to educate and inform parents. For example:

• children's learning-style profiles were shared with their parents during parent-teacher conferences;

• individual homework prescriptions explaining how each child should study and do homework based on his/her learning-style strengths were explained and given to parents;

• teachers developed class profiles that they shared with team members and special-area teachers;

• teachers re-designed their classrooms to accommodate the children's styles;

• all classrooms provided for some formal and informal areas;

• most teachers made some accommodation for lighting and sound;

• teachers developed and used tactile and kinesthetic instructional materials;

• teachers explained children's learning styles to them; and

• children were taught to make instructional materials that corresponded to their tactual or kinesthetic preferences.

In addition to the academic gains she noted, Mrs. Wellman saw attitudinal differences as well.

> All of my students enjoyed using materials geared to their learning styles. Those students whose style was best accommodated by Contract Activity Packages (CAPs) (Dunn & Dunn, 1992) liked sharing the Activity Alternatives they made with others. Students who used the Programmed Learning Sequences (PLSs) liked working independently and using the manipulatives that I created as part of them for reinforcement.

Susan urges that administrators appreciate that the most important first step is adequate inservice education for their staff. That initial, in-depth training should be followed by time for teachers to work, either individually or in groups, to create and develop units that are critical for success.

> It is important to begin the term with the CAP and PLS instructional materials that correspond to the units that will be taught and the different learning styles among the students. Therefore, teachers need to know *what* they will teach and *which materials will be needed* for those

units, and they need the *time* to make the materials in advance so as to coordinate them with the planned-for instructional units.

As for the costs, Susan sees this approach as supplanting traditional text-books that many schools have come to rely on. Therefore, book funds could be diverted for purchasing learning-styles-based materials and/or to provide teachers with the time to develop Multisensory Instructional Packages for poorly achieving students. She emphasizes that, once the instructional units have been identified and the materials created, they can be used repeatedly, year after year (like a book), with only minor adjustments needed for student variations. If teachers in a grade or in the same discipline each created one or two units, the work could be done easily and would not have to be replicated. In addition, St. John's University's Center for the Study of Learning and Teaching Styles has hundreds of units on all grade levels and subjects available for purchase, and permits their duplication within the same school district.

Susan Wellman's experiences as a classroom teacher and subsequent staff developer have given her insight into implementing a successful program. She values this approach that continually keeps both parents and teachers informed about how each child learns. Susan cautions others not to impose learning styles on teachers; rather, provide all staff with a quality inservice program and opportunities for teachers to meet, share ideas, and make materials. Through her knowledge and values, Susan Wellman has become a successful learning-styles practitioner and staff developer.

## REFERENCES

Dunn, R., & Dunn, K. (1992). *Teaching elementary students through their individual learning styles: Practical approaches for grades 3–6.* Boston: Allyn & Bacon.

Dunn, R., Dunn, K., & Price, G.E. (1975–1996). *Productivity Environmental Preference Survey.* Lawrence, KS: Price Systems.

*Chapter 30*

# Sherrye Dotson: "Learning Styles Is Just the Way We Teach!"

*Nancy Montgomery and Rita Dunn*

- Every child should be in a learning-styles program. It is wonderful!

- This is the best year he's ever had since first grade!

- Extend the learning-styles classes to every grade for every child. Children *want* to come to classes like this!

- This program has been great for my daughter. She became an avid reader. The combination of Whole Language and learning styles was key to her having a phenomenal school year.

- The choice of working alone or with a group was so much better for him than reading or listening to his teachers! He's a "new person!"

- My daughter talks constantly about her assignments and projects with such enthusiasm!

- My son was always very active and had trouble sitting still. We were thinking of asking the doctor if Ritalin would help. With learning styles, he behaves just as he should in his informal seating. He causes no problems. His teacher said he's "just fine!"

These were just a few of the comments from parents during Sherrye Dotson's eight-year tenure as Secondary Curriculum Director in the Jacksonville Independent School District (JISD) in eastern Texas. And those statements were representative of parents in Jacksonville's ethnically diverse population. Approximately 60 percent of the district is comprised of low socioeconomic-level families, many with non-English-speaking children. The remainder of the community enjoys high socioeconomic status; very few pupils are from middle-income homes. Thus, the district posed a challenge for educators required to meet the needs of learners from an array of diverse cultural and financial backgrounds.

## FROM THE MATH CLASSROOM TO THE LEARNING-STYLES PULPIT

Sherrye Dotson credits some of her staff development successes to the fact that she brought five years of intensive experience with applied learning-style strategies in high school math classrooms to her position as Jacksonville's Curriculum Director. Originally, she taught in a learning-styles high school in Corsicana, Texas under the leadership of principal T.Y. Harp (see Chapter 14). There, Sherrye had progressed through the ranks with the Dunn and Dunn Learning-Style Model (Dunn & Dunn, 1993) so that, when transferring to Jacksonville in 1989, she enjoyed credibility with its teaching staff. They appreciated that, since she had experienced their daily challenges firsthand, she was not sermonizing about a system with which she was unfamiliar. She honestly could say, "Let me tell you about the immediate successes your students will have!"

## THE SUPERINTENDENT'S DISTRICT GOAL

After attending an intensive workshop on learning styles in Dallas, Jacksonville's (then) superintendent became committed to bringing its instructional practices to his district and employed Mrs. Dotson because she was a certified Dunn and Dunn trainer and had conducted extensive staff development throughout Texas. He wanted her to be an advocate who "could promote, encourage, support, and preach learning styles to the entire district." Experience had taught Sherrye that it takes three to five years to get a viable learning-styles classroom established, and she anticipated that it would take at least that long to revitalize an entire school district. Nevertheless, with perseverance and patience, she accomplished the task.

By the time Sherrye transferred to a new district eight years later, things that were once shockingly unconventional in the district had become commonplace. Learning-style strategies in all of their stages were observable. In addition, several principals and trainers had been certified by St. John's University's Center for the Study of Learning and Teaching Styles in New York City. In addition to the Jacksonville educators having implemented the program in their own schools, many also had provided workshops in Dallas and its surrounding districts. How did Sherrye Dotson accomplish such a comprehensive and effective implementation of the Dunn and Dunn model?

*The importance of administrative support.* The success of JISD reflects on the cooperative efforts of a team of professionals consisting of curriculum directors, campus principals, teachers, counselors, and consultants. However, like many other learning-styles specialists, Sherrye Dotson cites the most important component as administrative support from the Central Office to the school campuses so that instructors feel comfortable, rather than threatened or misunderstood, when they experiment with non-traditional methods. What kind of support should the administration offer? Sherrye itemizes the following.

1. Do not mandate change; encourage and nurture it.

2. Actively voice support for the new program and demonstrate encouragement to staff by providing funds and personnel to assist in its implementation.

3. Sherrye provided assistance for the program personally and brought in others through the Texas Learning-Styles Center for Staff Development. She recommends that school personnel obtain certified specialists from any certified training center. (See Appendix A for a listing of learning style centers.)

4. Offer ongoing staff development for teachers and administrators specifically in learning styles:

   a. Provide gradual, but complete, training for new staff.

   b. Make available advanced and refresher training for experienced staff.

   c. Provide materials and time for instructors to develop ready-for-use-with-their-classes tactual and kinesthetic resources and Multisensory Instructional Packages.

   d. Allow adequate time for teachers to change at their own level of comfort.

   e. Schedule follow-up for coping with glitches, continued sharing, and the introduction of advanced resources like Contract Activity Packages (CAPs) and Programmed Learning Sequences (PLSs).

5. Establish good public relations

   a. Encourage networking with other teachers, schools, and districts. [Learning-style schools exist internationally.]

   b. Welcome visitors for campus and classroom observations.

   c. Allow teachers and administrators to visit other districts to inservice their staffs.

*Integrating and connecting innovative strategies.* Mrs. Dotson also recommends that teacher recruitment should focus on those who are committed to change and new ideas. Once a learning-styles program is in place and has produced achievement and attitudinal improvement, the previously more recalcitrant staff becomes eager to participate in something that has proven its effectiveness. Supervisors easily identify the energetic teachers who are unafraid of challenge. Once those instructors are successful, their colleagues *want* to jump onto their bandwagon.

## ENERGIZING RECRUITMENT

To initiate recruitment efforts in Jacksonville, teachers who accumulated 30 hours of staff development became eligible for a stipend, which led to positive attitudes and a readiness to participate in the six strands of concentration, *one* being learning styles. To avoid staff development that was "hit or miss" and provided little follow-up, Sherrye designed a program with a variety of different areas, but tied them all together into interdisciplinary units for relevance and continuity. For example, when a teacher chose to develop a learning-styles lesson in math for gifted and talented students, she also could incorporate knowledge she had acquired about technology, particularly with both tactual and kinesthetic keyboarding.

## COLLABORATIVE PLANNING OF CLASS-READY LESSONS

Mrs. Dotson believes that, whereas most teachers plan lessons to organize themselves, greater emphasis should be directed toward organizing for their students. She encouraged teachers to bring their plan books to workshops and assisted them in analyzing one week's worth of lessons and assignments. They each were asked to compare the number of lessons that had been planned to include (1) global or analytic components and (2) tactual- or kinesthetic-modality resources as opposed to auditory and visual emphases.

That was an "eye-opening" exercise that required teachers to tally the activities they actually had youngsters become involved in. Typically, each teacher's lesson plans fell strictly into one category—the standard linear lecture supplemented by readings—or the reverse. What to do? If a teacher focused inequitably on the analytic and the auditory, then his/her next week's plans had to include at least one global and one tactual activity daily.

Teachers often nod along at workshops when spoken to about innovative practices, thinking: (1) I already do this, (2) I already know that, or (3) of course, students do not just learn by listening to me talk.

However, Sherrye's method actually insured that teachers targeted their specific and immediate lesson plans toward their students' characteristics. What if the teacher recognized that he did a bit too much lecturing but couldn't think of anything tactual to do? Sherrye noted that, after a workshop, even well-intentioned teachers who planned lessons by themselves easily fell back into their old habits. However, when they were allowed plenty of time in subsequent follow-up sessions to plan changes in small groups in which they and their peers could brainstorm ideas to round out each other's agendas, they left with lessons in hand, enthusiastic about the original ideas generated with, and supported by, their colleagues—who later asked them how successful that lesson had been.

## ALIGNMENT OF ASSESSMENT WITH STUDENT STRENGTHS

One issue that teachers usually bring up when implementing learning styles is that of fairness in evaluation.

> Is it right for a youngster, whose strength is visual and tactual, to earn a grade by answering a 25-question paper-and-pencil test and hereby compete with another student, whose strength is kinesthetic and who completes a project that took five hours to put together?

Although most teachers are dismayed when they tally up just how many paper-and-pencil quizzes and assignments they require, they struggle to match evaluation strategies to their students' strengths rather than to highlighting their youngsters' weaknesses. Working toward authentic assessment, Mrs. Dotson would have instructors consider whether they are more interested in the way they test, or in pupils actually demonstrating mastery of what they have learned.

## TIPS FOR TEACHER TRAINING

Critical to successful staff development is the patience to allow for gradual change as teachers continually reflect on their evolving practices as they implement learning styles. They need to examine how and why they teach the way they do and then be given time to make substantive changes. Ms. Dotson's nuggets of wisdom for teacher training include the following:

- Explain learning styles fully to students.
- Carefully prepare them for the *Learning Style Inventory* (LSI) (Dunn, Dunn, & Price, 1975–1996).
- Thoroughly interpret Individual Profiles with them.
- Provide ample opportunities for them to experiment with their learning styles in nurturing, equitable environments.
- Encourage pupils to try out many different classroom areas and materials.

## A WORLD OF DIFFERENCE: THE IMPACT OF LEARNING STYLES

*TAAS exit learning-styles program shows exciting results in JISD.* This was the headline for a press release in 1993, documenting a typical example of the increased achievement resulting from Mrs. Dotson's system of implementing learning styles through staff development. Texas requires that all high school students pass a series of exit examinations, the *Texas Assessment*

**Figure 30.1**
**Comparison of Summer 1993 Jacksonville ISD Learning-Styles Program**
**TAAS Results with State of Texas TAAS Results**

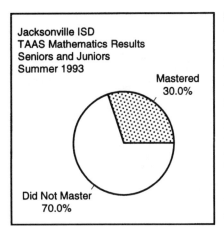

Jacksonville ISD
TAAS Mathematics Results
Seniors and Juniors
Summer 1993
Mastered
30.0%
Did Not Master
70.0%

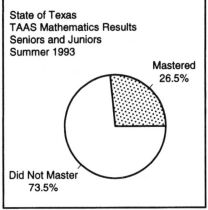

State of Texas
TAAS Mathematics Results
Seniors and Juniors
Summer 1993
Mastered
26.5%
Did Not Master
73.5%

*of Academic Skills* (TAAS). With many of its seniors in danger of not passing the TAAS, Jacksonville trained reading, writing, and math teachers in the Dunn and Dunn model. A summer remediation program was provided for juniors who were preparing for the TAAS test, as well as for seniors who had failed it. By the end of the summer session, the district's percentage of mastery *exceeded the state percentage on every test!*

• In math, 30 percent of Jacksonville pupils mastered the exit test compared to 26 percent at the state level (see Figure 30.1);

• In writing, a whopping 81 percent passed in JISD compared to 48 percent state-wide (see Figure 30.2);

• In reading, while 27 percent mastered TAAS in Texas, 67 percent did so in JISD for an increase of 40 percent (see Figure 30.3); and

• Similarly, from 1993 to 1994, the number of students needing remediation dropped substantially in both grades 11 and 12 (see Figure 30.4).

Free to any student in the district who has taken the TAAS exit exam and not mastered an area, the summer program's emphasis is placed on teaching students through their perceptual strengths, which very often are tactual and kinesthetic. Youngsters choose the time of day that they will attend classes and the amount of time each day they will attend. During the *18* days of instruction offered in that initial summer of 1993, many students accomplished a goal—passing the statewide test mandatory for receiving a high school diploma—that *12 years of traditional instruction had left unattainable.* This hugely effective learning-styles remediation session continued

Figure 30.2
**Comparison of Summer 1993 Jacksonville ISD Learning-Styles Program
TAAS Results with State of Texas TAAS Results**

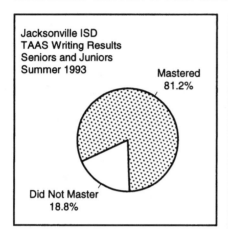

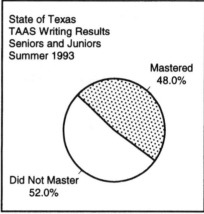

through the 1990s and has served as a model for many other Texas schools. It is recognized across the state for its novel approach and impressive results.

## SEVENTY-ONE PERCENT OF PARENTS REPORTED READING-LEVEL INCREASES DUE TO LEARNING STYLES

*Only the beginning.* Without time and effort devoted toward helping families understand the advantages of an active, sometimes noisy learning-styles classroom, some parents often do not understand that the way they learned does not necessarily meet the needs of their own offspring. Parents question:

• Why aren't kids doing 25 paper-and-pencil math problems in a row?

• What kind of misguided permissiveness allows students to lounge on beanbag chairs while donning headphone sets and enjoying a breeze through an open window in a dimly lighted classroom with carrot sticks in hand?

• When *we* went to school . . . ; why is it different now?

Contrary to the old assumption that if school is fun, they can't be learning the basics—parents "in the know" are amazed at the gains their children achieve in a learning-styles classroom, basics and beyond. They have been heard to tell questioning newcomers: "Learning styles is just the way we teach here!"

How does Jacksonville engage the cooperation of parents, thanks to Mrs. Dotson's tutelage?

**Figure 30.3**
**Comparison of Summer 1993 Jacksonville ISD Learning-Styles Program**
**TAAS Results with State of Texas TAAS Results**

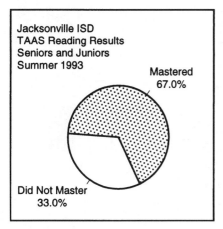

Jacksonville ISD
TAAS Reading Results
Seniors and Juniors
Summer 1993

Mastered
67.0%

Did Not Master
33.0%

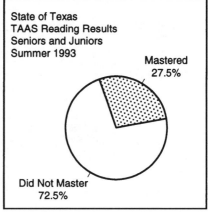

State of Texas
TAAS Reading Results
Seniors and Juniors
Summer 1993

Mastered
27.5%

Did Not Master
72.5%

1. At Open House each year, a session on learning styles is offered.

2. Parents can participate in learning about and making tactual and kinesthetic resources to help their school-age or younger children on Saturdays.

3. Counselors stage an annual "Parent-Fest" during which mini-sessions feature learning-styles information and concrete advice for supporting class work and homework—with Homework Prescriptions based on each student's learning style fully discussed (Dunn & Klavas, 1990) and

4. The local newspaper highlights learning-styles programs.

So what are the rewards of the efforts to include parents in the process of educating their children through the Dunn and Dunn model? A pilot program, including five fourth-grade and five fifth-grade teachers in 1992–1993, exemplified significant gains in achievement, attitude, and behaviors that documented the success of Sherrye Dotson's own model for staff development. Results of the survey, which was administered in English or Spanish, showed what happened when parents were partners.

In response to a combined learning-styles/Whole-Language approach to reading, parents were questioned about whether their children had benefited from an informal environment: 72 percent answered with a resounding "Yes!" Did youngsters like to come to school more than they had in previous years? "Yes" from 62 percent.

Only the beginning, this pilot program expanded to the entire school in 1993–1994, with norm-referenced scores supporting achievement gains. No wonder involved parents sang the praises of learning styles in Jacksonville!

**Figure 30.4**
**1993–1994 TAAS Comparison for Number of Students Needing Remediation**

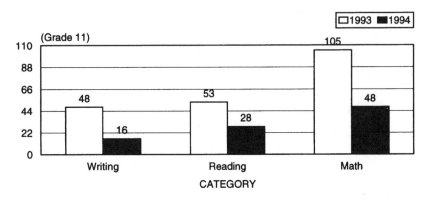

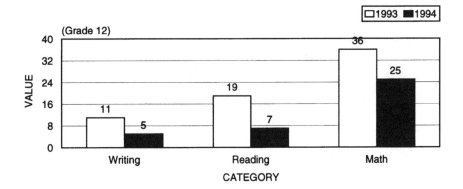

## EVERY CHILD IS SPECIAL: THE CLIMATE FOR LEARNING STYLES

Sherrye Dotson concluded that Howard Gardner's work on multiple intelligences and the brain-based research of the last 10 years only provides further corroboration for the Dunn and Dunn Learning-Style Model—which pre-dates the others by two decades or more. It may take more time to plan for learning styles initially, but Mrs. Dotson believes that it is more necessary to do that today than even before. Current national interest in authentic assessment, varied learning activities, inclusion, and an increasing acceptance of individual differences mandates teachers' responsiveness to student diversity.

Teachers who use learning styles in their classrooms become much more in tune with the needs of special youngsters. Special Education, Title I, and Section 504 modifications are much easier to make in a learning-styles environment. With learning-style activities underway, far fewer children with disabilities need to be channeled to Resource Rooms. Students neither feel disabled nor different because the individual needs of all pupils are being met. In fact, it has become unacceptable *not* to address student differences.

## DOING WHAT'S RIGHT FOR THE KIDS: THE LEGACY OF DR. T.Y. HARP

Principals in JISD reported that discipline problems were far fewer once learning styles was in full force. Pupils become confident and aware of their strengths, expressing openly that "school is fun!" Mrs. Dotson has found that "students and parents become the biggest supporters." Families rejoicing over the achievements of happy, accomplishing children who once struggled and hated school are invested in continuing with the program.

The focus, of course, is on "doing what's best for kids," something Sherrye learned from her former principal, Dr. Harp, back in those early 1980s when she was teaching through learning styles in her math classroom. An excerpt from an unsolicited letter from the parents of one middle school boy demonstrates how she has passed on the legacy of the Dunn and Dunn Learning-Style Model in east Texas:

> During this sixth-grade year, Chad's self-esteem and his attitude toward school have changed dramatically. He is so much more responsible, especially about homework. Partner learning and a relaxed, informal atmosphere have been a boost for him. His test scores and grades have improved greatly. We attribute all this to the willingness of his teachers to help Chad adapt his learning style to their classrooms. Since we know this is extra work for teachers, we can't tell you how much we appreciate your concern and help. It has made a world of difference.

## INTO THE FUTURE: GROUNDBREAKING LONGITUDINAL STUDY IN LEARNING STYLES DOCUMENTS SOARING ACHIEVEMENT!

Although currently enthusiastic about the opportunity to impact another district, Burleson, Texas, through the implementation of the model, Mrs. Dotson remains committed to researching the mature growth of learning styles in Jacksonville. She continues to trace the progress of 44 third-graders who started kindergarten; each ensuing group of kindergartners becomes part of a six-year study that will continue through the year 2001 when the children have completed the fifth grade. Staying with the same instructional design each year, this group of 50 percent native Spanish-speaking, and 50 percent native English-speaking students receives instruction in English in the morning and in Spanish in the afternoons.

Teachers trained in learning styles were taught to observe and test the children through the LSI to identify their perceptual strengths and create an accommodating environment. With guidance from a knowledgeable bilingual/ESL (English as a Second Language) guru, students are immersed in a total multisensory experience, including elicitation of physical responses—because such an approach is thought to be the best way to teach second-language acquisition.

*Preliminary findings.* Although these pupils were selected randomly from the regular student population with no attention to a facility for using diverse modalities, it appears that such a program may actually *develop* multiple perceptual strengths. Norm-referenced data demonstrate a phenomenal achievement in speakers of either language learning the other! With activities in motion all day to meet the needs of all preferences and with particular attention paid to the global processing of young children—staff have been able to present at language and curriculum conferences tremendous gains in achievement levels through a learning-styles/multisensory approach. These youngsters who, in fact, are not gifted as far as IQ is concerned, are evidencing strong characteristics generally associated with gifted children!

## SHERRYE DOTSON'S SUCCESS STORY

With this ambitious research agenda in Jacksonville, Sherrye Dotson exemplifies how a reflective classroom practitioner of the Dunn and Dunn model can blossom into a nationally recognized learning-styles leader and scholar. Having trained JISD staff to implement an instructional program based on the Dunn and Dunn Learning-Style Model, Sherrye Dotson finds herself eager to compare how a similar program will fare in her new district, which is demographically quite different.

Beginning the 1998–1999 academic year as the Assistant Superintendent for Instruction in the Burleson School District in the Dallas/Ft. Worth metroplex, Sherrye Dotson looks forward to continuing Jacksonville's first longitudinal study in learning styles and simultaneously following up implementation in Burleson with program evaluation and research into this model's impact on achievement. She's hoping that, before long, teachers in Burleson also will be saying, "Learning styles is just the way we teach here!"

## REFERENCES

Dunn, R., & Dunn, K. (1993). *Teaching secondary students through their individual learning styles: Practical approaches for grades 7–12.* Boston: Allyn & Bacon.

Dunn, R., & Klavas, A. (1990). *Homework disc.* Now York: St. John's University's Center for the Study of Learning and Teaching Styles.

Dunn, K., & Price, G.E. (1975–1996). *Learning Style Inventory.* Lawrence, KS: Price Systems.

*Chapter 31*

# Julia Kron: Empowering Teachers to Become Instructional Leaders in North Carolina

*Nancy Montgomery and Rita Dunn*

She never intended to have a career as an educator. As a zoology major at the University of North Carolina at Chapel Hill, Julia Kron went directly into laboratory research, which was "fun and challenging," with nary a thought to teaching school. However, a few years later, she became attracted to the profession because, she says modestly, she thought she "might be able to do a really nice job" of working with young people.

She went on to teach high school science for 20 years—from the mid-1960s through the 1980s. At that time, she had only a vague knowledge of individual differences—but a lot of dissatisfaction with the status quo. That dissatisfaction led to her receptivity to learning styles two decades later. What was it about teaching experimental science that led her to appreciate a model that focused principally on how students learn rather than on how teachers teach?

## THE CORNERSTONE OF EFFECTIVE TEACHING: TEACHING STUDENTS TO TEACH THEMSELVES— AND EACH OTHER

Early in her career, Mrs. Kron found that one way to get diverse students interested in, and able to master, science was to use lab activities as a cornerstone of teaching. She experimented with different ways of generating concepts and thinking skills among youngsters through participation and involvement, and found that they learned best when *they* considered what they were doing and how they were learning. When Julia found that the Dunn and Dunn Learning-Style Model advocated direct hands-on and experimental learning for tactual and kinesthetic students who needed mobility, she knew that she was face-to-face with a kindred philosophy! When she became aware that research based on that model had shown that many young students learned that way, but that some did not, she became intrigued with how to identify who did, who did not, and why.

## THE KRON PHILOSOPHY OF TEACHING AND LEARNING RESPONSIBILITIES

Julia Kron concluded that it is the teachers' responsibility to help students take ownership over their own learning; they need to learn how to teach themselves. To do that, they need to understand how they actually begin to concentrate, process, internalize, and retain new and difficult academic information. To her perception, the ultimate goal is to teach youngsters "how to learn without teachers" and, eventually, to become independent learners.

## ADMINISTRATIVE RESPONSIBILITIES: THE NORTH CAROLINA ASSOCIATION OF EDUCATORS AND THE NORTH CAROLINA TEACHER ACADEMY

In 1989, Mrs. Kron was elected president of the North Carolina Association of Educators (NCAE), an NEA affiliate comprised of 46,000 active members and another 30,000 retired teachers. From 1993 through the present, she has served as director of the North Carolina Teacher Academy funded by the General Assembly with a budget of over $4.1 million a year for all its programs, operations, and salaries. Most of that budget is reserved for summer workshops and trainers' salaries.

The academy provides staff development in:

- pedagogical processes and methods;
- the content areas;
- technology;
- balanced literacy (reading and writing);
- site-based decision management; and
- mentoring.

Julia's responsibilities include the development and delivery of staff development programs for K–12 teachers and the overall administration of the North Carolina Teacher Academy. One of the main thrusts of the Teacher Academy program is learning styles.

## RECOGNITION OF WHAT WORKS

The Teacher Academy's interest in learning styles evolved from a reform movement undertaken in North Carolina during the early 1990s. Mrs. Kron visited numerous schools at every level and type in many locations in the state to discuss the educational needs of the schools and the teachers in them. She also attended national conferences to develop a broadened perspective of research concerned with effective approaches for increasing student achievement. She found that:

• few of the programs receiving national attention had the research base that the Dunn and Dunn Learning-Style Model did; and

• two of the schools in North Carolina that were receiving a great deal of State Education Department attention because they had statistically increased the achievement of poverty, minority students had both used the Dunn and Dunn model exclusively (Andrews, 1990, 1991; Klavas, 1993; Stone, 1992). It became apparent to Mrs. Kron that, if North Carolina schools were to improve, (1) excellent and extensive staff development would be critical to any effective reform and (2) learning-styles instruction should be a primary consideration.

## ASSIGNMENT TO TASK FORCE LEADERSHIP

Mrs. Kron was hired to direct a task force appointed to design the Teacher Academy—summer training and fall/spring follow-ups—based on North Carolina legislation passed in 1993. Having contracted with an outside provider to do mailout surveys and conduct focus groups throughout the state, Julia and her colleagues listened to their constituency and pinpointed broad solutions to address the greatest number of identified problems.

Similar to a total quality skills, team-building approach to resolving conflicts about school issues, Academy staff have helped educators create visions of what their school *should* be like, and then designed mission statements and action-plans-for-improvement.

## LEARNING STYLES: THE CONTENT AND THE PROCESS

Because trainer training is the Teacher Academy's first priority, no expense is spared. For each new endeavor, the best-recommended consultants in each field are brought in to provide staff development for the in-the-trenches teachers. Those teachers then are required to use the new approach and demonstrate their skill with it in their own classroom with "real children." Successful teachers then are employed by the Teacher Academy to provide training for North Carolina educators throughout the state.

In 1994, Drs. Kenneth and Rita Dunn were invited to conduct a one-

week summer workshop to train potential trainers. Seventy-five North Carolina teachers, who worked with the Dunns that first summer, then
assisted them during the following summer to provide the same training for 200 more teachers who comprised school-based management teams with their principals. With costs shared by the school districts and the Academy, 26 of those trainers later earned sought-after certification through the Annual Leadership Certification Institute of St. John's University's Center for the Study of Learning and Teaching Styles.

Since that time, eight one-week sessions have been offered during each summer by the Teacher Academy certified trainers who provided staff development sessions for 75 more teachers and principals each week. Additional time is provided during follow-up workshops for extensive hands-on activities such as the designing of Programmed Learning Sequences (PLSs) and Multisensory Instructional Packages (MIPs). All Academy sessions use learning-styles strategies to teach learning-styles approaches to the educators who attend.

Participants' learning styles are identified with the *Productivity Environmental Preference Survey* (PEPS) (Dunn, Dunn, & Price, 1975–1996). Their individual profiles are analyzed to identify their perceptual and processing strengths. The group then is divided into subgroups (analytic versus global, and tactual versus kinesthetic versus auditory learners) to learn in ways that are most responsive to their styles. Participants are invited to work within their sociological preferences, to practice mobility and whole-body/experimental learning if they so choose, and to actively manipulate and experiment with resources—just as Mrs. Kron used to encourage her science lab students to do several decades back.

Of course, the credibility of the trainers is crucial. This begins with their having demonstrated proficiency with the inventories and profiles of their "students"—in this case, the school-based teams of principals and teachers. Each participant team experiences five full days of active involvement in which they:

- review their own profiles;
- learn how to determine their students' styles and interpret them to parents;
- learn about, and are tested for, the 21 elements and basic theory of the Dunn and Dunn model; and
- create and use tactual manipulatives, such as Flip Chutes, Electroboards, Task Cards, and Pic-A-Holes, as well as design kinesthetic resources such as body-action floor or wall games.

During the past few years, the Teacher Academy has provided staff development for many schools that now have site-based trainers—highly skilled teacher professionals who have been taught by Teacher Academy trainers how to teach to students' learning styles—but through their own learning styles.

## BACK TO SCHOOL: PARTICIPANTS' RESPONSES AND IMPLEMENTATION

Echoing the advice of other learning-styles supervisors, Julia Kron suggests that teachers leave workshops with class-ready tactual and kinesthetic materials in their hands! If these resources are not completed as group projects, when will they be finished? The response from participants is an eagerness to converse with, share, and learn from peers, an enthusiasm for team-building through learning styles, and an excitement engendered to go back and share what they have learned with others.

Follow-up is built into the program since it is required to obtain full continuation credit. Taking the credentialing a step higher, teachers can become trainers in their own buildings, subject to re-certification every five years. Principals do not necessarily need to follow up. However, they do need to understand that the learning-styles classroom appears and operates differently from traditional classrooms. They also need to supply resources and provide support for their teachers who are initiating learning-styles programs. They also are required to become involved in the process by seeking information and debriefing:

- What have you done with learning styles to date?
- Which approaches have you tried?
- How did they work?
- Were there any barriers?
- What were the successes?

Teacher colleagues offer suggestions to their peers for overcoming challenges. As a group they engage in problem solving, often through inquiry techniques (again, effective in a model of scientific investigation).

Another follow-up idea, after sharing progress to-date, is to offer another new learning-styles approach, such as the PLS, MIP, or CAP. The Academy staff has learned, through experience, as have most individuals and organizations implementing learning-style strategies, that teachers should not be overwhelmed. Instead of cramming too much into a workshop, they should be encouraged to return to their classrooms and try one of the new strategies they learned. Then they should be invited back to share the results and, once again, be exposed to something a bit more complex—that they then should try.

### Unanticipated Benefits

One benefit of the Academy's work is that, not only do teachers learn learning-style strategies, theory, and practice, but they also enjoy the fellowship and collaborative efforts of mixed teams from the entire state—the coast to the mountains. Summer sessions are held at 10 different college sites in North Carolina with none so close to home that participants are tempted to go there during a break to put in a load of laundry or see what the kids are up to. Fully funded by the Academy, the focus of this residential week is on learning to teach through learning styles in a nurturing environment.

## CLASSIC COLLABORATION

Mrs. Kron reports that the Academy's five-year program is working superbly, with the next step being more of an outreach into the schools with an emphasis on developing a local trainer to work with the entire staff. This new shift is well begun, with trainers hard-pressed to meet an inundation of requests.

Because trainers are classroom teachers, everyone's cooperation is needed. The Academy pays to cover class substitutes; administrators graciously allow trainers' occasional absences; and trainers usually are happy to do local staff development without charge—since the Academy and the state paid for their own training with national consultants. This would seem to be a classic collaborative effort to implement learning styles at every level.

## ADVENTURES IN LEARNING STYLES

With learning styles being the Teacher Academy's most popular program, the Dunn and Dunn model is a major thread woven throughout its divisions. Julia finds the new model for curriculum integration in grades 9–12, based on three years of preparation and planning, to be particularly promising. "High schools have been content silos with walls 30 feet thick and a mile high," she laments. "Don't you get into my content area, and I won't get into yours!" Learning-styles approaches provide ways to reach all students so that they can succeed academically regardless of the content.

Another venue for learning styles is the fledgling mentoring program based on coaching and conferencing. Experienced teachers receive training in how to work with beginning teachers on their instructional practices and encourage them to join school teams for summer sessions to enhance their "teacher bag of tricks" to add to their teaching skills.

Another facet of planning for the future is to institute a more formal gathering of data analysis and evaluation. With the Academy understaffed at present, Mrs. Kron intends to hire someone to work with the learning-styles trainers to create survey questions with which to begin gathering "hard" data.

Teacher surveys will be administered to determine the extent to which various learning-style practices have contributed to student achievement gains. The next step will be to initiate testing to document improved achievement scores. Pre- and post-tests are being prepared, and the same students will be tracked through consecutive years for evidence that their increased achievement is attributable to the learning-styles program. As is, anecdotal evidence has been mounting steadily and teacher testing has provided extensive support.

Another exciting new venture in the application of the Dunn and Dunn model was begun in 1998–1999. One nationally certified, learning-styles trainer and one balanced literacy trainer joined forces with one principal to open a charter elementary school devoted entirely to the implementation of learning styles. Testing was begun immediately to measure changes in achievement, attitudes, and behaviors as learning-styles approaches gradually were introduced.

## LEARNING ABOUT LEARNING STYLES FROM TEACHERS IN THE TRENCHES

Why is the Teacher Academy so successful? Mrs. Kron attributes some of the positive responses from participating instructors to the basic reality of learning from one's peers. Once the national consultants "got the ball rolling," training was continued by classroom teachers who were selected to become certified. Untrained teachers invented fewer excuses for not trying something new when the trainer was a tenth-grade English teacher just like themselves—with the same course load, the same student population, and the same restraints on budget and time. When trainers are working in the same daily circumstances in classrooms alongside their "mentees," they gain instant credibility.

## PRACTICE WHAT YOU PREACH

Well-trained trainers are the cornerstones of the Academy. They are taught adult learning theory through the use of media and engaging presentations. Knowing that we usually teach the way we are taught, Mrs. Kron is certain to see that trainers and trainees are never: (1) required to sit for more than one hour without active participation and movement; and (2) asked to conduct after-school workshops from 4:00–6:00 P.M. when they are exhausted and ready to go home.

As a staff developer, she knows that teachers are in the role of customer; "We provide what they need." The attitude should not be, "I know what will fix you," but rather, "within the parameters of what you can do, we'll tailor training to meet your needs." Hence, staff development should be teacher-driven because teachers want what will help them do a good job with their students. Teaching, then, should hinge on students' needs and how they learn. Trainers' work should hinge on teachers' needs and how to use learning styles to teach all their students, all the time, in ways that help them learn everything they can!

## WHAT MAKES THE ACADEMY TICK?

Mrs. Kron reminds us that "A large group of committed people can do anything!" To date, 1,404 teachers have gone through the Academy's Learning-Styles workshops. While things are in a state of constant change—as they are in any living organization, she happily states that "We seem to have a hit!" She urges other districts to spend enough resources to develop a small cadre of well-trained trainers to provide a solid delivery system that participants will want to buy into.

Trainers need to be experienced in using learning styles in their classrooms to be able to guide other teachers toward successful implementation! Teachers who have been shown how to create Floor Games and Task Cards, for instance, need to develop their own to match the students with whom they work every day. And they need to see how the students react and learn through them. As learning-style gains become increasingly evident, teachers become sufficiently confident to take further risks. Julia Kron finds middle school teachers extremely willing to try new and creative approaches, "because they are so desperate" and their youngsters are so tough to teach. Even high school teachers, who tend to be fairly traditional, become interested when other teachers offer them strategies to help their students perform better. Once youngsters begin achieving higher test scores, and even become eager to get to class, teachers enjoy their own work more. "Nobody wants students talking about how boring the class was."

## LEARNING FOR A LIFETIME

Mrs. Kron began her career with rigorous academic preparation in her content area. Before long, she wanted to impart that love of her discipline to young people and to instill in them the habits of independent, intellectual endeavor and the understanding of the scientific method and the systematic processes of experimentation. We appreciate how she used these tenets as director of the North Carolina Teacher Academy—particularly in providing exemplary staff development practices that resulted in a statewide implementation of the Dunn and Dunn Learning-Style Model.

Julia Kron has used the principles of learning styles to train top-notch trainers who have worked throughout the state to allow implementation to reach critical mass. Her trainers teach teachers through their learning styles;

teachers, in turn, teach their pupils through theirs. The goal is to develop independent thinkers who will teach themselves to learn effectively throughout their lives. Julia Kron's hunch about the possibility of contributing to education proved right: indeed, she has "done a really nice job!"

## REFERENCES

Andrews, R.H. (1990, July–September). The development of a learning styles program in a low socioeconomic, underachieving North Carolina elementary school. *Journal of Reading, Writing, and Learning Disabilities International, 6*(3), 307–314.

Andrews, R.H. (1991). Insights into education: An elementary principal's perspective. In *Hands on approaches to learning styles: Practical approaches to successful schooling* (pp. 50–52). New Wilmington, PA: Association for the Advancement of International Education.

Dunn, R., Dunn, K., & Price, G.E. (1975–1996). *Productivity Environmental Preference Survey.* Lawrence, KS: Price Systems.

Klavas, A. (1993). In Greensboro, North Carolina: Learning style program boosts achievement and test scores. *The Clearing House, 67*(3), 149–151.

Stone, P. (1992, November). How we turned around a problem school. *The Principal, 71*(2), 34–36.

*Chapter 32*

# Denise Stephenson: A Southern Lady Brings Learning Styles to Davidson County, North Carolina

*Karen Burke and Rita Dunn*

For northerners and southerners alike, images of Southern women often emanate more from the myth and fantasy engendered by the pages of *Gone with the Wind* than from history books or academic works. That novel and the acclaimed film were effective precisely because Margaret Mitchell drew her stereotypes so well and set them in such drama. Melanie Wilkes was the classic "Southern Lady"; Scarlett O'Hara was the primary "Southern Belle"; and Mammy was the typically strong, loyal black woman.

Attractive and comforting as such a simplistic perception may be, it reveals little about many present-day, Southern women. It also obscures the position of individual women, their goals and identities, and their professional endeavors. A host of all-but-invisible, accomplished women are politicians, writers, teachers, administrators, artists, and business leaders whose stories have been neglected. Constructing their reality is a necessary task if role models are to exist for young Southern girls who may aspire to joining their ranks some day.

We begin this task by introducing you to a real Southern lady in Davidson County, North Carolina. Denise Stephenson may be described as a veteran classroom teacher, an educational staff developer, and a school administrator. At one time, a former student described her as "a strong woman set in her own beliefs." Mrs. Stephenson is all of the above but, in addition, she is an elegant, beautiful professional who dresses attractively, is energetic, and is dedicated to a mission—that of improving education for teenagers who learn differently from conventional schooling practices. These characteristics may explain why Denise Stephenson became the first Certified Learning-Styles Trainer in the state of North Carolina. Her influence began in East

Davidson High School but it did not take long for her to inspire teachers throughout the state.

## LEARNING STYLES COMES TO EAST DAVIDSON HIGH SCHOOL

Learning styles was first introduced to East Davidson High School when the assistant principal, Dr. Russ Gobble, sent Stephenson to a learning-styles workshop in Durham, North Carolina. Immediately following that workshop, Stephenson agreed to introduce learning-style strategies into three of the eleventh-grade English classes she taught. That implementation was part of a multi-tiered experiment focused on student tracking.

The criteria used to track students at East Davidson High School included classroom performance, teachers' appraisals, and the results of standardized testing. Two of Stephenson's classes were labeled "accelerated"; one officially was classified as "basic"—indicating that its population was comprised of underachievers.

Students in all three classes were assessed for their individual learning styles. New and difficult academic information then was introduced by using the youngsters' primary learning preferences. All students in these three classes were accountable for mastering the same curriculum, text, and tests.

In the beginning of the semester, many students in the basic class became disgruntled when they realized that they would be required to take the same tests as the accelerated classes. Then they became curious about the unusual teaching techniques they were experiencing in their English class. Interest and motivation gradually replaced their concerns when they noticed their grades improving. Before long, the basic students discovered that most of them were scoring equally as well as and, in some cases, better than students in the accelerated classes. Intense pride in themselves emerged and, with it, intense competition. The basic students began studying to outperform those in the accelerated groups!

At the end of the year, student averages were calculated and a mean for each class was established. The class that began the year in the basic track and had not had the benefits of the accelerated preparation enjoyed the second highest class average—outscoring one of the accelerated classes!

| Class Label | Class Mean |
| --- | --- |
| Accelerated 1 | 80.9 |
| Basic | 78.0 |
| Accelerated 2 | 77.4 |

The results were conclusive—rather than tracking being the issue it was how information was presented to, and then processed by, the students. In her evaluation, Stephenson wrote, "Learning style has released me from the bondage of tracking. Teaching students through their learning styles eliminates the need for tracking students into classes that falsely label them and destroy their self-respect."

The following September, Chris Gearren, a student from the "basic" class, conveyed some of his thoughts about the experience of being in Stephenson's English class.

> I was a problem in high school. School was where I felt dumb and out of place. I never felt good about myself. Then Mrs. Stephenson changed my life. In her class, I actually started learning—and liked it! By the end of the year, I had gone from a D- to an A. At that point, she suggested that I go to college.
>
> I am proud to say that I am now a student at Guilford Community College. I plan to make a dream come true that I never thought possible—Chris Gearren getting an education! One teacher can make an impact on a person's whole life. Mrs. Stephenson can teach us all a valuable lesson—never give up on kids because they can all learn. After all, Chris Gearren did!

This anecdote is just the beginning of the story of learning styles and Denise Stephenson. Her impact continues beyond the walls of her own classroom. Through her students, she experienced the negative effects of traditional teaching on students with non-traditional learning styles and needed to share the message with other teachers and administrators.

## LEARNING STYLES AND STAFF DEVELOPMENT

Denise Stephenson attended St. John's University's sixteenth Annual Learning-Styles Certification Institute in New York City during the summer of 1993. Her enthusiasm, professional knowledge born of the year of implementation she had experienced in her English classes, and the excellent results she shared prompted Professor Rita Dunn, the Institute director, to invite Stephenson to be on staff the following year. During the next five years she showed hundreds of teachers who attended the Institute how to teach their students through the youngsters' individual learning-style strengths.

Stephenson's staff development began at the New York City Learning-Styles Certification Institute but it has taken her to many classrooms, schools, districts, states, and even halfway around the world. She has trained approximately 500 Davidson County teachers, and countless more throughout the states of North Carolina, South Carolina, and Alabama. Her expertise as a classroom teacher and a staff developer encouraged Alan Cooper, headmaster at St. George's School in Wanganui, New Zealand, to invite Stephenson to provide staff development to his school district. But this was only the beginning of the journey. Since 1993, Stephenson has participated in more than 90 learning-styles workshops as a consultant, staff developer and, at times, as the keynote speaker.

## LEARNING STYLES AND ADMINISTRATION

Stephenson knew that she was impacting on her students, but she thought it was equally important to share learning-style strategies with other teachers. She hoped that, by influencing colleagues through staff development, she could affect many more students. It was this realization that led her to accept an administrative position in the Davidson County Transitional Youth Education Program. She believed that her best contribution to education might be in influencing teachers who work with at-risk adolescents.

Mrs. Stephenson was instrumental in developing Project LEARN—a transitional academic and behavioral program for students aged 13–15 who were experiencing difficulty in a traditional school setting. The cornerstone of the program emphasized academic goals, but recognized that individuals' physical, social, and emotional needs needed to be met for students to function productively in school and later in life. Project LEARN incorporated the philosophy that most students could master the same content; how they mastered it was determined by each individual's learning style. Accordingly, Stephenson stressed that successful interventions take into account each student's learning-style strengths, skill deficiencies, and interests.

The qualitative effects of this program were evidenced by increased student motivation, self-concept, on-task behaviors, self-discipline, awareness of their unique learning-style strengths, and positive conflict resolutions— all crucial to the smooth functioning of a school. Quantitatively, students performed better during their single year in the program than many had ever done before. It did not take long for administrators to recognize how well Project LEARN was working with previously unproductive adolescents, and Stephenson was invited to become the assistant principal in the middle school.

She began this new position with the clear understanding that administrators wanted her to move toward a mutually understood goal. In the spirit of the expression "what goes around, comes around," Stephenson worked at modeling, through staff development, those same learning-styles strategies that she—and they—hoped teachers would incorporate into their daily teaching. Initial emphasis was placed on short, global introductions that related the subject content for each lesson to the students' lives. Stephenson then required teachers to document this new thrust in their daily lesson plans. Throughout the year, she modeled this and other learning-style strategies for teachers who expressed an interest.

At the end of the first year of modeling and gradual implementation, Stephenson was encouraged by the results of statewide writing and standardized tests. In addition, she felt a great sense of accomplishment in her own office when learning-style interventions were used as she counseled students who were discipline referrals. In this scenario, you might have observed Stephenson conferring with a student while classical music played softly in the background, the lighting was soft and indirect, and the students' learning-style profile was being examined by both—but held in the youngster's hands.

## CONCLUSION

A pioneering beginning has been made, and the schools in at least one part of North Carolina are beginning to incorporate learning styles as a basic component of instruction. Overall, this case study adds to our understanding of how to improve education through the successes of some of the people who have been instrumental in producing pioneering gains. It is not easy to be a different kind of teacher in a system that promotes carbon copies rather than diversity. Denise Stephenson's is an impressive example because we see how one person's convictions and personal devotion can make a documented difference. Perhaps this example will inspire others to exercise professional inquiry and instructional experimentation. Perhaps it will promote many similar studies which, when examined together, gradually will permit accurate generalizations.

Southern women come in many varieties and exemplify many success stories in terms of both personal accomplishments and service to others. Reality is neither as simple nor as glamorous as myth. Modern people have a disconcerting ability to defy historians' classifications and avoid reflecting the legends their descendents often relate. Reality, when it emerges, is no less interesting, and far more helpful toward understanding professional women than the myths and fiction ever were.

If *Gone with the Wind* educated and reinforced another generation's image of Southern women, let this vignette aid in segregating the stereotype from this vivid written and pictorial characterization. People may be impressed from afar, but their lives normally are best impacted upon up close.

*Epilogue*

# Alabama Mary and Learning Styles:
# "This Ain't the Army, Mrs. White!"

*Karen Burke and Rita Dunn*

The United States Army recruiting slogan states: *Be all that you can be—join the army.* Mary White knew that was not what her colleague was referring to when she posed a question to her. With great hesitation, for fear of offending Dr. White, she approached her with this perplexity. "Mary, for years I have heard from the children and faculty members something I would like to have clarified. Is it true that you were a Sargent in the army before you became a teacher?" White responded negatively, but said that she understood why both students and teachers viewed her in that manner.

Much like what was expected in the army, every student in White's class was expected to march to the beat of the same drummer. Every student was expected to learn in exactly the same way. The desks were lined up in straight rows, marked by masking tape. The lines were so straight that they easily could match the exactitude of any roll-call line-up in the service. General Patton would have been proud of the conformity in her classroom—and so was Mary White, until a transformation occurred in her life.

White describes how the transformation began with an eight-day training institute sponsored by St. John's University in New York. It was top-heavy with research showing that students actually achieved better on standardized tests when they were shown how to study and concentrate in their own learning styles. She attended that institute in 1987 and you probably could say that she has been AWOL from the army ever since.

## HOW SCOTT CARTER CHANGED HER LIFE

The month following her attendance at the Annual Learning-Styles Certification Institute in New York, White received a visit from the parent of one of her former mathematics students. This mother requested that she fill out a recommendation for her son, Scott, to enter a private school the following year. "I would appreciate this greatly! You see, I don't believe public education has anything to offer my son." Having contributed significantly to this mother's frustration by failing Scott in math, White realized she had to make one last effort to undo whatever harm she may have done.

Reflecting on the previous eight days of training in New York, she felt that, for the first time, she could impact on this child's life. She consented to write the recommendation but made one final plea. She asked the mother to consider giving her the opportunity to teach Scott one more time. She told Mrs. Carter that she believed she now had an understanding of Scott and others like him who had previously gone unnoticed.

White was uncertain as to whether she would see Scott when school began in the fall. She was pleasantly surprised and has a picture of him etched within her mind as she thinks of him. He invariably would sit in the most dimly lit section of the room on an old, ragged beanbag with sunglasses and a walkman headset across his head. Putting into application what she had learned about "global" learning styles, she found Scott to be most intelligent. He went from Fs to As and developed a newfound love for learning. White knew that the opportunity she was given with Scott that year couldn't undo the harm that had been inflicted on those who had previously been in her classes. However, she realized that she could never look at students again with that same "lock-step" mentality that had been part of her attitude for so long. Scott gave her an opportunity that year to regain her dignity and respect as a teacher, but for a long time she had no idea of how much this one child would change her life!

In 1994, on a Sunday afternoon, White received an unexpected telephone call. Her principal was notifying her of Scott Carter's untimely and tragic death in a car accident. Immediately, White called the family to express her sympathy for the loss of that sweet child who had so deeply touched her life. Although nearly seven years had passed since Scott had been in Mary White's class, his mother proceeded to make one final request in her time of need.

> Mary, had Scott lived to be an adult, he would have been one of those students who frequented your door to express his appreciation for the difference you made in his life. Would you do him one last favor and deliver his eulogy?

Dr. White still wonders how she ever responded to this parent's heart-breaking request. She knew she had the opportunity to do one last deed for Scott. It gave her the moment to say "Thank You Scott," for helping her realize the potential that it is possible to unleash in every child through learning styles.

## HOW ONE "BABY" STEP LED TO A GIANT LEAP

The writer C.S. Lewis once said, "A warm heart does not mean a soft head." Amidst her efforts to increase academic standards, Mary realized that, as she affirmed her commitment to children as unique individuals, she simultaneously had to help them live up to their maximum potential. Given these considerations, she became more sensitive to the needs of others.

As she experienced that gradual transition, Mary also developed a deeper acceptance of people who were different from herself. Apparently, that philosophy was contagious, for suddenly other teachers in the school began to perceive children in a different way too. Incredibly, many recognized how much talent actually existed in children once they had been shown how to capitalize on their individual strengths.

## IMPACT ON TEACHER TRAINING

While teaching mathematics to middle school students, Dr. White also served as adjunct faculty in the Teacher Education Program at the University of Alabama in Birmingham. She altered her teaching at the university by requiring her "methods" classes to attend her mathematics classes in the public school as she taught. She thought it essential for those aspiring future teachers to spend time in a real learning-styles classroom and observe how to teach children through their learning-style strengths. She admonished higher education strongly:

> We professors frequently *tell* young teachers how to teach, but we never actually teach them the way we say they ought to teach. That has to stop! The teachers-in-training assigned to me will *experience* learning-styles teaching so that they understand how *good* it feels to the student and how easy it is for the teacher!

For years, newspaper reporters wrote about the hands-on experiences she provided for students who previously had been unable to pass mathematics and for Teacher Education registrants who were just learning how to become good teachers. University students would clamor to get into her courses and parents never again criticized how Mrs. White was teaching their children.

## FIRST ADMINISTRATIVE STEPS

Dr. White's developing enthusiasm, knowledge, and practical applications in learning styles led to her appointment as assistant principal of the newly opened Oak Mountain Middle School. Mounting community and State Department of Education expectations to improve instruction for the diversity of students found within today's classrooms was demanding. Alternative teaching strategies were emphasized particularly for schools in which the inclusion of Special Education students virtually required a strong knowledge of learning-style instructional techniques. Mary quickly was thrust into a leadership position precisely because she could assist faculty in re-examining the teaching-learning process. That opportunity enabled her to equip the staff with skills and resources necessary to build a school that responded directly to the needs of each student. To her amazement, almost all staff were interested in developing new strategies as long as a colleague was willing to demonstrate the method, help translate the related theory into practice, and assist with caring whenever the "going got rough."

## BEGINNING A LEARNING-STYLES PROGRAM

Many Oak Mountain Middle School faculty members were essentially unfamiliar with learning styles, but were willing—almost eager to learn. That required Mary to model various instructional strategies to show how to involve students more in active learning and less in lecture-dominated listening. Further modification of their teaching required some classroom redesign to respond better to students' diverse needs. In any given class not grouped by learning-style similarities, children need to be identified by their ability to concentrate in:

* sound versus quiet;
* soft, rather than bright light;
* informal rather than conventional seating; and
* passivity versus mobility—suggesting that some youngsters periodically must move from one area to another as required, but with "the two Ds—discipline and decorum."

Mary demonstrated how to use small-group instructional techniques like Team Learning, Circle of Knowledge, Brainstorming, Case Studies, and simulations for peer-oriented middle school students. She also introduced CAPs and PLSs as alternatives to conventional instruction (Dunn & Dunn, 1992, 1993). Gradually, she initiated a graduate-level course in the local university to develop regional teacher awareness. Implementation began in the sixth-grade mathematics classes and expanded to other subject areas in that grade, as well as throughout the school—with various levels of implementation as its benefits became evident. Mary also undertook a research project to determine the relative effects of encouraging students to study and do their homework through their learning-style strengths (White, 1996).

Dr. White and a colleague conducted a study using learning styles within math on algebraic equations. The unit was conducted for a period of three weeks with concepts that are not introduced until grade 8. A repeated-measures design was used to examine the interaction between groups and pre- to post-gains. Group 1 consisted of students in Teacher 1's class. These students were taught the math subject matter on algebraic equations using a traditional approach. The instruction included reading the textbook chapter, teacher-directed presentations, and completing assigned worksheets. Group 2 consisted of students in Teacher 2's class. These students were taught the math subject matter on algebraic equations by matching the instructional resources that accommodated the needs of the individual learning styles in the class. Anecdotal observations revealed that Teacher 2 taught consistently with strategies congruent to the students' learning-style preferences and introduced the students to resources such as Flip Chutes, Pic-A-Holes, Task Cards, or Floor Games.

Both groups ranged from the gifted to Learning Disabled (LD) or at-risk. The initial analyses of the mean scores for both groups at the time of pre-testing achievement indicated that the students in Group 2 scored significantly lower than the students in Group 1. Twenty-six percent of the Group 2 students were classified as LD. Yet post-test scores for Teacher 2 were similar to the other groups. The post hoc analysis of variance indicated significant difference ($p < .05$) between the math gains of students in the classroom of Teachers 2 and 1.

Dr. White concluded that the significant gains in Group 2 must be attributed to the global teaching style of Teacher 2 and the matching of instructional resources with students' learning styles. As the school administrator, she realized that the teacher's focus on teaching through students' learning-style strengths rather than on their perceived intelligence allowed these students to achieve the success that they rarely experienced before.

Over a three-year period, Mary began to notice significant changes on the students' standardized test scores. The progression of the average grades of the students in the learning-styles classes revealed significant gains as the implementation of learning styles continued. The eighth-grade students' scores increased in every subject area by the third year of learning-styles implementation (see Figure E.1).

## RIPPLING EFFECTS

Exposure of students at Oak Mountain Middle School to learning styles influenced schools beyond the boundaries of Alabama. The first year the school opened, it had a gifted sixth-grade student who was introduced to learning styles for the first time. Before the end of that first semester, the boy was transferred to Tennessee. Coincidentally, staff at that school system in Tennessee were just beginning to consider adopting the Dunn and Dunn Learning-Style Model. Inadvertently overhearing several teachers in his

Figure E.1
Eighth-Grade Progression of Students Using Learning Styles

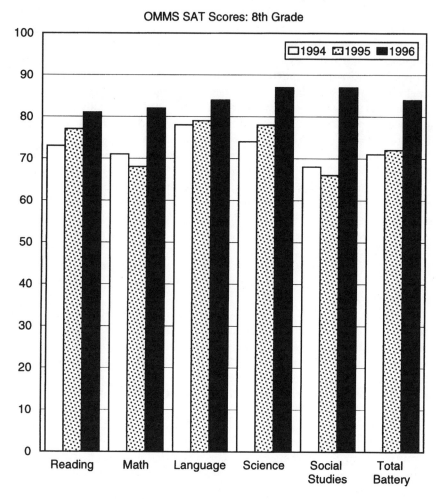

OMMS SAT Scores: 8th Grade

school discussing this approach prompted Jeremy to offer personal accolades describing his experiences at Oak Mountain Middle School. Jeremy suggested that the school contact Dr. White for permission to visit and "see for yourself!" Jeremy believed in learning styles so strongly that he consented to address the Board of Education to elicit support for teachers to visit the school. Subsequently, the Board members provided the necessary funding for inservice in learning styles for volunteers in that school system. As that school's students began performing better on standardized achievement tests, Dr. White received many more requests from both Tennessee and Alabama schools for additional staff development in learning styles.

## REVEILLE IN THE SOUTH

Mary White's story cautions all educational leaders to remember the unique challenges that students face and the profound struggles they must overcome to grow into well-balanced, confident, able human beings. In addition to our concern about preparing them for a secure future, it is time to reaffirm the critical importance of individual learning styles, talents, and interests. It is only then that teachers will be able to honestly say to each student, *"We are helping you to become all that you can be!"*

## NOTE

For the survey that initially provided demographic information on the schools described herein, see Appendix B.

## REFERENCES

Dunn, R., & Dunn, K. (1992). *Teaching elementary students through their individual learning styles: Practical approaches for grades 3–6.* Boston: Allyn & Bacon.

Dunn, R., & Dunn, R. (1993). *Teaching secondary students through their individual learning styles: Practical approaches for grades 7–12.* Boston: Allyn & Bacon.

White, M.E. (1996). Effects of homework prescriptions based upon individual learning-style preferences on the achievement and attitudes toward mathematics of sixth-grade students. (Doctoral dissertation, University of Alabama at Birmingham, 1996). *Dissertation Abstracts International, 57*(08), 3384.

For additional research on the effects of homework prescriptions based on individual learning-style preferences on achievement and attitudes, see:

Brand, E. (1999). Effects of learning-style based homework prescriptions on urban 11th-grade low-achieving students in vocabulary. (Doctoral dissertation, St. John's University, 1999).

Geiser, W.F. (1998). Effects of learning-style awareness and responsive study strategies on achievement, incidence of study, and attitudes of suburban eighth-grade students. (Doctoral dissertation, St. John's University, 1998).

Lenehan, M. (1994). Effects of learning style knowledge on nursing majors' achievement, anxiety, anger, and curiosity. (Doctoral dissertation, St. John's University, 1994).

Lenehan, M.C., Dunn, R., Ingham, J., Murray, W., & Signer, B. (1994). Learning style: Necessary know-how for academic success in college. *Journal of College Student Development, 35*, 461–466.

Marino, J. (1993). Homework: A fresh approach to a perennial problem. *Momentum, 24*(1), 69–71.

Turner, N.D. (1992). A comparative study of the effects of learning style prescriptions and/or modality-based instruction on the spelling achievement of fifth-grade students. (Doctoral dissertation, Andrews University, 1992). *Dissertation Abstracts International, 53*(04), p. 1051.

Turner, N.D. (1993, summer). Learning styles and meta-cognition. *Reading Improvement, 30*(2), 82–85.

*Appendix A*

# International Learning Styles Network

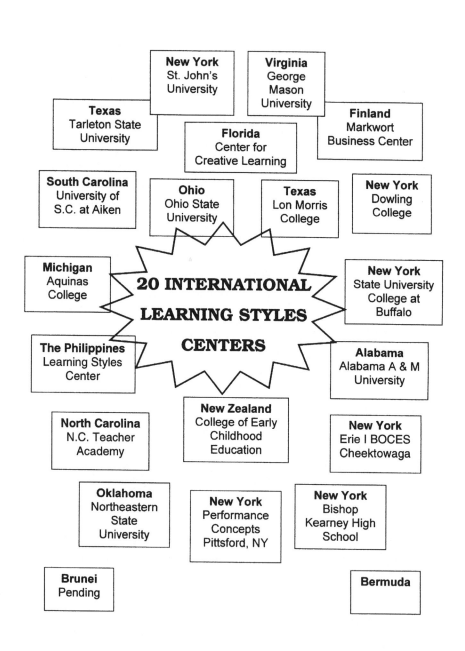

**New York**
St. John's University

**Virginia**
George Mason University

**Texas**
Tarleton State University

**Finland**
Markwort Business Center

**Florida**
Center for Creative Learning

**South Carolina**
University of S.C. at Aiken

**Ohio**
Ohio State University

**Texas**
Lon Morris College

**New York**
Dowling College

**Michigan**
Aquinas College

## 20 INTERNATIONAL LEARNING STYLES CENTERS

**New York**
State University College at Buffalo

**The Philippines**
Learning Styles Center

**Alabama**
Alabama A & M University

**North Carolina**
N.C. Teacher Academy

**New Zealand**
College of Early Childhood Education

**New York**
Erie I BOCES Cheektowaga

**Oklahoma**
Northeastern State University

**New York**
Performance Concepts Pittsford, NY

**New York**
Bishop Kearney High School

**Brunei**
Pending

**Bermuda**

# Supervisor's Success Story
# Survey and Implementation Chart

Last Name: _____    First Name: _____

School and District Name: _____

School Address: _____

City: _____    Country: _____

School Telephone: _____    Home Telephone: _____

Is the school community (check one):   urban _____    suburban _____    town _____
rural _____    farm _____?

**In One or Two Sentences Describe:**
1. The most unique things about the community in which the school is located.

2. Anything unique about your school district.

3. Some of your staff's qualities.

4. Your school's enrollment in terms of numbers:
   (a) more than _____    (b) fewer than _____    (c) between _____ and _____

5. The school or district socioeconomic level:
   (a) high _____    (b) low _____    (c) varied _____    (d) mixed _____

6. The student population in terms of:
   reading and math achievement before implementing learning styles:

7. (in numbers) The average class size: _____

8. The number of teaching faculty: _____

9. The number of support staff: _____

10. Approximate teacher/student ratio: _____

11. The cultural background of your students:

(a) ____% Asian  (b) ____% Asian-American  (c) ____% African

(d) ____% African-American  (e) ____% Hispanic  (f) ____% Hispanic-American

(g) ____% Caucasian  (h) ____% Caucasian-American  (i) ____% Mid-Eastern

(j) ____% Mid-Eastern-American

**Please Examine Figure B.1 and:**

- Check each of the learning-styles items that visitors would see if visiting your school.

- Place the #1 next to the first items that were introduced.

- Place the #2 next to the second items that were introduced.

- Continue the pattern of numbering those items that currently exist that can be seen in your school/district. Do not be concerned about anything that was not introduced.

**Briefly Describe:**

12. How your learning-styles program began.

13. When your staff first began working with learning styles.

14. How your staff decided which steps to implement first.

15. Plans for program expansion (if any).

16. How you knew your staff was accepting learning styles.

17. How and when your staff was trained in learning styles.

18. Who provided the staff learning-styles training.

19. How you contributed to the training.

20. Why you implemented the Dunn and Dunn model.

21. How the learning-styles perspective influenced you as an administrator or supervisor.

**Answer Only Those Questions That Apply:**

22. Can you document ACHIEVEMENT GAINS because of the learning-styles program? (Attach charts, graphs, tables, or anecdotes)

23. Can you document ATTITUDE GAINS because of the learning-styles program? (Attach charts, graphs, tables, or anecdotes)

24. Can you document BEHAVIOR or ATTENDANCE GAINS because of the learning-styles program? (Attach charts, graphs, tables, or anecdotes)

25. Can you cite any incident or anecdotes that demonstrate the effectiveness of learning-styles instruction?

26. What resistance or difficulties did you have to overcome and how did you do it?

*If you care to do so, collect and add teachers' and students' anecdotes (and their names and/or grades) and we'll add them to your story.*

Figure B.1
Learning-Styles Implementation Stages

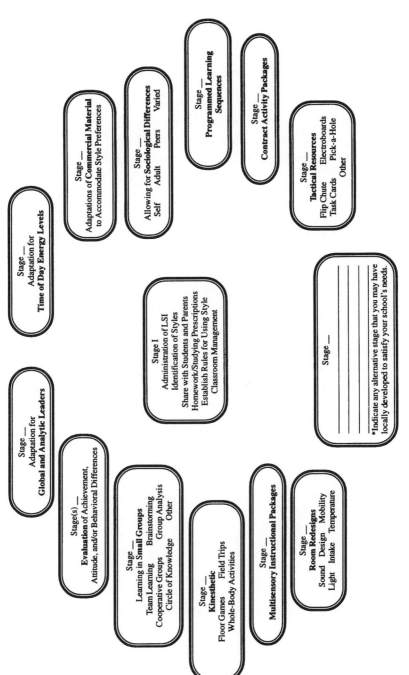

Please use this graphic to respond to survey question Number 1 and return it with your response. You may wish to copy this page to track your school's progress.

*Developed by Drs. Rita Dunn and Thomas C. DeBello.

# Index

# About the Editors and Contributors

RITA DUNN is professor, Division of Administrative and Instructional Leadership, and director, Center for the Study of Learning and Teaching Styles, St. John's University, New York. She is the recipient of more than 20 national awards for the quality of her research and teaching and is the author of 22 books and more than 300 published articles and research studies.

THOMAS C. DeBELLO is principal, Setauket Elementary School, Setauket, New York, and the author of many practitioner-oriented articles on successful school-based learning-styles practices. He is co-director of Dowling College's Learning Strategies Center.

KAREN BURKE has been an elementary school teacher and assistant principal, but currently is assistant professor, Child Study Department, St. Joseph's College, Brooklyn, New York. She is the author of several published chapters and articles on learning-styles theory and applications.

ROGER J. CALLAN has been a high school principal and teacher, but currently serves as director of the International Learning Styles Network's Bishop Kearney High School Demonstration Center in New York City. His many publications have appeared as chapters in several books and in *Educational Leadership, Clearinghouse,* and *Educational Psychological Review.*

ANDREA HONIGSFELD is teaching assistant to Dr. Dunn and a candidate in St. John's University's Instructional Leadership Doctoral Program. She is the author of several published articles on learning-styles theory and application.

MARYANN KIELY LOVELACE has been a high school science teacher at Northern Valley Regional High School in Demarest, New Jersey, for six years and is a candidate in St. John's University's Instructional Leadership Doctoral Program.

NANCY MONTGOMERY is assistant professor, Division of Administrative and Instructional Leadership, St. John's University, New York City, where she also is a learning-styles staff developer.

JEANNIE RYAN is a high school English teacher and teacher-trainer at Northern Valley Regional High School in Demarest, New Jersey, and is a candidate in St. John's University's Instructional Leadership Doctoral Program.

**Previous Books by Rita Dunn**

*Practical Approaches to Individualizing Instruction: Contracts and Other Effective Teaching Strategies* (with K. Dunn, 1972)

*Educator's Self-Teaching Guide to Individualizing Instructional Programs* (with K. Dunn, 1975)

*Administrator's Guide to New Programs for Faculty Management and Evaluation* (with K. Dunn, 1977)

*How to Raise Independent and Professionally Successful Daughters* (with K. Dunn, 1977)

*Teaching Students Through Their Individual Learning Styles: A Practical Approach* (with K. Dunn, 1978)

*Situational Leadership for Principals: The School Administrator in Action* (with K. Dunn, 1983)

*Teaching Students to Read Through Their Individual Learning Styles* (with M. Carbo and K. Dunn, 1986)

*Learning Styles: Quiet Revolution in American Secondary Schools* (with S.A. Griggs, 1988)

*Hands-on Approaches to Learning Styles: A Practical Guide to Successful Schooling* (1991)

*Teaching Elementary Students Through Their Individual Learning Styles: Practical Approaches for Grades 3–6* (with K. Dunn, 1992)

*Teaching Secondary Students Through Their Individual Learning Styles: Practical Approaches for Grades 7–12* (with K. Dunn, 1993)

*Bringing Out the Giftedness in Your Child: Nurturing Every Child's Unique Strengths, Talents, and Potential* (with K. Dunn and D. Treffinger, 1992)

*Teaching and Counseling Gifted and Talented Adolescents: An International Learning Style Perspective* (ed., with R.M. Milgram and G.E. Price, 1993)

*Teaching Young Children Through Their Individual Learning Styles* (with K. Dunn and J. Perrin, 1994)

*Educating Diverse Learners: Strategies for Improving Classroom Practices* (1995)

*Multiculturalism and Learning Style: Teaching and Counseling Adolescents* (with S.A. Griggs, 1995)

*Everything You Need to Successfully Implement a Learning-Styles Instructional Program: Materials and Methods* (1996)

*How to Implement and Supervise a Learning Style Program* (1996)

*Learning Styles and the Nursing Profession* (ed., with S.A. Griggs, 1998)

*Practical Approaches to Individualizing Staff Development for Adults* (ed., with K. Dunn, 1998)

*The Complete Guide to the Learning Styles Inservice System* (with K. Dunn, 1999)

ISBN 0-89789-687-4

9 780897 896870

90000>

HARDCOVER BAR CODE